Policing Images

Policing Images

Policing, communication and legitimacy

Rob C Mawby

WILLAN
PUBLISHING

Published by

Willan Publishing
Culmcott House
Mill Street, Uffculme
Cullompton, Devon
EX15 3AT, UK
Tel: +44(0)1884 840337
Fax: +44(0)1884 840251
e-mail: info@willanpublishing.co.uk
website: www.willanpublishing.co.uk

Published simultaneously in the USA and Canada by

Willan Publishing
c/o ISBS, 5824 N.E. Hassalo St
Portland, Oregon 97213-3644, USA
Tel: +001(0)503 287 3093
Fax: +001(0)503 280 8832
website: www.isbs.com

First published 2002

ISBN 1-903240 71-9

British Library Cataloguing-in-Publication Data
A catalogue record for this book is available from the British Library.

Printed by T J International Ltd, Trecerus Industrial Estate, Padstow, Cornwall
Typeset by PDQ Typesetting, Newcastle-under-Lyme, Staffordshire

Contents

Acknowledgements

This book has its roots in ideas and questions which came to mind in 1994–95 when I was researching media aspects of police management. In its development from a nagging idea to a potentially interesting area of research, then into a PhD thesis, and now into a book, I have benefited from the support of a number of people and organisations and I would like to record my grateful thanks for their encouragement and assistance.

Ian Loader supervised the PhD thesis on which the book is based. I owe Ian an enormous debt; not only for his exemplary supervision, but also for agreeing to go through it all again by commenting on the book proposal and, later, painstakingly reading and commenting on the final manuscript. I would also like to thank Robert Reiner and Richard Sparks, who examined the thesis and provided valuable comments and guidance.

The research detailed in the book would not have been possible without the cooperation of the police service and at various stages I have benefited from the access facilitated by the Association of Chief Police Officers (ACPO) and the support of the Association of Police Public Relations Officers (APPRO). I would like to acknowledge the help provided by these organisations, and by the police forces and individual police officers and civilians who contributed to the research. They variously enriched the study by agreeing to answer interview questions, by filling in questionnaires, and by allowing me to observe their everyday work. In particular I am grateful to Tony Coe, former chief constable of Suffolk Constabulary, who initially opened many doors whilst chair of the then ACPO General Purposes Committee. Thanks also to the former chief constable of South Yorkshire Police, Richard Wells, and his successor, Mike Hedges, for allowing me unbridled access to observe and subsequently write about police 'image work' in one force. During the case study fieldwork, Gillian Radcliffe, then South Yorkshire Police's head of press and public relations, was a consistent source of support. She has remained equally supportive whilst chair of APPRO. Collectively the members of South Yorkshire Police made the fieldwork a genuinely enlightening experience and I am grateful to them for their spirit of openness. Whilst I benefited from the cooperation of many police personnel, the analysis and arguments presented in this book are mine, as are any errors, and I readily accept that those who contributed would not necessarily agree with my conclusions.

I have also benefited from the support of former and current colleagues. Ellis Cashmore and the late Mike Collison provided vital early encouragement. Gary Lynch-Wood, Geoff Berry and Lynne Walley provided encouragement in times of doubt, and my momentum and spirit was maintained through countless discussions with Alan Wright, often killing time at airports or in late-night bars in Budapest. I won't forget his generosity and support.

Throughout the process of planning and preparing the book, Brian Willan has provided timely and practical advice and I would like to thank him for showing faith in the idea.

Book-writing inevitably takes its toll on weekends and family life and, last, but never least, thanks to my wife Angie and daughters Sally, Harriet and Lucy for their tolerance and unconditional support.

Rob C Mawby
December 2001

List of figures and tables

Introduction

The police image, though an enduring cultural symbol, is complex. It is multi-faceted, changes over time and in content and it is different to different people. It encompasses not only physical appearances, but also the character and attributes of the police institution, its non-visual representations and its social meanings. This book is about how this image is constructed and communicated by the police themselves. It does not address the reception or perception of the police image by those on the receiving end – that would be a very different book. It is, therefore, a study of police 'image work'. By image work I mean all the activities in which police forces engage and which project meanings of policing. These include overt and intended image management activities such as media and public relations work, but also the unintended, the mundane practices of police work which communicate images of policing, and through which the social meanings of policing are produced.

Why is police image work worthy of research? Since the late 1980s new terms have become part of the language of British policing, including 'corporate identity' and 'corporate image', 'media and public relations' and 'marketing'. All these terms are more commonly associated with the worlds of business, commerce and the private sector. The emergence of these terms and their associated activities suggests that the police service has become active in image building. But is this new and does it represent a significant shift in policing with implications for twenty-first century policing? Or is it a re-labelling of what the police have always done and if so why have they always done it?

In this book I argue that police image work has always existed, though it has taken different forms to meet different organisational needs at different times and, furthermore, image work has always been related to the legitimation process, entwined with the seeking and retaining of legitimacy. At the inception of the modern police in 1829, Peel and the first commissioners, Rowan and Mayne, engaged in image work as one mechanism to encourage policing by consent and, equally, the modern police service utilises image work in its efforts to maintain legitimacy. Yet, despite the consistent presence of image work, a new policing context emerged in the 1990s in which image work was to take on a greater significance. The conditions of this context were created by a combination of managerialist government policy, widespread concern with police performance and misconduct, and a realisation by police elites that change was necessary. At the same time there existed what appeared to be an insatiable demand for policing services within a climate of 'fear of crime'. Added to these conditions, rapidly changing media developments ensured that during the 1990s the visibility of policing was high, compelling the police service to address the management of its visibility. These conditions generated challenges to police legitimacy and increased the profile of police image work. Given this context the purpose of the book is to explore, drawing on empirical research at national and local levels, how the police seek to construct and communicate their image and to examine how this image work is related to police legitimacy.

The first three chapters consider questions of history, context and theory. In chapter 1 I trace the emergence of police image work from the creation of the modern police in 1829 up to 1987. In tracing the history of image work I demonstrate that although there has always been a concern to promote certain images of the British police, image work falls into phases in which it has progressively become more active and purposive. Chapter 2 sets out the contemporary policing context and the triggers which generated the distinguishing features of the most recent phase of police image work. Chapter 3 introduces the theoretical concerns, considering the concepts of legitimacy, communication and the public sphere. Drawing on social and political theory it examines what it entails for the police to legitimate their power. It considers also the nature of police communications in a highly mediated society.

Chapter 4 charts the terrain of contemporary image work across the police service nationally. It examines image work at a number of levels; from the perspective of chief constables, the three primary staff associations and force media and public relations departments. The chapter draws on interviews with policy makers and practitioners. It also draws on two comprehensive surveys of police force press offices conducted in 1996–97 and in 2000–01. This chapter therefore presents and discusses original data on the extent and activities of image work across the police service. It identifies convergence and divergence in intentions and practices, examines how forces have responded to the pressures which have compelled them to address image work through media relations, public relations, marketing and corporate identity activities. By doing so, this chapter provides a systemic perspective on image work.

Chapters 5, 6 and 7 comprise a case study of the image work of one force – South Yorkshire Police. Chapter 5 provides the historical background of the force and outlines two axial events, the 1984–85 Miners' Strike and the 1989 Hillsborough tragedy, which impacted on the force image. The force of 1997, the year of the fieldwork, is described and force documentation is analysed to illustrate the image which the force was seeking to promote in the late 1990s. Whilst Chapter 5 considers the recent history of South Yorkshire Police and the image that it was aspiring to project at the turn of the century, Chapters 6 and 7, in contrast, analyse the practice of image work. Drawing on time spent with police officers and civilian staff undertaking a range of policing functions, these chapters provide an account of police image work at various sites 'on the ground'.

Chapter 6 focuses on the work of media relations in the force, examining news management and the planning and delivery of set piece promotional events. The work of the headquarters press office staff (civilian professional communicators), and the district press officers (uniformed part-time media officers), is compared and contrasted, mapping convergence and divergence. However, the image of a police force will develop not only through active media and public relations, but also through the routine undertaking of police work, involving countless police-public encounters which create impressions of the police. Therefore Chapter 7 examines how image work operates on the ground in routine policing. Three areas of practical policing are scrutinised – public order policing, routine operational police work and community involvement. These areas of policing differ from media and public relations work in that their primary focus is not, on the face of it, image work. However, for different reasons, each of these spheres of policing is shot through with image implications and the chapter explores the images which each creates, and analyses to what extent image work is permeating operational police work.

In the final chapter, I consider the extent to which image work pervades contemporary police work and the implications for policing in the context of a highly mediated society. I consider the relationship between image work and the legitimation process, arguing that at different times in varying circumstances image work will support and demonstrate legitimate policing, but equally it will be used to mask, or compensate for, problems of legitimation. I conclude that image work is now embedded in police work and despite divergence in practice has become significant in the shaping of police work. Situating image work within wider transformations in policing and society in which the mass media today occupy a prominent role, I conclude that image work and the legitimation of policing will continue to be closely entwined.

Chapter 1

A history of police image work 1829–1987

The Police are reminded of the great importance of not using any irritating language or expressions…the more good temper and coolness shown by the Police whenever they are called upon to act, the more readily will all the well disposed assist them in preserving the public peace. (*Metropolitan Police General Regulations, Instructions and Orders*, 1851 edition)

Numerous examples were found in all forces visited of poor behaviour towards members of the public and colleagues alike… Every time an officer abuses the trust placed in him or her by the public, the collective image of the Police Service is damaged. (Her Majesty's Inspectorate of Constabulary 1999: 3)

Policing in Great Britain has always been as much a matter of image as substance. (Reiner 1994a: 11)

Activities which fall under the umbrella of 'image management' or 'promotionalism' have been brought to bear in recent years on the British police service, including corporate identity, marketing, press and public relations activities.[1] However, image *management* is not exclusively a modern practice; police image *work* has always existed. By 'image work' I mean all the activities in which police forces engage and which construct and project images and meanings of policing. These include overt and intended image-management activities, but also the less obvious, the unintended, the mundane practices of police work which communicate images of policing. This chapter traces the emergence of police image work from the establishment of the modern police in 1829 by Robert Peel through to the appointment of Peter Imbert as Metropolitan Police Commissioner in 1987. In doing so the chapter considers the origins of the police image and the key shifts in its management. The character of image work changes during the period. Initially it is piecemeal and concerned with the design and establishment of an appropriate image, whilst later, reflecting developments in the media, image work is closely connected to press and public relations activities and the establishment of systems for communication. Throughout the period, however, image work is related to legitimacy, initially its fostering, latterly its maintenance.

Four historical phases encapsulate particular characteristics of image work. The first period, that of *informal image work* runs from 1829 to 1919. In this period there were no formal mechanisms, though image was uppermost in elite minds and its communication was important. Image making was at work in the design and presentation of a force with a specific and not wholly welcomed role in society. The second period is one of *emergent public relations* and runs from 1919 through to 1972. It starts with the establishment of the first police force press bureau, marking the formalisation of police-press relations. This period sees greater resources dedicated to establishing formal channels for image and information management, though developments remain sporadic. The third period, *embedding public relations* starts with the appointment of Robert Mark as Metropolitan Police Commissioner in 1972. Mark embarked upon a policy of what he called 'open administration' (Mark 1978: 135) which included a radical revision of the Met.'s relationship with the news media. This policy was continued by Mark's successors, David McNee (1977–82) and Kenneth Newman (1982–87). The fourth period, that of *professionalisation of police image work*, begins with the appointment of Peter Imbert as Metropolitan Police Commissioner in 1987 and runs through to the present day. During this period Imbert commissioned the advice of corporate image consultants and, outside the Metropolitan Police Service (hereafter the Met.), in many forces communication of the police image became a discrete activity resourced by trained professionals.

The following sections of this chapter discuss the first three of these phases, the fourth phase is discussed in Chapter 2 within the context of wider developments in contemporary British policing. In this chapter discussion focuses on the national context and the Met. as this is the best documented and the Met. has been the barometer in terms of image promotion. The Met. is not typical in terms of image work, indeed as later chapters demonstrate, there is an uneven pattern of convergence and divergence in the organisation of image work. Nevertheless, historically, significant shifts have focused on the Met. and set the pattern for developments elsewhere.

Informal image work 1829–1919

During this initial phase which commences with the establishment of the Metropolitan Police in 1829, the modern language of image management was not in existence and activities now recognisable within the spheres of corporate identity, marketing, press and public relations were not distinct activities with their own objectives. Yet the fore-runners of these image-making activities existed, wrapped up within the approach taken and the policies adopted by the architects of the modern police. In this sense image-building activities were inseparable from the raft of measures which were designed to establish an acceptable police service. As such, image making infused all activities aimed at legitimating the police service. This is a significant point. As this and later chapters explore, this was not always to be the case.

In *The English Bobby: An Indulgent Tradition*,[2] Clive Emsley addresses the origins of the image of the 'Bobby' and suggests how the 'indulgent tradition' developed and was maintained (Emsley 1992). Like others (Critchley 1973, Tobias 1975, Reiner 2000a), Emsley notes that in the 1820s there was opposition to the creation of a police force as the continental model of policing, which cast the police as overt and covert agents of the state (Chapman 1970), was alien to the English way of life. The historian E.P. Thompson (1980: 204) has noted 'the peculiar jealousy of the British people towards the central powers of the state, their abhorrence of military intervention in civil affairs, their dislike of state espionage and of any form of heavy policing'. This was part of 'Englishness' as an 'official identity' and 'cultural ideology' forged during the eighteenth and nineteenth centuries and by the years of Empire (Haseler 1996: 2). Included within this identity was a commitment to such ideals as liberty, expressed, for example, through the campaigning, if self-serving, activities of John Wilkes (1727–97) (Pringle 1955: 169–82). The English were also suspicious of large standing armies and if a police force was to be established it required an image that disassociated itself from both the continental model and the military.

These ideals of 'Englishness' were initially an obstacle to the establishment of the modern police, yet policing was later to become an important ingredient in the construction of Englishness, officially and popularly represented as one of its 'best in the world' institutions. As Tobias points out:

> The Metropolitan Police itself was born into a suspicious world full of people looking sharply for signs of a threat to liberty, and certainly its first leaders were constantly alert to suppress or prevent conduct likely to put the force in bad odour with the public. (*Tobias 1975: 100*).

To counter this suspicion, Critchley believes the most important founding principle for the new police was that they 'must go out of their way to win the goodwill and cooperation of the public, *advertising* themselves as a service rather than a force' (Critchley 1973: 30, emphasis added). Suspicion of the police, and the need for legitimation, has been and remains a consistent problem for the police to address.

Robert Peel and the first Metropolitan Police Commissioners, Richard Rowan and Charles Mayne, made a conscious contribution to the creation of a police force that was acceptable to the policed (Emsley 1992: 115–16, Reiner 2000a: 50). The image of this force was considered carefully and designed for specific purposes. The police were uniformed, to communicate the message that they were not spies, and the uniform was deliberately a different colour (blue) from military uniforms (black) (Reith 1943: 36, Ascoli 1979: 90). Secondly, the police were unarmed, again to distinguish them from the military, and the truncheons they carried were discretely positioned out of view in the tunic (Reith 1952: 152, Waddington 2000: 170). Thirdly, the low pay discouraged 'gentlemen and commissioned officers' from joining thus avoiding again the 'taint of militarism' (Emsley 1992: 116) and encouraging the incorporation of the working class. As Critchley puts it 'the police and those with whom they were mainly likely to come into contact would have similar backgrounds and experience and, it was hoped, a degree of mutual sympathy, even forbearance, would develop' (Critchley 1973: 31).

Image considerations run through the original Metropolitan Police Instructions of 1829 devised by Rowan and Mayne and issued to each recruit. These have a general tone of creating and maintaining a particular image. There are many references to the importance of being properly dressed in full uniform at all times and officers are instructed to give their names and divisions when so requested and are warned against concealing their numbers to prevent identification by members of the public (Metropolitan *Police Orders*, 11 October 1829, p. 55).[3] There is an emphasis on officers using appropriate language and projecting a demeanour of civility and respect towards members of the public. For example, attention is drawn to the importance of treating visitors to police stations with 'civility and attention' (*ibid*, 6 August 1830, p. 66; 17 July 1831, pp. 75–6). Moreover:

> The Police are reminded of the great importance of not using any irritating language or expressions...the more good temper and coolness shown by the Police whenever they are called upon to act, the more readily will all the well disposed assist them in preserving the public peace'. (*ibid*, 20 August 1842, p. 109).

Ascoli has noted that this is 'a classic statement of the art of public relations in its widest sense' (Ascoli 1979: 86). Officers are also exhorted 'at a time when an attempt is made to create a strong prejudice against them, that they should do their duty with every possible moderation and forbearance' (*Metropolitan Police Orders*, 1 November 1830, p. 71). They should act with '...utmost temper and forbearance...with good humour and civility' (*ibid*, 26 October and 1 November 1830, p. 71). Image making then was present at the very inception of the modern police.[4]

Emsley argues that a favourable police image was able to develop through the non-political and locally accountable character of the police service operating within the 'political stability and political structure of Victorian Britain' (Emsley 1992: 118, 121–2). This was underpinned by the successful policing of such events as the Great Exhibition of 1851. Reiner puts forward eight characteristics that were used to foster legitimacy: a bureaucratic organisation; the rule of law; a strategy of minimal force; non-partisanship; accountability; the service role; preventive policing and police effectiveness (Reiner 2000a: 51–8). Approximately 25 years after the 1829 Metropolitan Police Act, through the use of such measures, the opposition to the new police was ebbing away:

> Here was an institution which Englishmen could boast of as being particularly English in that, in contrast to European police organisations, it was generally unarmed, non-military, and non-political; it suited well the liberal Englishman's notion that his country's success derived from institutions, ideas and practices which provided models for the world. The police constable, to many middle-class Victorians, became the personification of an idealized image of the English legal system. (Emsley 1992: 118)

The acceptance of the police and the development of popular police images was aided by the growth of the media in the middle of the nineteenth century. During the 1840s, Britain experienced 'the effective establishment of a popular Sunday press...the growth of new kinds of periodical...development of minor theatres...the rise of the music halls' (Williams 1961: 72–3), all of which helped to develop and spread popular images of the police. Emsley (1996: 62–3) quotes favourable police character sketches from *Punch* (1851), *The Times* (1863) and *The Quarterly Review* (1856). In the same period a body of popular literature emerged providing positive representations of policing to the reading public. This comprised the reminiscences of police officers, accompanied by 'a tide of fiction posing as genuine memoirs' (Cox 1992: xiv), whilst, in contrast, Charles Dickens and Wilkie Collins based fictional characters on real police officers.[5]

Focusing on a particular aspect of English culture, namely theatrical entertainment, it is evident that by the early 1880s, favourable images of the police were being conveyed. In productions such as Gilbert and Sullivan's *Pirates of Penzance* (1880), the police were characterised as 'decent, dutiful, well-meaning and incorruptible – even if not overbright' (Cannadine 1992: 27). However, the images developing in popular culture were not wholly positive and uncritical. *Punch* appeared in 1841 and initially targeted the police with 'ridicule and contempt' (Ascoli 1979: 119) later softening to 'joking and jibes' (Emsley 1992: 120). In ballad literature and, later, in the music halls the police were satirised for their association with strong drink, as well as to cast doubt on their competence and honesty. Robert Mark relates in his autobiography that the music hall song 'If you want to know the time ask a policeman' originates not from police officers' renowned time-keeping skill, but from the practice of police officers stealing watches from drunken 'toffs' (Mark 1978: 17; see also Reiner 1994a: 13–14). Steedman argues that police officers were ridiculed not only for their affinity to alcohol which conflicted with their duty to control drunkenness but also as working-class men that had 'sought entry to a wider sphere...to become among those who govern and manage' (Steedman 1984: 162). Indeed scholars have differentiated the acceptance of the police by the various sections of Victorian society, suggesting working class resentment of the new police remained after influential sections of the middle classes had been won over (Storch 1975, Brogden 1982: 180–1). In an examination of policing Islington in London, Cohen argues that police/working-class relations comprised 'outright physical confrontation' until around 1920 where-upon 'an unwritten system of tacit negotiation' emerged in its place (Cohen 1979: 123).

Cannadine notes that the positive depiction of the police in *Pirates of Penzance* was a recent innovation and in addition to reflecting changed attitudes, the theatrical images may have helped to create the new attitude (Cannadine 1992: 22). Traces of the 'indulgent tradition' are identifiable in this operetta. The image of the police officer was being conveyed affectionately, contributing to the establishment of the popular 'Bobby' image, joining other national symbols such as the Jack Tar and John Bull. This was the age of Empire, a time of national success, when the English identity had been established and the Empire had 'added, to an already pretty elevated self-image of Englishness, the crucial ingredient of superiority.' (Haseler 1996: 37). In Emsley's words, 'part of the success of Victorian society was rubbing off on its new guardians' (Emsley 1996: 64).

In the late nineteenth century the social and political conditions of Victorian England had allowed the police to consolidate their role and image and by the early 1900s the Met. were being described as the 'best police in the world'. *Hansard* records several occurrences of the police being described as the world's best at the turn of the century and there are other similar references in contemporary books and newspapers (Emsley 1996: 94). By 1908 a *Times* editorial was describing the 'policeman in London' as 'not merely guardian of the peace; he is an integral part of its social life ... the best friend of a mass of people who have no other counsellor or protector' (cited in Critchley 1978: 326). Although this sentiment might not have been held in all sections of society it is apparent that by the early twentieth century the police had gained a measure of legitimacy. In doing so the construction and communication of an appropriate image had been a significant factor in building support and acceptance, but the image work was informal, concerned with presentation, the inculcation of modes of behaviour for police officers and emphasising the distinct role of the new force as concerned with 'the prevention of crime ... the security of person and property, the preservation of the public tranquillity' (*General Instruction Book*, 1829). In the period that followed, from 1919 to 1972, more formal arrangements for police image work were to emerge.

Emergent public relations 1919–1972

For 90 years the Met., and provincial forces for a shorter period, existed without a specialist department to represent them to the outside world and to liaise directly with the press. William McAdoo, a former New York

City Police Commissioner, following a visit to London in 1909, noted with astonishment that the press praised the police 'on every occasion' but that they were not allowed into Scotland Yard (cited in Emsley 1992: 123). Emsley believes the lack of 'continual press investigation and criticism probably contributed to the "indulgent tradition" in the early years of the twentieth century' (Emsley 1992: 123). However, times were changing. In the second period of police image work the growth and influence of the popular press and the potential for police conflict with the middle classes, their traditional supporters,[6] compelled the police to address formal mechanisms for image-management. This second phase of police image work begins with the establishment of the Scotland Yard Press Bureau in 1919 – the harbinger of formal police public relations activities.

In his study of crime reporting Chibnall documents that as popular journalism expanded and competition increased around the 1920s, the police were a crucial, if uncooperative news source. Consequently, informal arrangements for the acquiring of information often consisted of police officers selling information in pubs to reporters (Chibnall 1977: 49–51). When concern over this informal system reached the level of parliamentary complaints, the Commissioner, Sir Nevil Macready, took the first step towards formalising police–press relations by establishing the Scotland Yard Press Bureau on 1 October 1919. The motive for this was one of control – to stem the leaks and to create an official channel for the release of information (Macready 1924: 416–17, Chibnall 1979: 136). At the very moment of origin of a bespoke office and channel for police-press relations, the *raison d'être* was control of the external environment rather than transparency of the police organisation. The Bureau consisted of one civil servant, initially Macready's secretary, who collected information from all Scotland Yard's departments and issued two press releases each day (Macready 1924: 416–17, Chibnall 1979: 136). This source of information proved insufficient to meet all the requirements of the press and to obtain the stories they required the informal system continued. Nevertheless, this modest initiative by Macready signalled the start of a formal means of managing the police image through the active use of an official bureau to liaise with the press. Hitherto image-making had been bound up in the entirety of policing activities that had fostered legitimacy. From this point on image work would at least partly be undertaken by an office established for precisely the purpose of managing the police image.

This pioneering step did not lead immediately to a significant growth in the scope or extent of press and public relations activities by the police service. A review of the literature from the period yields little information concerning formal press and overt public relations during the late 1920s through to the mid-1940s. For example, writing in 1934, Sir John Moylan (Receiver for the Metropolitan Police District and Courts for over 25 years), described the Press Bureau as having a simple liaison role. The press applied for accurate information through the Bureau or conversely the Commissioner, through the Bureau, asked the press to publish or not publish for reasons of assisting police investigations. 'Many are the occasions on which the press can and do assist in this way' (Moylan 1934: 140). Chibnall has also acknowledged the lack of comment on press relations in the literature of the period, though he notes that police attitudes towards journalists remained generally suspicious, even hostile, despite a number of journalists being selected to work closely with the police on occasions to encourage warmer relations (Chibnall 1979: 136–7).

Police suspicion of the press is evident in an episode described by H.M. Howgrave-Graham, Secretary to the Metropolitan Police from 1926–47. He relates that whilst Commissioner between 1928 and 1931 Lord Byng became concerned that the press were sensationalising routine discipline cases, damaging the reputation of the force. The matter came to a head through Byng addressing the Newspaper Proprietors' Association and requesting that they report responsibly and give less attention to discipline cases. To the clear surprise of Howgrave-Graham, the proprietors complied with the request and for over two years their papers made no references to such cases. Thereafter Howgrave-Graham rebutted all claims that the press 'have no sense of public duty and about as many scruples as a Nazi boss' (Howgrave-Graham 1947: 16–17). This example both shows the police suspicion of the press and at the same time illustrates the potential for cooperation. Byng's successor, Lord Trenchard (Commissioner from 1931 to 1935), subsequently took to explaining to Fleet Street editors the reasons for his reforms before making them public – 'the mere fact of the Commissioner of Police taking editors into his confidence is calculated in itself to create a sympathetic attitude' (Howgrave-Graham 1947: 181). These examples illustrate the nature of attempts by the police during this period to influence the way in which the press portrayed them. They are essentially sporadic interventions by senior officers, rather than systematic plans to promote consistent images of policing.

These insights into police image work through the actions of senior officers are counterpointed by a street-level perspective. Brogden's oral history of the policing of Liverpool between the wars provides an indication of the character and image of policing during this period:

> ...there were two images of policing. On one hand, there was the ubiquitous picture of the officer plodding the beat: a figure armed with omnipotent powers and, as such, to be deferred to or to be avoided. Then there was the mass impression...occasions to admire the police as they marched in serried ranks to patriotic tunes from the Police Band. Displays of police horses, motor cycles, dogs, and dress marching were a dominant image of policing as a uniformed institution...Police pageantry was a symbolic rite... The second image reinforced the first. (Brogden 1991: 61–2)

Brogden sketches impressions of respect for the uniform with locals seeking the advice of officers on matters such as the education of their children (*ibid*: 114) and at the same time brutality and ritual in the realities of street level policing (*ibid*: 98) – a paradoxical mixture of consent and antagonism (*ibid*: 104). By providing examples of both the symbolism of policing that had developed and also the toughness of policing working-class areas, Brogden captures well the respected image of the 'indulgent tradition' co-existing with the harsher side of policing. The imagery, the symbolism, had taken hold.

Towards the end of the 1930s there is evidence, derived from memoirs, of greater cooperation developing between police officers and (crime) journalists (Chibnall 1979: 136). This cooperation was developed further by Sir Harold Scott, Metropolitan Police Commissioner from June 1945 to 1953. His appointment was a significant development for image work. In his memoirs, Scott explains that on becoming Commissioner he was immediately struck by the level of interest from the public and the press in his job and the force. He subsequently took every opportunity to lecture clubs and organisations on the work of the police and to form mutually beneficial relationships with newspaper editors (Scott 1954: 91, 92). Aware of the role of the press in the formulation of the public image of the police (Chibnall 1979: 137), he immediately increased the functions of the Press Bureau. This included the appointment of a 'Public Information Officer'. Scott was critical of the fact that the existing members of the Press Bureau were not experienced journalists and felt that the appointee to the new post must know Fleet Street well if satisfactory relationships were to be built with the press. He also emphasised that the post was information based – 'for the distribution of information' – it was not intended to create a 'Public Relations Officer' who existed 'only to praise or excuse their ministers or departments' (Scott 1954: 92). Mr P.H. Fearnley, an experienced press officer and former employee of the BBC and the War Office, was appointed.

Scott extended the size of the Bureau – at the time a 'small office in the basement' (Howgrave-Graham 1947: 178) – and created a new press and public relations policy which was a move towards rolling back the atmosphere of secrecy which he felt surrounded Scotland Yard. The policy was announced by Scott to a gathering of London's news editors. It was, he said, a policy:

> to give the fullest and earliest information to the press on police activities, subject only to the necessity to avoid publication of information which might interfere with an inquiry in progress or with the course of justice. (Scott 1954: 92)

The moves towards employing a professional journalist in the Bureau, building relationships with the press and providing more information about the police to the public through the press are precursors of the policies later deployed by Robert Mark in the 1970s and a number of chief constables in the 1990s (discussed in Chapter 4). As Scott himself recorded, 'publicity became an indispensable part of our armoury' (Scott 1954: 99).

The period that followed (1945 through to the end of the 1950s) has been called the 'golden age' of policing (Reiner 1994a: 12; 1997a: 1035–6; 2000a: 144), when police folk heroes such as Fabian of the Yard (Fabian 1955) and PC George Dixon (first introduced in *The Blue Lamp* in 1950) were established as police icons, symbolic of the British police officer and an idealised police/public relationship.[7] Reviewing *The Blue Lamp*, C.H. Rolph proclaimed it to be 'the first time the police of this country have been adequately presented on the screen...Jack Warner is an entirely convincing Metropolitan Policeman' (*Police Review* 27/1/50). The former Commissioner, Sir Harold Scott, concurred that the film was a 'faithful picture of the policeman's life and work' (Scott 1954: 91). Not all commentators agreed, as the previously quoted 'indulgent tradition' *Times* review shows, yet this imagery achieved a significance as the years have passed that it never wholly represented at the time of first transmission. For example, *The Blue Lamp* is not remembered for its depiction of a society fearful of a post-war crime wave (Berry *et al.* 1998: 213–14; see also Loader and Mulcahy 2001a: 44) or for the way the children who recover the gun used to kill Dixon suspiciously regard the police constable who questions them – the children clearly regard him as the 'tangible "or else" of society' (Bittner 1990: 10). Similarly the television programme *Dixon of Dock Green* in its run from 1956 to 1974 never achieved top ten viewing status until 1973–74 and Sgt. Dixon became an anachronism long before he bade his last 'Evening, all'. Cashmore (1994: 156) has argued that this was the case even in the 1960s and that by the 1970s the series and by implication its portrayal of the police was irrelevant. Sparks (1993: 88) concurs that by the mid-1970s Dixon 'seemed to speak from another age'. Nevertheless the character of Dixon 'began to be used as a benchmark against which the behaviour of the police later in the century was to be measured' (Emsley 1996: 170).[8] Whether these icons were a true representation of the British police at that time is another question altogether.

This period has been the subject of research by Weinberger which suggests that if a golden age of police–public relations did exist then it was during the 'blitz spirit' of the (1939–45) Second World War (Weinberger 1995: 129–31). Scott has also recorded that during the blitz 'for the first time people who had looked on the police as their natural enemies found that the police were in fact their best friends' (Scott 1954: 22). Thereafter, in the post-war years the relationship became more problematic due to several factors. These included concern with rising crime (Weinberger 1995: 144); changes in attitude amongst the post-war recruits (ibid: 132); a number of highly publicised minor scandals (ibid: 197); and a better educated and less malleable public (ibid: 144). Together these constituted 'a new public consciousness that eventually altered for good the existing relations between the police and the public' (ibid: 197). The public were less respectful, especially young people, and the police no longer enjoyed the position of 'enforcing standards generally acceptable to the majority' (ibid: 197). This suggests one important pre-condition of police legitimacy (discussed in Chapter 3), that of shared values (Beetham 1991). Prior to Weinberger's research, Tobias argued that the police–public relationship was born out of the aforementioned Victorian social and political conditions and good relations will not necessarily perpetuate if these conditions no longer hold true (Tobias 1975: 104–5). Critchley also questioned the relevance of Peel's original principles following changes in society and the possible realignment of police and public values (Critchley 1973: 34–7). Weinberger's research confirms these points.

Certainly, by the turn of the 1960s cracks in the image were appearing. Whilst Reiner has argued that the 1960s were glowing years for the treatment of the police by the press (Reiner 2000a: 144–5), Chibnall believes that changes in the media towards 'newness, vitality and irreverence symbolised by youth began to undermine the acceptability of the established police image' (Chibnall 1977: 69). Reiner points to the success of the gangbusting Yard and the reflected glory for the police image as crime fighters. Chibnall points to the aura of glamour surrounding the Krays and the Great Train Robbers, eclipsing the police. Media changes, Chibnall believes, not only undermined the police image in the 1960s but changed it. The 1960s themes of popular journalism – 'speed, vigour, change, technology' – rubbed off on the media representations of policing, remoulding the image such that 'the dominant image of the honest, brave dependable (but plodding) "British Bobby" was recast as the tough, dashing, formidable (but still brave and honest) "Crime-Buster"' (Chibnall 1977: 71). As Chibnall remarks the image was 'less lovable, but better equipped' (ibid: 71). The developments Chibnall identified in the media during the 1960s are pertinent – a sign of things to come. As later chapters demonstrate, organisational and technological developments in the media during the 1980s and 1990s would impact on the police image and influence police forces in the ways they attempted to communicate and manage their image.

During the 1960s, media representations of policing increased in number and diversity.[9] American influences were prominent, a progression from the popularity of American detectives and investigators in the movies and novels. Commercial television stations had been introduced in Britain in 1955 and television became available to a mass audience from the mid-1950s. Between 1957 and 1960 the numbers of viewers with television sets capable of receiving both BBC and ITV tripled to almost 75 per cent of the population (Laing 1991) and the impact of this emerging medium was not lost on those concerned with managing the police image. It is notable that 1940s' and 1950s' books by Howgrave-Graham (1947: 186–7), Scott (1954: 92–3, 99) and Coatman (1959: 166) commend the restraint and even-handedness of the press. In contrast by 1973, commentators are theorising the damaging effects of television coverage of policing, both in factual coverage of public order events – 'the largest outside influence on the service is doubtless television' (Stansfield 1973: 90 providing a chief constable's view) – and fiction – 'does no one mind about the police "image" now built up, I suppose indestructibly, by carte-blanche television producers?' (Rolph 1973: 154). This is a further indication of the influence of the changing structure of the media on the way the police image has been, and is, communicated.

Whilst Chibnall emphasises the impact of media changes on the police image in the 1960s, other elements were also at play including changing social conditions, changing policing methods and a number of police scandals involving corruption and malpractice. Emsley (1992: 128) and Reiner (2000a: 59–61) note that the decline of the police image occurred towards the end of the 1950s and early 1960s as crime rates increased and the police became distant from the community as they moved from beat foot patrols to car patrols. This change to motorised patrols is widely felt to have distanced the police from the public (Coatman 1959: 153, Critchley 1973: 34, Bittner 1990: 6, Emsley 1992: 128, Weinberger 1995, Emsley 1996: 147, Reiner 2000a: 76). At the same time there were an increasing number of confrontations with middle-class sections of society at demonstrations with the potential for disorder, an indication of the changing constituency of protester seen later at Greenham Common, Newbury and Shoreham.[10] These situations with the potential for confrontation were increasingly taking place in a society which was becoming more questioning of policing and more generally of the powers of the state and its institutions, threatening an 'exhaustion of "consent"' (Hall *et al.* 1978: 218–19).

The combination of these factors resulted in a loss of public confidence in the police and by the late 1960s police relations with the media were worsening at a time when wider interest in policing was developing. Press reporters were looking beyond crime to report on changes in procedure and on technological change. In addition, academic interest in policing began to make an impact by placing policing studies in the public domain. Hitherto, books on policing had largely comprised historical studies (Reith 1938, 1948) or memoirs of retired senior officers and civilians (for example, Moylan 1934, Howgrave-Graham 1947, Scott 1954), but in 1964 the publication of Ben Whitaker's *The Police* and Michael Banton's *The Policeman in the Community* heralded a steady flow of sometimes critical studies of the police which were often sociologically rooted and which examined diverse aspects of policing. Whitaker felt there was 'a readiness in Britain today to take a fresh look at institutions which we have long taken for granted' (Whitaker 1964: 11).[11] Reiner credits Banton's book as 'the first study of policing by an academic social scientist in Britain and virtually the first in the world' (Reiner 1995a: 121). Works which became classics of the sociology of policing appeared in subsequent years from Skolnick (1966) and Bittner (1967) in the USA, and in the late 1960s and early 1970s from British researchers including Maureen Cain, Mike Chatterton, Simon Holdaway, Maurice Punch and Robert Reiner (Holdaway 1979, Reiner 1995a, Shapland and Hobbs 1989: 3–6).

At the same time that academics, the press and the public were coming to look at policing more critically, recent research suggests that in turn within the ranks of the chief officers there were stirrings of the politicisation of policing that became a prominent feature of the 1970s. Loader and Mulcahy's analysis of the forewords of force annual reports from 1945 onwards found that from the mid-1960s the commentary of chief constables shifts from the parochial to wider issues 'of "the state of the nation" and the advent of a more strident articulation of the police perspective' (Loader and Mulcahy 2001a: 46). In the next phase of image work (see below) these stirrings were forcibly articulated on a national stage by a number of chief constables (most notably Robert Mark and James Anderton) who chose to contribute their views regularly and directly through the media, unlike predecessors (for example, Byng and Scott) who rarely gave press interviews and instead sought to influence proprietors and editors behind the scenes. But at this time these police voices were essentially local and with the police increasingly under the spotlight at a national level, the existing image-making activities appeared anachronistic. The characteristics of this phase of image work – the establishment of rudimentary channels of communication with the media, backed up by the forays and haphazard innovations of individual chief officers – were no longer appropriate. Writing as early as 1947 Howgrave-Graham had remarked (emphasis added):

> ...it is perhaps curious that a service which depends for its success...on the understanding and support of the people should have been content to carry on for so many years *with no proper provision* in its organisation for maintaining contact with the world and ensuring that people understood in some measure what their police were trying to do for them and why. (Howgrave-Graham 1947: 178).

This was echoed in 1959 by Coatman who noted with surprise 'the importance of reasonable publicity is now appreciated by the police almost everywhere, but it is strange to note how recent a development this is, at any rate as a regular part of police work' (Coatman 1959: 167–8). In fact there had been only limited developments since Harold Scott's time and by the turn of the 1970s, as the police became beset by continuing crises (Reiner 2000a: 59–80), there was a need to implement *proper provision* for rebuilding the image. A more systematic approach to image work was required. Attempts were made to provide this under the Metropolitan Police Commissioner appointed in 1972.

Embedding public relations 1972–1987

The third phase of police image work dates from Robert Mark's appointment as Metropolitan Police Commissioner in April 1972 and is characterised by Mark's attempts to implement his blueprint for improved relations with the news media. Mark's initiative had far-reaching implications for the police image and its management.

On becoming Commissioner, Mark began to develop his 'character-istically personal style of press relations' (Chibnall 1979: 140). Some of the groundwork had been done with the appointment of Mr G.D. Gregory in 1967 as head of public relations at Scotland Yard – interestingly in the same year Robert Mark arrived at the Met. as assistant commissioner responsible for 'D' department which included the public relations department. Gregory had a public relations background and was brought in from industry after putting the 'Schhh' in Schweppes. He immediately set about 'a task of image reconstruction' (Chibnall 1977: 72), appointing a number of experienced journalists to the staff and sponsoring the investigations of a freelance journalist, Peter Laurie, who was given unbridled access to the Met. Laurie spent eight months at Scotland Yard and in 1970 published his findings in book form. Despite being sponsored by Gregory, the work of the Press Bureau receives only a few lines which inform that the Bureau provides news and enables articles and books to be written and films to made about the police and publishes a fortnightly newspaper, The Job (Laurie 1970: 21). The stature of the Press Bureau in 1970 is signalled by Laurie's use of a footnote to explain that it previously had a 'low position in the hierarchy and was not geared to positive explanation of the police problems and activities' until 'more recently' it had become a stand-alone department with a civilian head of equivalent rank to an assistant commissioner (Laurie 1970: 21).

By the time of Mark's appointment, it is apt to consider again William McAdoo's 1909 comment concerning the lack of press criticism of the police being a factor in maintaining a favourable image. Since this observation about police-press relations in 1909, as noted above, technological advances had changed the way both the police and the media worked and the press (and other media) had become influential and constant commentators on the police. At times the relationship had become severely strained. Whilst chief constable at Leicester between 1957 and 1967, Mark recognised the influence that the local papers, the Leicester Mercury and the Evening Mail wielded and he took steps to build cordial relationships with the editors, resulting in the papers' support for his initiatives. The Mercury later published extracts from Mark's lectures – 'a new dimension in police–press relations which thereafter continually improved on a basis of mutual trust and confidence' (Mark 1978: 67). On his subsequent move to the Met. and appointment as Commissioner, Mark made it a priority to use the media to better effect as part of his reforms to rebuild the police image, which had been damaged by allegations of police corruption and alleged links of senior officers to organised crime. The press, in particular *The Times*, had played a prominent role in bringing these issues into the public domain (Cox *et al.* 1977).

In a different media age Peel and the first Commissioners had faced the dilemma of establishing a force with a role to regulate social conflict, yet which could achieve legitimacy and they approached this through presentational and tactical measures. Mark sought to re-establish police legitimacy both through far-reaching reform of the CID, but also through a new press policy. In relation to the news media, Chibnall notes that 'control agencies' usually have three goals: 'i) to protect the public reputation and image of the control agency; ii) to directly facilitate the work of the control agency in controlling and apprehending deviants; and iii) to promote the particular aims, ideologies, and interests of members of the control agency' (Chibnall 1977: 173). Although success in all three areas will have implications for the police image, it is Mark's impact in the first and third areas which are of prime interest here.

Mark has stated his belief that 'acceptability of the police in a free society depended, amongst other factors, on our willingness to be an accountable and open administration. A free and open relationship with the Press was, in my view, the best way to demonstrate this' (Mark 1978: 135). Yet at the time of becoming Commissioner he describes the relationship between the press and the Met. as one of 'mutual distrust and dislike' (*ibid*: 123). Concluding that he needed the help of the press to increase public accountability (*ibid*: 133) he embarked upon the new press policy which, he later claimed, transformed police–press relations (*ibid*: 135). Mark described the policy as a 'radical revision of our relationship with the press...the principle "tell them only what you must"...reversed to..."withhold only what you must"' (Mark 1977: 50, 1978: 134). The new policy was laid down in an internal memorandum of 24 May 1973 which was circulated to the news media and also appeared as appendix 27 to that year's annual force report. The memorandum comprises 14 paragraphs which make the case for a new policy and outline its components. It notes that good press relations are important to encourage the support and cooperation of the general public, to provide full and fair information on police activities for those who infrequently encounter the police and to act as a means of accountability of the police as a public service. The memorandum goes on to outline the new guidelines for releasing information to the news media and for supplying information to the Press Bureau. It then outlines the new procedures for issuing 'press cards' to journalists and the facilities to be made available to card-holders. This memorandum is significant in that for the first time police officers, as a matter of policy, were being openly encouraged to disclose information to the media and in increasing numbers – the memorandum encouraged the involvement of officers of the rank of inspector and also officers of lower rank providing they had been given authorisation by a superior officer. The memorandum also encouraged special arrangements for liaison with the local press.

These guidelines for disclosing information appear commonsensical and uncontroversial, yet to a police force whose officers were traditionally suspicious of liaising with the media, they were challenging. In this respect it is notable that the content of this 1973 memorandum is similar to a number of media guidelines produced by police forces in the 1990s which encouraged 'openness' and devolved media liaison (discussed in Chapter 4). Proponents of a proactive media strategy within ACPO continue to preach the same message as the 1973 memo and the policies of some forces replicate it. For example, addressing the operational commanders' course at the Bramshill Police staff college in 1996, the chief constable of South Yorkshire Police (and the then chair of ACPO's Media Advisory Group) spoke of the need for a paradigm shift from withholding to disclosing as much information as possible. Later chapters examine how far these principles and practices have become embedded in contemporary police image work and consider their implications for legitimating police work.

Despite Mark's advocacy of the new policy on the grounds of transparency and accountability, it was not solely about the democratic ideals of free speech and participation. Just as the establishment of the Press Bureau had the motive of controlling the release of information in 1919, this latest policy also had its element of control. The new 'openness' was balanced by the strict control of 'Press Identification Cards'. Information facilities were only available to card-holders and the cards were issued at the discretion of the Met., thus ensuring that they controlled the flow of information (paragraphs 10 and 11 of the General Memorandum of 24 May 1973; see also Bunyan 1977: 91–2, Schlesinger and Tumber 1994: 111–12). Chibnall (1979: 143) emphasises that the new press relations policy was not 'a simple opening of the door to the news media with the invitation to look around. The policy was essentially active rather than passive and very much a means to clearly defined ends.' To Chibnall the main thrust of the policy was propagandist. Mark was clearly aware of the propaganda aspect of managing the media. In a post-retirement television programme, *Top Cop* (12 July 1977), he was interviewed by the BBC's Desmond Wilcox and admitted that it was sometimes necessary to mask intentions with words. He confirmed that his comments denying any connection between Met. corruption and pornography in the 1973 Dimbleby Lecture had been one such occasion (Chibnall 1979: 147, Reiner 1992a: 178).

In this respect, it should also be remembered that Mark coined the phrase 'win by appearing to lose'. He used the phrase in the *Top Cop* interview with Desmond Wilcox, saying 'the real art of policing a free society or democracy is to win by appearing to lose; or, at least, to win by not appearing to win' (*Sir Robert Mark on villainy, virtue and 'Vanessa's loonies'* in *The Listener* 4/8/77). Mark provided his own example of winning whilst appearing to lose, describing a key member of the Met.:

> We have a singularly attractive horse – she is the Brigitte Bardot of the 230 horses that we possess – and she is trained to simulate death on the word of command, in front of a television camera. This is the way to make sure that the police image which the British people like to have is maintained.

In this one phrase Mark identified a core police dilemma, that of having to maintain order in difficult and emotive public order situations whilst at the same time retaining the support of the public at large. Examining the history of policing public order generates a number of examples which illustrate his maxim in operation. One example of winning whilst appearing to lose was an image created during the 1977 Grunwick industrial dispute (which saw daily public order problems involving at its height over 2,000 pickets and 1,500 police officers). A photograph depicted an unarmed uniformed officer lying in the road bleeding from a head wound – PC Trevor Wilson had been struck by a flying milk bottle, allegedly thrown by a demonstrator. This image appeared both on the television news and the front pages of the following day's newspapers. It won sympathy for the police and has been credited as a turning point in the dispute, shocking official pickets and instrumental in the down-scaling of the daily disorder (Clutterbuck 1980: 213–15). The photograph was used for a subsequent Police Federation publicity campaign (Reiner 1992a: 177). The vulnerable image of the wounded officer had gained the sympathy not only of the public but also the parties involved in the dispute and facilitated the resolution of the public order problem. The police had won whilst appearing to lose.

In contrast during the 1984–85 Miners' Strike, at the disturbances around the Orgreave coking plant, by using heavy handed tactics – thousands of officers, horses, cavalry charges, against striking miners – the police arguably lost whilst appearing to win. Images of heavily protected police officers charging into miners were broadcast to the nation through the national news and did the police image no favours.

Winning whilst appearing to lose requires a delicate balance between maintaining order and sympathy – the police cannot afford to lose too badly as it will undermine their authority and influence perceptions of their effectiveness and competence. For example, at Broadwater Farm in 1985, although there was great sympathy for the family of the murdered PC Blakelock, there was also concern with police competence and management of the disorder (Gifford 1986, Graef 1989: 77–9). As these incidents suggest, Mark's cynical yet incisive maxim is particularly apt in relation to maintaining the image of the police during high-profile, widely-mediated incidents and the communication of the police role in these incidents became a central task of force press officers during the 1990s.

Mark retired as Commissioner in March 1977 and his legacy in terms of image work was to have laid down a template for police-media relations, which (the restrictive issuing of press cards apart) 'opens' the police service in that it advocates the free flow of information about the force through the media to the public. Secondly, it sets a framework for devolving media liaison to police officers of all ranks, rather than liaison being the preserve of the managerial ranking officers or of a headquarters department. Such a template, at its best can be used by a force to demonstrate transparency and to foster legitimacy.

Mark's new media policy and his own skill in managing the media saw greater cooperation and reduced levels of hostility in police-media relations during his tenure as Commissioner. However, Chibnall's research suggested that despite the efforts of Mark and the additional support given to the Press Bureau, it did not have the trust of either officers or reporters (Chibnall 1977: 147–9; see also Mark 1978: 134). Mark's successors as Commissioner, David McNee (1977–82) and Kenneth Newman (1982–87) were unable to consolidate the gains. Police–media relations became particularly strained during McNee's office. McNee later acknowledged that the police service needed to 'improve its performance in the sphere of public communications' commenting that he had eschewed television appearances but had made countless speeches and even granted several interviews (McNee 1983: 235). Newman re-emphasised the importance of good relations with the media and used the 'self-same rhetoric of "openness"' (Schlesinger and Tumber 1994: 112). In 1986 he introduced regular briefings with crime and home affairs correspondents which were to be continued by his successor (Schlesinger and Tumber 1992: 194).

Police–media relations deteriorated, then, not so much because Mark's successors were less skilled media spokesmen but rather as a symptom of the politicised state of policing (Reiner 2000a: 145). In this respect both McNee's and Newman's terms of office coincided with the years of the

Thatcher government and their attendant social and industrial unrest, including riots (Bristol 1980, Brixton, Toxteth, Moss Side and elsewhere in 1981, Handsworth, Brixton and Broadwater Farm in 1985), the 1984–85 Miners' Strike and disturbances at the News International plant at Wapping in 1986–87. The police were deployed in force at industrial disputes and utilised aggressive responses to disorder, raising fears of police alignment with the Thatcher government (Graef 1989: 46–84, Emsley 1996: 182, Reiner 2000a: 145–6). These fears had been precipitated by similar 'law and order' messages being communicated in the run-up to the 1979 general election by the Conservative Party and by increasingly high profile police officers (Reiner 2000a: 71–2). As E.P. Thompson observed 'wherever one looked in the media, Mr. James Anderton or some other over-mighty chief constable was holding forth' (Thompson 1980: x). The suspicions of politicisation were confirmed by the knowledge that following the election of the Conservative government they proceeded to set in motion cuts across the public sector including education and social services but excluding the police who, in contrast, were supported, receiving substantial pay rises as recommended by the Edmund-Davies committee (Committee of Inquiry into the Police, 1978; see also McLaughlin and Murji 1997: 86, Reiner 2000a: 72).

In addition to the politicisation of the police during this period, Waddington identifies two converging trends which damaged the image of the police. The first trend, the 'increasing, and increasingly public, use of firearms' transformed officers from 'Unarmed Bobby to Armed Cop' (Waddington 1991: 13–28). This trend saw mounting public concern about police competence following the shootings of innocent members of the public – first in 1980 an expectant mother in Birmingham, Gail Kishen, followed in 1983 by the shooting in London of Stephen Waldorf, a freelance television producer who resembled a wanted armed robber. These were followed in 1985 by the shooting of five-year-old John Shorthouse in Birmingham and a few weeks later of Mrs Cherry Groce in London. Both were mistakenly shot as armed police searched their family homes. These tragic shootings called into question the competence of the police during armed operations and added to the damaging charges of incompetence in crime investigation which arose from high profile murder investigations such as the case of the 'Yorkshire Ripper' (Home Office 1982, Bland 1984: 203–4).

The second trend, the 'progressive paramilitarization of policing civil disorder' transformed 'Bobbies on the Beat' to 'Riot Police' (Waddington 1991: 28–39). During the disorder at the 1976 Notting Hill Carnival police officers were seen defending themselves with dust-bin lids and milk-bottle crates – generating images of vulnerability. Five years later, after the 1981 Toxteth riots in Liverpool, the police took steps to 'improve their capability of dealing with serious public disorder' (*ibid*: 34). These included the provision of new equipment such as protective riot shields, crash helmets with visors and flame-proof overalls. Other steps included improved training, the establishment of dedicated public order units, and the authorisation of mainland police forces to acquire CS gas and plastic baton rounds (Northam 1988). No longer would the police appear vulnerable in public order situations. Waddington's analysis places the two trends converging in 1985 when the shooting of Cherry Groce was followed by riots in Brixton which claimed two lives and projected televised images of rioters clashing with police fully equipped in their specialist gear.

In the post 'Marksist' (Reiner 2000a: 71) years up to 1987 dissatisfaction with the police service and unease about the state of policing arose from a number of quarters. Crime statistics continued to rise and the issue of police corruption and malpractice refused to go away. The police relationship with ethnic minorities was consistently tense (Smith, Gray and Small 1983) despite the recommendations of the Scarman Report following the 1981 Brixton riots (Scarman 1981). A 'passionate and extensive' public debate raged over police accountability (McLaughlin 1994: 1) and there was concern over deaths in police custody. Police legitimacy was once more an issue, just as at the conclusion of the previous phase of image work. One strand of the police attempt to regain legitimacy and to rebuild the faltering image was to re-examine the existing image-making activities and to embark on innovations in image work.

Notes

1 I use the concept of image work in general terms in this initial chapter to mean the custodianship and communication of the characteristics and attributes of the police service. In later chapters more precise formulations are introduced.

2 The term is derived from a review in *The Times* (20/1/50) of the 1950 film *The Blue Lamp*. This stated that the central characters (one of them was PC George Dixon) were not 'policemen as they really are but policemen as an indulgent tradition has chosen to think they are' (cited in Emsley 1992: 114). This indulgent tradition has subsequently been perpetuated in the public imagination by television cops such as Inspector Morse (Sparks 1993).

3 *General Regulations, Instructions and Orders, for the Government and Guidance of the Metropolitan Police Force* (1851), London: W Clowes and Sons for HMSO. This document contains the original Regulations and Instructions (parts I and III) and also Orders (part II) issued from 1829 to 1851.

4 Prior to the establishment of Peel's police, earlier upholders of law and order indulged in promoting their reputation. The Fieldings, for example, in the 1750s spread news of their crime-fighting successes through pamphlets and their newspaper, *The Covent Garden Journal*, 'keeping their names before the public and the government' (Rawlings 1995: 140).

5 Two of the original detectives appointed to work from Scotland Yard in 1842 were used as models for Dickens' Inspector Buckett and Collins' Sergeant Cuff (Ascoli 1979: 119). Dickens introduced Inspector Bucket in *Bleak House* in 1853, making him the first police detective in English literary fiction, Sergeant Cuff appears in 1868 in *The Moonstone*.

6 One concern was increasing contact with the middle classes as the use of the motor vehicle developed. Fears that encounters between police officers and the newly motorised middle classes might harm relationships led to the Home Secretary writing to all chief constables in 1928 counselling them to urge their officers to treat such encounters cautiously, utilising the 'Bobby's unique qualities, his good humour and impartiality' (Emsley 1996: 147).

7 In *The Blue Lamp*, PC Dixon is first seen 'directing a Scotsman to Paddington railway station, then admonishing with humour a street urchin who has kidded a probationer that he is lost, before enforcing the law by firmly but fairly moving on a street trader. The epitome of the British Bobby – providing service to the public, guidance to inexperienced colleagues and enforcing the law of the land' (Berry *et al.* 1998: 213).

8 In confirmation of Emsley's point, in 1998 the then Home Secretary, Jack Straw, outlined his vision of police officers of the future and urged the adoption of a *Dixon of Dock Green* model 'the most reassuring policeman ever depicted on British television' (*Sunday Times* 8/2/98).

9 Robert Reiner, Sonia Livingstone and Jessica Allen recently analysed changing representations of crime and criminal justice in films and newspapers (1945–91) and television (1955–91). Their research found an 'increasing prevalence of professional police heroes, especially after the late 1960s' (Allen *et al.* 1998: 67). The representation of the police became less positive over the whole period, but remained mostly positive. The police tend to be represented most positively from 1945–63; from 1964–79 the image is more negative, from which there is some recovery in the final period 1980–91 (Allen *et al.* 1998, Reiner *et al.* 1998, Reiner 2000b: 60).

10 Critchley has commented that 'before protest marches began to involve all sections of society...[the police] rarely dealt with and, hence rarely offended, members of the middle and upper classes, and it is they who tend to mould public opinion' (Critchley 1973: 37).

11 Whitaker lamented the failure of police forces to use press and public relations to improve communication with the general public (1964: 159–64). Shortly after the publication of Whitaker's book, the Met. appointed (in June 1965) press liaison officers in each of its (then four) districts with the task of disseminating information to the news media and by the late 1960s the Scotland Yard Press Bureau had over 20 staff (Berkley 1969: 164, 167).

Chapter 2

The professionalisation of police image work since 1987

Your police are making a difference, by doing things differently.
(ACPO Policing Factsheet No. 4. 1996)

In the late 1980s there was a discernible shift in police image work. The period from 1987 onwards is characterised by the application of language and techniques more often associated with the business and commercial world than with policing. The phase begins with the appointment of Peter Imbert as Metropolitan Police Commissioner (1987–93). Imbert was instrumental in the introduction of such practices, notably the dropping of the name 'force' in favour of 'service' and the appointment of the corporate identity[1] consultants, Wolff Olins. Prior to introducing the distinctive features of image work that emerged during this period, this chapter examines the political and social context of British policing in the 1980s and 1990s and recent media developments. These conditions compelled the police service to address matters of image and communication in a more proactive manner than hitherto.

The managerialist context

In 1979 a Conservative government was elected under the leadership of Margaret Thatcher and immediately set about challenging 'much of the received wisdom of the post-war consensus' (Brown and Sparks 1989: x). With a commitment to rolling back the state, an ideological belief in the rule of the market and convinced of the superiority of private sector management principles and practices, the Thatcher government vigorously embarked upon a programme of reforming the public sector (Brown and Sparks 1989, Clarke *et al.* 1994). Convinced that the public services were poorly managed, unaccountable and under-performing bureaucracies which placed an unjustified burden on government expenditure, Thatcher and her colleagues considered that nothing less than fundamental reform would do. The general thrust and direction they adopted has been identified as 'managerialist' or 'new manage-rialist' (Pollitt 1993, Clarke *et al.* 1994, McLaughlin and Muncie 1994, Loader 1996: 14–22, McLaughlin and Murji 1997: 82). Within this approach McLaughlin and Murji have identified 11 characteristics of a 'new public sector management model' which 'force public institutions to reconceptualize the financing and delivery of their services in ways which in turn trigger and drive further transformations' (*ibid*: 84). The 11 characteristics are:

1. The appointment of professional managers held accountable for specific tasks, resources and results.
2. Business-like operations management.
3. The setting of clear measurable standards and targets.
4. Explicit costing of activities.
5. Development of performance indicators and league tables.
6. Emphasis on outputs and results rather than processes.
7. Rationalisation of purpose and scope of the organisation and the shedding of peripheral activities.
8. Competitive environments – service contracts, client-contractor relationships, customer service.
9. Reconfiguration of recipients and beneficiaries of public services as customers and consumers.
10. Overhauling the working culture of organisations to improve productivity.
11. Fragmentation – the monolithic state bureaucracy is replaced by local, flexible organisational configurations.

(Summarised from McLaughlin and Murji 1997: 84–5).

Leishman *et al.* place the radical reform of the public sector within the 'rise of new public management' and identify five key elements: belief in the private rather than the public sector; commitment to the benefits of competition; control of policy-making from the centre combined with local control of service delivery; and fragmentation of service provision (Leishman, Cope and Starie 1996: 11).

In the run-up to the 1979 general election 'law and order' became a heated issue. This highlighted and crystallised a trend from the mid-1960s which witnessed law and order becoming a party political issue (Downes and Morgan 1997: 87, 98). The previously 'bipartisan consensus' in relation to the police, which had been evident in the post-war reconstruction years, began to fall away (Newburn 1995: 54). During the 1970s there had been increasing numbers of public disagreements between members of the Labour Party and senior police officers and at the same time the Conservative Party projected itself as the party of 'law and order'. The Conservatives' 1979 election manifesto had promised 'the next Conservative government will spend more on fighting crime even while we economise elsewhere' (Conservative Party 1979) and for most of the next decade it appeared that the police service would be spared the most painful reform processes and managerialist 'solutions' that were imposed on other parts of the public sector (Clarke *et al.* 1994). Indeed the new government immediately confirmed its 'law and order' credentials by implementing fully the Edmund-Davies pay recommendations (thereby linking police pay to average rather than basic earnings), and throughout the 1980s, in contrast to other public sector organisations, funding to the police increased. At the same time that pay and equipment improved, the police were used regularly and in force to counter disorder at industrial disputes. Any criticisms of 'over-robust' policing tactics were defended by the government and it appeared that the police were being favoured by the government as they were needed to contain dissatisfied workers and the populations of inner-cities (Davies 1992: 28, McLaughlin and Murji 1997: 87).

Although the police may have been privileged, they were not exempt (Brake and Hale 1989: 147–8, Emsley 1996: 182, McLaughlin and Murji 1997: 87–9, 2001: 110–13). They were subjected to greater scrutiny and attempts were made to encourage them to be more efficient and financially accountable. In 1982 the 'Financial Management Initiative' (FMI hereafter) was introduced across government departments targeting financial and resource efficiency through objective setting, performance measurement and performance indicators. The Home Office was included within the FMI, which impacted upon the police through such instruments as Home Office circulars, Her Majesty's Inspectorate of Constabulary (HMIC hereafter) and the Audit Commission.

Two Home Office circulars are worthy of comment in relation to police image work. First, circular 114/83, *Manpower, Effectiveness and Efficiency in the Police Service* encouraged the recruitment of civilians in favour of officers for reasons of cost – 'the Home Secretary will not normally be prepared to approve increases in establishment if police officers are occupying posts which could properly, and more economically, be filled by civilians' (Home Office 1983). This facilitated the recruitment of professional communicators to resource press and public relations offices. Secondly, circular 105/88, *Civilian Staff in the Police Service,* invited chief officers to review the scope for further civilianisation and included a check-list of favoured areas. The check-list included 'Press office and other public relations duties' (Home Office 1988).

Home Office circular 114/83 signalled a more important role for HMIC. Authorised by the 1964 Police Act to inspect and report to the Home Secretary on the efficiency and effectiveness of police forces, during the 1980s HMIC was utilised as a tool for the encouragement of the government's FMI (Weatheritt 1993: 26, 29–32, McLaughlin and Murji 1997: 91–2, Oliver 1997: 71–84). The appointment of ACPO 'high-flyers' and the publication of its reports from 1990 enhanced its status (Reiner 2000a: 191–2). In 1993, the appointment of two lay inspectors, including a successful business executive, gave weight to the argument that HMIC was another expression of the managerialist intent of the Conservative government (Benke *et al.* 1997: 81–2).

Whilst the work of HMIC involves scrutiny by peers in the form (mostly) of ex-senior police officers, since 1988 the police have also been scrutinised by 'professional outsiders' in the form of the Audit Commission (Weatheritt 1993: 33). Blatantly managerialist in its purpose, the Audit Commission first turned its attention to the police in 1988 and early reports scrutinised the financing of police funding and budget allocation (for example, Audit Commission 1988). However, later reports focused on operational matters, including such sacred cows of the police service as crime management (Audit Commission 1993) and patrol work (Audit Commission 1996).

Policing also came under scrutiny from other sources. A number of reports from the Home Office's Police Research and Planning Unit (Clarke and Mayhew 1980, Morris and Heal 1981) brought into question the value of pouring more money into the police service as a means of countering crime, as the research evidence indicated that crime fighting work took up a relatively small proportion of police time (Brake and Hale 1989: 147–8, McLaughlin and Murji 1997: 88). Other reports suggested that the police were losing the support of sections of the community (Scarman 1981, Smith *et al.* 1983), and the British Crime Survey, introduced in 1982, indicated that actual crime levels were higher than the official crime statistics which were themselves increasing year on year.

This scrutinised yet protected status which the police service had enjoyed since 1979 was to change leading eventually to a discernible shift and the realignment of relationships between the police service and the political parties during the 1990s. From the early 1980s, as the Home Office circulars illustrate, the police were being encouraged to improve their management and allocation of resources, but they were supported by the government who had been elected on a law and order ticket and who were prepared to make funds available to the police in the fight against crime. However, the politicians' expectations were high (it transpired, also, that the implications for the police image were great) and despite the police playing their part in successfully, from the government's viewpoint, enforcing the law during difficult and politicised industrial disputes, the disturbing reports of the loss of public support for the police and the mounting evidence of police failure to reduce crime embarrassed the government who had pledged police resources for this purpose.

If the government restricted police reform to pruning in the 1980s, by the turn of the decade it was apparent that it was preparing for root and branch overhaul. The response of the police service was to include attempts to rebuild their image, through such activities as a series of quality of service initiatives and by improving communications through media and public relations management.

Rumblings of government dissatisfaction with the police, in relation to their management, their all round performance and particularly crime figures, were being expressed at cabinet level by 1990. The government concluded that significant additional resourcing of the police had failed to control crime and the service was not providing value for money. This view was reflected in the mood of the country – the police reputation was at a low ebb. This resulted from a build up of critical activities during the 1980s. As the police clashed with trade unionists, inner city youth and ethnic minorities, their image became more oppressive as they donned paramilitary equipment. Corruption remained an issue, as did police misbehaviour in a series of now infamous miscarriages of justice (Guildford Four released 1989, Birmingham Six released 1991) and the wholesale dismantling of the West Midlands Serious Crime Squad (1989). On top of this recorded crime continued to rise (by 111 per cent between 1981 and 1993). Whilst policing was certainly controversial during the 1980s, there was a consensus held together by the Conservative government and those sections of the public normally sympathetic towards the police (generally referred to, at least by journalists, as 'middle England') that policing should be supported. By the turn of the 1990s, this consensus was eroding and the new challenge was to the structure and functions of policing – what public policing should comprise, who should do it and under what terms of contract, its accountability, its management and its alignment with business practices. In short the battle for policing came off the streets and emerged instead in the politics of police reform. As Reiner wryly points out there was good news in that there was again consensus on policing, the bad news was that 'the new consensus view [was] that the police were failing badly on almost every front, and in need of drastic reform' (Reiner 2000a: 11).

In this climate the government launched a number of inquiries and an associated legislative programme committed to fundamental reform of the police service. The first example of the sea change was Home Secretary Kenneth Clarke's announcement in May 1993 of an inquiry to examine the rank structure, remuneration framework and the terms and conditions of service of police officers. Sir Patrick Sheehy's Inquiry into Police Responsibilities and Rewards was a clear manifestation of managerialism, tackling perceived internal management deficiencies, and recommending a flatter rank structure, fixed-term appointments, performance-related pay and the abolition of allowances and perks (Sheehy 1993). The language and practices of the private sector and the market were being applied to produce an organisation driven by cost and efficiency indicators rather than by need and service. The Sheehy report indicated according to a *Guardian* leader that policing was 'in an anarchic mess: too many tiers, too little management, too ready to leave the incompetent in place, and too reliant on ancient and absurd perks' (*Guardian* 6/10/94).

Hot on the heels of Sheehy was the 1993 Posen Inquiry – The Home Office Review of Police Core and Ancillary Tasks – which aimed to make recommendations about the most cost-effective ways of delivering core police tasks and to assess the scope for relinquishing ancillary tasks. In its quest for efficiency and effectiveness of fulfilling tasks the inquiry was firmly in the spirit of the managerialist drive. The establishment of this inquiry fuelled much speculation about the potential privatisation of traditional police functions and raised fears (particularly within the police staff associations) that it would result in the removal of the service functions and restrict the police to catching criminals and enforcing the law. This issue has obvious implications for the police image as its effect could be to leave the police only with confrontational tasks projecting negative images. During its inquiry period Posen was vilified as strongly as Sheehy by policing pressure groups but the great threat materialised as a damp squib when the committee reported (late) in June 1995, concluding that no major police functions should be hived off to the private sector or local authority control (Posen 1995). The threat of both the Sheehy and Posen inquiries was perceived to be so great that it succeeded in uniting previously disparate policing voices in coordinated campaigns to denigrate both inquiries. The influence of the growing organisation of the police 'voices' should not be underestimated and is discussed below.

In addition to these inquiries, the government redefined the tripartite structure of police governance in a managerialist style through the 1994 Police and Magistrates' Courts Act (hereafter PMCA). Under the PMCA the Home Secretary determined key national policing objectives (which were superceded by 'Ministerial Priorities' in 1998),[2] directs police authorities to establish performance targets, determines the cash grant to police authorities and issues codes of practice to local police authorities. Local police authorities were established as precepting bodies responsible for budget and resource allocation. They are responsible for the appointment of chief constables and the negotiation of fixed-term contracts and performance-related pay of senior officers. Chief constables in conjunction with the local police authorities are responsible for producing annually a costed policing plan determining local policing priorities following consultation with their local communities. Chief constables retained responsibility for direction and control of their force and also gained greater day-to-day financial control and responsibility for civilian staff. In sum the PMCA comes 'as near as has been possible to date to establishing a framework for more "business-like" police forces, with clear measures of inputs and outputs' (McLaughlin and Murji 1997: 98).[3]

One strand of the new public sector management model identified by McLaughlin and Murji involves the 'reconfiguration of recipients and beneficiaries of public services as customers and consumers' (1997: 85). This 'consumerism' is identified by Loader (1996: 15) as coming to the fore under John Major's Conservative administration after the 'overthrow' of Margaret Thatcher in 1990, signalling a subtle shift in the application of managerialism to the public sector. Major launched the Citizen's Charter in 1991 confirming that the police would fall within its scope, thus making it incumbent upon the police to consider standards of quality of service and customer responsiveness (Weatheritt 1993: 39–41, Loader 1996: 17, McLaughlin and Murji 1997: 97). Consumerism is evident in the publication of performance indicators and response times, in the improved reception areas of police buildings as well as in the public consultation exercises and satisfaction surveys undertaken by police forces.

The flaws of accepting the police–public relationship as one of supplier–consumer have been well-documented, not least in relation to the consumer's (in)ability to choose a public policing provider or whether to accept or reject some aspects of the policing product – 'considerable violence has to be done to the meaning of the word "consumer" for it to fit the realities of police work' (Loader 1996: 20; see also Heward 1994: 249–50). Unsurprisingly this language and imagery of consumerism does not always sit easily throughout the police service and at the 1996 Police Federation conference it was denounced by the chair of the constables' central committee as 'commodity policing' based on 'point of sale law and order' (*Police Review* 17/5/96). The commodification of policing relates to the situation where policing is seen as a commodity that is not the prime reserve of the public police but is something that can be modularised and undertaken by others if it can be done lawfully, efficiently and effectively. This commodification strand of managerialism can be seen in the debate over core police tasks and the possible privatisation of traditional police activities such as the patrol function (Audit Commission 1996, Cassels 1996). It is also a reflection on contemporary society which has an apparently insatiable demand for policing services and a not inconsiderable 'fear of crime' (Loader 1997b).

The managerialist framework with its strands of consumerism and commodification has implications for the role of the police and consequently for the police image. Running through the Conservative government's 1990s police reform programme was the issue of the role of the police, something that has direct implications for images of policing. The traditional debate has been over whether the police are primarily a police 'force' or a police 'service' (Punch 1979a, Reiner 2000a: 109–15; see also Waddington 1999a: 4–20), a debate focusing on functions that project contrasting images and have implications for legitimacy. As Chapter 1 has argued, during the early years of the modern police, the service role was emphasised for the purposes of securing policing by consent and to achieve legitimacy (Reiner 2000a: Ch. 2). The service or force dilemma faced Peel as it faced later policing policy makers and Reiner notes that Peel, Mayne and latterly Scarman reinforced the 'preservation of public tranquillity' as the fundamental goal, above law enforcement (Reiner 1994b: 153). Equally Skolnick (1966), Bittner (1980), and Ericson (1982) have shown that the police play a key role in order maintenance, preserving the status quo, and the key element of this is their power to use legal force. The debate recurs. For example, the 1994 Stephens and Becker book *Police Force, Police Service* takes its title from this debate. The central theme of this edited work is the police as carers or controllers – in the editors' views both can be paths to legitimacy, though they suggest that the then Conservative government's preference, the internal culture and the popular (mediated) image is of controllers. The debate is obviously simplistic in that providing service to one sector of the community often involves executing force against another sector of the community. Equally some police functions, for example, public order policing, include force as part of the service. The police must combine both roles and it is the balance between the two which is really at issue.

The impact of media developments

High visibility policing

The managerialist climate of the 1980s which developed into full-scale police reform in the early 1990s impacted on police image work, but this managerialist trend converged with influential developments in the communications media which increased police visibility and compelled the police to manage this visibility.

Policing now operates in a society which has become highly mediated (Ericson 1994, Poster 1995, Thompson 1995, Ericson and Haggerty 1997). This raises issues of what Thompson calls the 'management of visibility' (Thompson 1995: 74, 134–40). Thompson argues that the development of communications media was an integral part of the rise of modern societies (*ibid*: 3) and he identifies three major trends in the development of the media industries since the nineteenth century. These are: transformation of media institutions into large scale commercial concerns; the globalisation of communication; and the development of electronically mediated forms of communication (*ibid*: 82–5). These developments have led to the situation which has increased the capacity of individuals to experience phenomena which they are unlikely ever to encounter (*ibid*: 208–9). In this situation it is easier than ever before to acquire information about organisations such as the police.

Mathiesen (1997) similarly recognises that it is now easier than hitherto to know about organisations in his discussion of the panopticon (the few watch the many) and synopticon (the many watch the few).[4] He acknowledges the influence and role of the mass media and argues that although Foucault made an important contribution towards our under-standing of modern surveillance systems in his discussions of Bentham's panopticon, he neglected the influence of the opposite process by which the mass media, particularly television, enable the many to see the few. He asserts that it is in fact the synopticon principle rather than the panopticon that fulfils Foucault's vision of surveillance and its role in controlling society. Mathiesen's position has great relevance to the police service in that it is amongst the most watched institutions in our contemporary society. Public policing is the subject of fictional and documentary-based television programmes, is guaranteed media coverage if it fails to perform and occupies a high visibility position in news programmes featuring stories which might have policing as its subject or the police as participants/observers/mediators in stories where they are not the main subject, for example, in coverage of public order events.

Across the media, newspapers, radio and television all have a consistent interest in the police, both for the purposes of news reporting and also for features and series.[5] There are several reasons for this. At a mundane level, the police are a regular and readily available source of information for news gatherers. In addition police stories and in particular police television programmes are popular with audiences, attracting high viewing figures. A further factor is that police programmes can be made comparatively cheaply, for example, the extremely popular *Police, Camera, Action* series consists of police-supplied video footage of car chases. These are introduced by a well-known newsreader, who stresses road safety messages as he prefaces the video clips. This results in economic programme making and a pro-police series which is popular with viewers.

In this context of high visibility there are clearly implications for the police image and its management. Media treatment of the police has always played a role in mystifying the police (Allen *et al.* 1998, Reiner 2000a: 138–162) and in fostering favourable imagery which along with the motivation of police history and tradition has bestowed a symbolic status upon the police service (Emsley 1992, Manning 1997). One aspect of this is illustrated by the central position which policing occupies in popular culture. Particularly through media representations of policing, 'the police remain one of the principal means by which English society tells stories about itself' (Loader 1997a: 2).

The media developments since the mid-1980s which have compelled the police to re-assess the way they communicate through the media are both organisational and technological. Organisational changes in the media industry have led to an explosion of media outlets, particularly news based, which places greater demands on media personnel to find more stories. During the ten years from 1989 to 1999 there was an 800 per cent increase in the supply of television news alone. This in turn places more demand upon the police, as an established source, to supply copy to meet the increased need. One example is the growth in weekend news-reporting; previously television outlets only gathered news from Monday to Friday and radio stations and newspapers were also far less active in their weekend news-gathering. In more recent times the growth of the number of outlets in the traditional terrestrial arena has been supplemented with the growth of cable and satellite television. These developments are not restricted to television; the growth in the number of commercial radio stations also increased the number of news gatherers and the demand for stories. Consequently the number of 'customers' for police news has expanded. This demand has also increased through changes in news distribution formats including 24 hours rolling news. The changes in media capacity and in demand place additional pressure on police forces to provide a flexible service to the media.

Technological advances in the media have also had an impact. The use of lightweight cameras (and camcorders used by amateurs) has increased the level of scrutiny to which the police are subjected. This has impacted on the potential accountability of the police, for example, through the use of hand-held camcorders by protesters during the policing of environmental issues and a number of companies now specialise in training protesters in film-making techniques (Harding 1997). There have been examples of such 'amateur' footage being used on national news, the most obvious example being the beating of Rodney King by officers of the LAPD in 1991 (Thompson 1995: 247–9, Manning 1996, Barak 1997). The police have also used lightweight cameras for their own purposes, for example as surveillance tools during the policing of public order. These different uses to which the lightweight technology is put vividly demonstrate the balance and tension between panoptic and synoptic power to which Mathiesen alludes. These same technological advances also present opportunities to the police to communicate to their advantage, for example, film crews accompanying 'live' dawn raids to publicise proactive policing and the instantaneous coverage of police patrol activities on live Saturday night television specials (*Police Action Live*, ITV network 18/11/95). Arrangements for such filming are formally negotiated and bound by regulations set out by the police, including the signing of contracts and indemnity forms.[6]

These media developments therefore provide for high visibility policing and both subject the police to scrutiny but also present more opportunities for the police to communicate messages and promote their public image. The importance of the media both as a threat and opportunity to the police is underlined by research which suggests that up to two-thirds of people find out about the police through the media rather than personal contact (Skogan 1990: 18–19, 1994: 13–14). If this is true, then communication through the media is a critical issue for the police service.

The mediation of public order policing

One area in which the visibility of the police has increased is public order policing which attracts considerable media attention, particularly when disorder occurs. As noted in Chapter 1, Waddington had cited the 'progressive paramilitarization of policing civil disorder' as a damaging influence on the police image (1991: 28–39). Public order policing is connected with maintaining the status quo and the police image of neutrality can be threatened as was the case during the 1984–85 Miners' Strike (Green 1990: 79). Fielding (1991: 30) has observed that public order has been at the heart of the sustained controversy over police powers and actions in a way that crime control seldom has. Waddington (2000: 156–9) has noted that in role terms public order policing is more morally ambiguous than crime fighting as criminals are outside and preying on the moral community whereas rioters (civil rights protesters, pickets, strikers, political protesters) are the moral equals of other citizens (including the police). The police and government can pursue a 'war against crime' but there is a legitimacy issue, not to mention an image problem, in engaging in battle with protesting fellow citizens. The issue of public order policing has become a central part of managing the police image. This has less to do with the number of events or the incidence of violence, than with the issues at stake and the 'protester profile'. The protesters are no longer only the 'other' who could be explained away as roving hippies, disaffected youth or inner city trouble-makers, but are just as likely to be local middle-class families demonstrating against road or runway building, the use of the motor vehicle or the export of live animals. Such groups constitute 'challengers' or 'disarmers' who can 'weaken or neutralise police work' (Holdaway 1983: 77).

The police image can be damaged by the saturated media coverage which attends public order events and protests with moral and environmental dimensions have raised problems for police image work. One example involved the export of live animals from ports in Essex, Kent and Sussex during 1995. The export operation united a cross section of local residents (and outsiders) to stage protests which included in Brightlingsea groups of old age pensioners and Brownies sitting in roads blocking the passage of the animal transporters. Whilst the police had a duty to keep the roads open they did not wish to alienate local relationships and damage their image by becoming involved in clashes with middle-class protesters in the full glare of the nation's media. To manage their image through these operations, Essex (Operation Gunfleet) and Sussex (Operation Ferndown) operational police officers worked closely with their media officers to devise media strategies. These aimed to maintain the support of the local residents and to avoid negative images of policing in the media. Waddington has praised the ability of the British police to communicate and cooperate with protesters (1994: Ch. 4), but despite their efforts, the police did receive criticism as articulate middle-class professionals from whom the police would normally hope to attract support, experienced the realities of front-line protesting and subsequently relayed their disillusionment with the attitude and behaviour of the police to observing media representatives. As the animal export protests illustrate, in public order situations the police image always has the potential to be controversial. This dilemma is explored empirically in later chapters.

Equipping the police for public order operations has obvious image implications. Waddington acknowledges that the riot gear 'symbolise[s] a relationship between police and public that is the antithesis of the "Dixon of Dock Green" Myth' (Waddington 2000: 171). The debate over police equipment was present in the 1980s when the police requested suitable equipment to deal with the mainland riots, and remains current. Protracted debates have been instigated in recent years by moves to routinely equip the police with self defence sprays and long-handled batons. In the course of these debates, the traditional image of the unarmed, helmeted police officer remains a touchstone. One example of this was the attention given to the 1996 debate on whether the traditional helmet should be replaced by a more functional one. This question was discussed in national newspapers and on national television. In addition, the Police Federation commissioned a national survey of forces and the public on whether the helmet should stay and its uniform project group debated the helmet against terms of reference which included image. At the 1996 Police Federation conference the chair of the constables' central committee stated that 'the British police uniform is a brand every bit as strong as the logo of your favourite cola or burger' (*Police Review* 17/5/96). The symbolic importance of appearances should not be underestimated. Wright illustrates the influence of equipment on image and legitimacy with a Panamanian example. In post-Norriega Panama the new constitution established a civilian police to replace the old *Policia Militar*, the National Police of Panama, a military force with a reputation for institutional corruption. However, the new regime's police officers found it difficult to win the confidence of the people and achieve any legitimacy whilst wearing the uniform and using the equipment of the old national police. A change of image involving the replacement of the old uniforms with ex-Californian highway patrol uniforms had an immediate effect on the way the police were received and perceived by Panamanians. The presentation of the police 'had a vital and symbolic significance for public opinion and confidence' (Wright 1996: 8).

These examples from Britain and Panama illustrate the importance of presentation and image to the public police as a legitimation factor. In the context of the media developments discussed, where the visibility of public institutions is amplified, the arguments in favour of implementing organised and specialised means of managing image become compelling.

The police reaction

In the preceding sections I have examined the political conditions of the 1980s and 1990s and the managerialist policies which were increasingly brought to bear on the police service. These policies with the potential for the commodification of policing had implications for the role and image of the police. At the same time developments in the media industry exerted additional pressure on the police to consider how they communicated and projected their public image. These combined pressures contributed to a shift in police image work which can be dated from 1987.

At one level it might appear odd that the police service felt compelled to embrace image work more seriously than hitherto from the late 1980s as in some ways policing had less obvious problems than during the 1970s and early/middle 1980s. The inner cities were relatively quiet, government legislation had nullified the threat of industrial unrest and as the 1990s progressed, even recorded crime was to go down. Policing, it appeared, had entered a 'post-critical' period (Reiner 2000b: 62). Yet despite the absence of protracted industrial strife and serial urban rioting, the police image was still under threat. On one front the police still had to deal with difficult public order situations including the 1990 poll tax riots and stand-offs with 'eco warriors' including potential confrontations with middle Englanders. On another front the police had to deal with crises of the police institution arising from misconduct and incompetence including miscarriages of justice, the 1989 Hillsborough disaster and its aftermath, and also allegations of deep-seated sexism and racism. On top of these difficulties the police faced criticism relating to communities' fear of crime and an apparently insatiable demand for policing services. These are reasons enough to build a case for the police to address image work. Yet, with the addition of managerialist policies and media developments, the context of policing was less heated but different in that fundamental questions were being asked of the police service. These questions related not only to performance and efficiency, but also challenged the role and responsibilities of the public police as police conduct was increasingly visible and scrutinised under mass-mediated conditions. Within this context the police were to address image work as a defence to the reform programme, to engage with media developments and also as a genuine reaction by concerned police leaders to the state of the police institution and the police–public relationship – an attempt to maintain legitimacy. In the following sections I examine the police response to the detailed pressures and chart the shifts which characterise the fourth phase of police image work.

Imbert, Wolff Olins and PLUS

The fourth phase of police image work dates from the appointment of Peter Imbert as Metropolitan Police Commissioner in 1987. Imbert came to the Met. with a reputation for supporting organisational openness whilst chief constable of Thames Valley Police (1979–85). In particular, Imbert had allowed the film maker Roger Graef into the force in 1982 to produce a 'fly on the wall' style documentary. This series, simply entitled *Police*, remains the seminal police documentary. In respect of policing images, one programme featured the treatment of a rape victim, in which the police officers came across as insensitive and bullying. The resulting outcry was instrumental in the move towards changes in procedures for rape complaints (Blair 1985). Commentators subsequently suggested that Imbert's decision 'to allow that series of television documentaries to be made was probably more important in making police governance democratic than the whole apparatus established by the 1964 [Police] Act' (Jones *et al.* 1994: 311). The impact of this one programme lingered despite the scene not being broadcast again due to police sensitivity until September 1999 as part of Channel 4's *Coppers* series.[7] Imbert's apparently open attitude towards the media coupled with a 'populist personal style and a career rooted in the toughest aspects of operational policing' (Reiner 1992a: 264), augured well for relations with both the media and the work force.

Once at the Met., Imbert continued the 'openness' espoused by Mark and followed by McNee and Newman – addressing the 1989 International Police Exhibition and Conference he stated 'openness must be central to the policing of a democratic and pluralist society' (Schlesinger and Tumber 1994: 113). In contrast to his predecessors, however, he followed the example of commercial organisations and contracted specialists in communication and corporate identity to advise on image improvement. In addition to using the services of Saatchi and Saatchi for expensive advertising campaigns, Imbert took image work into a new phase in 1988 by commissioning the corporate identity consultants Wolff Olins to undertake an audit of internal and external attitudes towards the Met. At a cost of £150,000 this, more than anything else, heralded the professionalisation of police image work. The Met. requested Wolff Olins to 'look at the Met.'s current identity, to assess what people inside and outside the Force think works and what doesn't. And then to suggest areas in which improvements might be made' (Wolff Olins 1988: 4). Schlesinger and Tumber (1994: 108) comment that the Met. hoped that hiring Wolff Olins would lead to measures to boost support for the force, but this does not acknowledge the substantive as opposed to the visual content of the consultants' audit and recommendations.

The consultants' report, *A Force for Change*, was presented to the Met.'s Policy Committee in August 1988. It stated that the prime concern of the study was 'with identity, with what the organisation stands for, how it does things and how it is perceived' (Wolff Olins 1988: 3). Drawing on over 250 formal interviews and an audit of literature, police buildings, vehicles, uniforms and equipment, a series of issues was highlighted, two of which were 'communication' and 'presentation'. Notably the report highlighted the importance of not just external, but also internal, aspects of communication and presentation. In these areas the report concluded that the Met. needed to 'improve its communication techniques both internally and to the world outside' and to 'improve its appearance in terms of buildings, uniforms, equipment and associated matters' (*ibid:* 15). It suggested changes that would improve not only the public perception of the police, but also the self image of employees, for example one recommendation was to improve the appearance of police stations both on the front desk and behind the scenes. Other issues highlighted were 'purpose', 'organisation', 'management', and 'attitudes'. The report concluded that for the force to be effective in its 'difficult and complex job' culture change was necessary and that the force must clarify its purpose, improve its management systems and embrace the service concept.

The effects of the Wolff Olins report were far reaching. It resulted in the development of the PLUS programme which included the establishment of a marketing group responsible for looking at communications, both directly with the public and through the media (Schlesinger and Tumber 1994: 108–10). It also included the development of the *Statement of Common Purpose and Values* which was seen as integral to developing a common sense of purpose. PLUS emphasised the core business of the 'service', improved leadership and the importance of quality of service – and it attempted to win the hearts and minds of the work force through a series of seminars to all 44,000 staff members at a cost of £5.5 million (Fleming 1994: 448). Having changed the name of the Metropolitan Police *Force* to the Metropolitan Police *Service*, in the force annual report for 1989 Imbert confirmed the common purpose of the Met. was 'about changing the emphasis from a "Force" to a "Service" ethos'.

At the time of commissioning Wolff Olins, the Met. was concerned about its public image, its relations with the government, the media and sections of the public and the resulting measures were aimed at addressing the perceived poor image of the Met. and realigning the organisation with the needs of its public. Undoubtedly, components of PLUS were a serious and determined attempt to effect cultural change and to encourage 'openness', rather than superficial tinkering with visual considerations (Heward 1994: 248), yet it is significant that the 'public' were now seen as, and talked about in the language of, 'consumers, as the customers, and paymasters of policing' (Schlesinger and Tumber 1994: 109). In this respect the appointment of Wolff Olins and the implementation of the PLUS programme need to be seen in the context of the pressure of government policy on the public services. McLaughlin and Muncie regard the implementation of the PLUS programme as 'classic "new managerialist" philosophy' (1994: 131), making the connection between the Met.'s concern with its image and its reaction to the 1980–90s political context described above in which the police were subject to greater scrutiny and greater expectations from the government.

The more organised nature of image work during this phase is also evidenced by the increasing sophistication of the structures of police public relations within forces. Again taking the Met. as an example, it developed a large organisational infrastructure to support its media and public relations policies. At Scotland Yard Nevil Macready's one-person Press Bureau of 1919 had grown by 1997 into a Directorate of Public Affairs and Internal Communication (hereafter DPA) with a staff of nearly 100 and a £9 million budget. The resource allocated to image work by the Met. illustrates the commitment of one force with unmatched financial resources. With its high profile and central position, the Met. has often been a model for practice which has subsequently been adapted and used in provincial forces. In terms of media and public relations management, however, few other forces are subject to the same media scrutiny and pressure as the Met., they do not have such financial resources available and do not justify such an organisational commitment. Different forces have varying needs and the Met. model would not be appropriate for most provincial forces.

Nevertheless ex-Met. ACPO officers have propagated good practice at executive level as they have moved to other forces. At an operational level a number of press officers have undergone 'apprenticeships' in the DPA before moving on to manage media and PR offices in other forces and in the staff associations. The DPA has also seconded staff to assist other forces under pressure, for example during the live animal export operation in 1995. Other forces, for example, Thames Valley and Dorset, have developed innovative communications models and practice independently of Met. influence. Due to the circumstances described above, all forces have become more conscious of their image and consequently of the need to manage media and public relations. However, there is no uniform way in which each force organises for media and public relations, allowing each force to develop flexibly to suit local needs and conditions. This divergence and convergence is examined in Chapter 4.

The Quality of Service programme

As noted above, the Met.'s commissioning of Wolff Olins and the subsequent PLUS programme can be interpreted as a reaction to both declining public satisfaction and also as a consumerist expression of managerialist policy. The consumerist approach of PLUS projects the police as providers of a service, which has implications for changing occupational culture to accept and promote customer orientation. This force-based initiative was not an isolated example, there were also expressions at a national level arising not only through government pressure but also a realisation from within the police service that it needed to reconsider its relationship with the policed. Aware of apparent declining satisfaction with the police in public surveys (for example, the 1988 British Crime Survey), the service embarked in 1988 upon an ACPO inspired 'Quality of Service' programme which was also supported by the Police Superintendents' Association (PSA) and the Police Federation (Weatheritt 1993: 36–8, Waters 1996, 2000). This service-wide 'quality crusade' began with the *Operational Policing Review* (OPR hereafter), undertaken by representatives from all three of the staff associations and including surveys of the public and of serving officers (Joint Consultative Committee 1990). This review revealed declining levels of confidence in the police and a mismatch in police–public expectations about the role and priorities of policing (Stephens and Becker 1994: 224).

The OPR was published in March 1990 and an ACPO Working Group supported by the PSA and the Police Federation immediately began work (in consultation with the Home Office and HMIC) on a service-wide response. It was published in October 1990 – the ACPO *Strategic Policy Document: Setting the Standards for Policing: Meeting Community Expectation* (ACPO 1990). This built on the PLUS approach, emphasising a service-based orientation and incorporating a *Statement of Common Purpose and Values* which was intended to provide the police service with its corporate statement. The ACPO Working Group became the ACPO Quality of Service Sub-Committee in October 1990 with the brief to develop the quality of service initiative for the service. The sub-committee went on to identify five key operational service areas, namely: i) crime management; ii) handling/management of the public's calls; iii) traffic management; iv) public reassurance and public order mainte-nance;[8] v) community relations and community problem solving (ACPO Quality of Service Sub-Committee 1991). As Loveday (1994: 229) has pointed out, the Conservative government's law and order programme with its crime control focus did not align completely with ACPO's key areas of immediate interest. Similarly the chief constable of Gloucester-shire, Tony Butler, lamented the narrowness of the government vision which equated what the police do with crime rates. In support of a holistic service he referenced the OPR of 1990 as a positive response to the apparent decline in the police image in the public's perception, observing that the OPR surveys showed that the public highly valued the service functions whilst being realistic about what the police could do to control crime (Butler 1996: 228).

The Quality of Service momentum was maintained by the *Getting Things Right* initiative in 1993 promoting the principles of total quality management and subsequently forces have pursued various quality initiatives including *Investors in People* and the Business Excellence Model. In this crusade the service role has been foremost. The most obvious outward sign is in the change of names of specific forces to services. Other signs are the publication of mission statements, the seeking of Charter Marks, glossy leaflets promising standards of performance and visitor questionnaires situated in police station reception areas.

Contemporary police voices

One notable feature of this period has been the increasing prominence of a number of police voices. During the 1970s the Police Federation successfully made the transition from 'humble professional association' to 'media opinion leader' (Reiner 2000a: 71) and more recently the Association of Chief Police Officers (ACPO) and the Police Superintendents' Association (PSA) have also heightened their profiles. Each has lobbied behind the scenes seeking to influence policing policy and at the same time each has made increasing use of media and public relations activities to convey policing viewpoints, to engage and influence public opinion. In doing so the associations have at times formed strategic alliances (for example, the Operational Police Review 1990 and the series of promotional 'policing Factsheets' (ACPO 1993, 1994, 1996)) to defend and promote policing and at other times they have competed for the mantle of the most authentic police voice. I will briefly consider each in turn.

The Association of Chief Police Officers (ACPO)

Whilst individual ACPO officers can pursue communication and promotional strategies at force level which attempt to influence the image of local policing, during this latest phase of image work the collective influence of these officers combined within ACPO has grown (Savage et al. 2000).[9] The increased prominence of the policy making and lobbying role of ACPO was recognised by the decision in April 1996 to divide it into two bodies: ACPO who promote the professional interests of the service and the Chief Police Officers' Staff Association (CPOSA) – purely a staff association (Barton 1996).

Although Emsley (1996: 95) dates the beginnings of a police corporate identity from 1893 with the establishment of the Chief Constables' Association, one of the features of the 1990s and since has been the increased cohesiveness and unity of ACPO as a body and its greater influence on police policy making. This collection of senior officers increasingly projects 'a single police voice' (Wall 1998: 316). Recent research attributes this trajectory of ACPO to factors including: the political context of the 1980s and 1990s which both encouraged a common view from the police leadership and also galvanised the previously fragmented chief officers to unite in the face of threatening police reform; the increasingly complex policing environment which heightened the need for specialist ACPO committees to provide advice; and formative events including the Scarman report and the 1984–85 Miners' Strike (Savage and Charman 1996a, Savage et al. 2000: 69–80). Savage and Charman identify two influential shifts in the development of ACPO as a united police voice. First, during the presidency of Peter Wright from 1987–8, the principle of 'presumption in favour of compliance' was introduced. This meant that if chief officers decided not to conform to policy debated and agreed within ACPO, henceforth there was an expectation that they would justify their decision in writing to the ACPO president (Savage and Charman 1996a: 15). Secondly, in 1990 an expanded secretariat was established to service the body and this had a 'professionalising effect' on the decision making and information dissemination processes of ACPO (Savage and Charman 1996a: 17, 1996b: 52, Savage *et al.* 2000: 80–1).

As a collection of the most senior officers in the country, 'a powerful elite group of growing importance' (Reiner 1991: 3), ACPO spokespersons are influential in conveying the police view and constructing the police image. Through the principle of 'presumption in favour of compliance' and the thematic 'Business Areas' (which replaced the ACPO themed committees during 2001), the ACPO Head of Information can seek the coordinated ACPO view on issues and relate them to the media, or the Head of the Business Area can articulate the ACPO position. The structure also enables ACPO to pursue proactively its agenda rather than being purely reactive. This suggests that the way the senior officers as a group are communicating is becoming more organised. There is less room, at least in the public sphere, for diversity and public debate between chief officers. There is a more strategic view to communicating and this is reflected in the attempts to promote a (usually) united senior police image.

With specific reference to the media, this sits within the ACPO president's portfolio and in 2001 ACPO developed for the first time a media strategy. In addition there exists the ACPO Media Advisory Group (MAG hereafter) which was established in 1993 by a small, like-minded group of senior press officers and ACPO officers. This group was founded with the intention to discuss common media issues, to determine and disseminate good practice and to liaise with bodies such as the Society of Editors. The membership was revised around 1997 to make the group more representative in that each policing region now contributes a representative to MAG meetings. MAG fulfils a coordinating role and disseminates advice on policy and practice. For example circulars are distributed to forces on such subjects as pre-verdict media briefings in criminal cases and the release of police-held video footage to the media. In May 1999 a MAG circular (resulting from liaison with the Data Protection Registrar) advised forces that the names of crime and road traffic accident victims and witnesses should not be disclosed to the media without prior consent. At a local level this had the effect of antagonising forces' symbiotic relationships with the local media who depend on such 'bread and butter' information. Consequently a number of forces took the decision not to comply with the circular – a decision taken at chief officer level and not without some regret at noncompliance. MAG therefore has some influence in the conveyance of the police image as it provides advice on approaches to be adopted in managing the media.

The Police Superintendents' Association (PSA)

Just as ACPO became a more cohesive police voice in the 1990s, the Police Superintendents' Association also raised its profile. The PSA was established by the 1964 Police Act as a staff association, but now goes beyond that role, providing another police voice, acting as a policing pressure group and holding an annual conference attended by senior politicians. Of the three staff associations, the PSA probably has the lowest profile. Writing in 1982, Brogden suggested that the Association was powerless – 'the only weapon of the PSA – structurally and organisationally castrated – is publicity' (Brogden 1982: 162). In his view its powerlessness lies in it having no formal *raison d'être*, and the superintendent being neither the master nor servant in the police hierarchy. Even in respect of public relations, the PSA during the late 1990s had no press secretariat and no media and communications strategy. Until April 2000 the National Press Officer was a coordinator fitting in PSA duties around normal duties. However, after adopting a policy of never refusing an interview, coupled with, from the mid-1990s, a dynamic chairperson, chief superintendent Brian Mackenzie, the PSA became a frequent contributor to criminal justice debates held in the media. Mackenzie became a ubiquitous panellist on 'talk-ins' and current affairs broadcasts. Interviewed shortly before his retirement (and elevation to the House of Lords) in 1998, he opined that the PSA had succeeded in reinventing itself, moving from a fringe organisation to an influential authority that successfully lobbied politicians and regularly gave evidence to parliamentary Home Affairs Committees. The PSA, in his view, had come to represent 'the voice of the service' ('The life of Brian', *Police Review*, 20/3/98). Since Brogden dismissed the influence of the PSA, its profile has undoubtedly risen and in the contemporary policing context it has the capacity to influence the police image.

The Police Federation

In the politicised period of the 1970s, the Police Federation became a prominent police 'voice'. It campaigned to 'mobilise the "silent majority"', to influence politicians to support the "rule of law" and to reverse the liberalising trend in penal and social policy' (Reiner 2000a: 72). This was not a sudden incursion. McLaughlin and Murji (1998: 376) have traced the Federation's efforts to articulate the police voice, including its first press release and television appearances by its chairman in 1959, its first press conference in 1965 and its increasing confidence in running publicity campaigns. The prominence of the Federation voice when ACPO and the PSA had not yet found theirs did not meet universal approval (Robert Mark [1978: 151] is particularly scathing of them speaking out without 'experience or knowledge'.) Research carried out by Reiner in the 1970s addressed the influence that the Federation had on the public image of the police. He concluded that 'the Federation is not seen as effective in conveying a good public image of the police. It is not seen as the most suitable vehicle for this' (Reiner 1978: 74). This conclusion was based on interviews with police officers, who appeared to think that senior officers were more suited with their 'social polish and intellectual graces' to convey a favourable image of the police (*ibid*: 73). Interviewees also felt that the police image was influenced more by 'the appearance and actions of constables on the street than any public relations efforts by either the Federation or senior officers' (*ibid*: 73).

However, the Federation is an influential and effective pressure group, an organised and successful lobbyist and an active campaigner. On occasions, despite having its own Press Manager, it has abandoned 'normal public relations' activities when it found that such activities were not penetrating the corridors of power (McLaughlin and Murji 1998). It has stepped outside the normal channels of media communication to appeal direct to the public through advertisements. In doing so the Federation has drawn upon and motivated themes from policing's rich history including 'duty, loyalty, consent, trust, tradition,' which highlight the 'difference' and 'uniqueness' of the English police officer (*ibid*: 372). The Federation has also taken steps to keep police bad news out of the media, using the 'formidable weapon of libel actions to constrain reporting of police deviance' (*Observer*, 9/2/97, quoted in Reiner 1997b: 224). Although the emergence of the Black Police Association and the Lesbian and Gay Police Association has brought into question the capacity of the Federation to speak for *all* rank-and-file police officers, it nevertheless remains a significant contributor to the police image. Its national and local spokespersons are often seen on television and heard on radio reacting to law and order issues, commenting on new laws and trial verdicts, and generally presenting a police world-view on the society we live in.

Notes

1 Corporate identity has been described as 'the process of explicit management of some or all of the ways by which the organisation is perceived' (Olins 1988: 55). Others separate corporate identity into 'corporate image' (how an organisation is perceived by internal and external audiences), 'corporate personality' (the essential nature of the organisation), and 'visual identity' (the visual identifier(s) of an organisation, including its logo, livery and stationery) (Heward 1994: 241).

2 In August 1998 the government announced a new set of overarching aims and objectives for the police service. These specified three aims: a) to promote safety and reduce disorder; b) to reduce crime and fear of crime; c) to contribute to delivering justice in a way which secures and maintains public confidence in the rule of law. Within this overarching framework the Home Secretary sets 'Ministerial Priorities'.

3 The managerialist character of government policing policy continued under the Labour government elected in May 1997 and re-elected in June 2001 (see generally McLaughlin and Murji 2001: 114–18). The Crime and Disorder Act 1998 has been described as 'infused with a managerialist philosophy which is both output-fixated and driven by performance measurement' (Crawford 1998: 4). The Labour government also continued the established approach to public spending which emphasises 'the importance of target-setting, performance measures and evaluation of costs and consequences' (Stockdale *et al*. 1999: 1). The trajectory was confirmed by the 1998 Comprehensive Spending Review and has continued to be supported by the Inspectorate (HMIC 1998) and by the Audit Commission (1998). A prime vehicle of this managerialist strategy is the 'best value' programme which from April 2000 placed a statutory duty on local authorities to deliver services to clear standards by the most effective, economic and efficient means (DETR 1998). Local police authorities are included as 'best value authorities' and as such police forces are required to demonstrate 'best value' (Leigh *et al*. 1999).

4 In the late eighteenth century the utilitarian writer Jeremy Bentham produced a design for a prison which enabled all prisoners in their individual cells to be watched at all times from one central location by guards, who could not be seen by the prisoners (Bozovic 1995). Foucault subsequently used Bentham's panopticon as a metaphor for the state's maintenance of social discipline through surveillance (Foucault 1977).

5 In an interview reviewing his role as Metropolitan Police Commissioner between 1993 and 2000 Sir Paul Condon expressed his surprise at the 'public recognition of the Commissioner as a personality...the Commissioner is so much more visible in a way that even Peter Imbert and Kenneth Newman did not experience', '21st Century Paul', *Police Review* 21/1/2000.

6 Preparation for the television programme *Police Action Live* involved months of studying legal implications and gaining the confidence of lawyers, politicians and police forces. The programme was transmitted on 18 November 1995, almost live – it had a built-in 13 seconds' delay prior to transmission, allowing the programme to cut to other locations if necessary.

7   Guy Davies, the writer of the Channel 4 programme *Coppers: a job for the gentle sex*, has recorded his difficulty in securing agreements to broadcast the rape interview scene again. 'Thames Valley had an unprecedented veto – and the BBC had placed it under lock and key, with a file note that it could never be shown again'. The film was released to Davies following an appeal to the chief constable of Thames Valley Police ('Watching the detectives', *The Independent* 7/9/99).

8   One of the core functions within this area was to 'market reassuring and positive image[s]' of police forces (ACPO Quality of Service Sub-Committee 1991: 17).

9   Loader and Mulcahy characterise the period from 1987 to the present as one in which chief constables moved from individual profiles to a more collective identity, from 'the policeman as hero' to 'a corporate (more liberal) voice' (Loader and Mulcahy 2001a: 51).

Chapter 3

Police legitimacy, communication and the public sphere

> If people believe in the legitimation of power, is this not because the powerful have been successful in the public relations campaign, because they have managed to convince people that they are legitimate? (Beetham 1991: 9)

The legitimacy of the public police is potentially held up for scrutiny when any policing activity is engaged in. Each event which brings into question police integrity and competence, for example, ill-disciplined public order police or alleged racist behaviour, communicates particular images and threatens to undermine police legitimacy. Proven miscarriages of justice and allegations of corruption receive national media coverage and project images of the police. Converging from a different direction, in the gaze of government-led managerialist policies, police performance in terms of effectiveness, efficiency and economy is held up for public approval or disapproval. These processes are facilitated by the communications media. League tables are drawn up, typically focusing on the index of success in the 'war against crime', encouraging regional populations to compare and contrast their local police force with others.

As documented in the previous chapter, senior police officers and other policing stakeholders have recognised that the police service needs to justify its worth as a public sector organisation and state institution, needs to find a 'role' in a changing society and to satisfy public demands which show no sign of diminishing (Loader 1997b). In short the public police have had to act to maintain their institutional position, their acceptance by a more questioning, less malleable society. They have been forced to address the question of what an institution can do to render itself 'deserving of respect rather than compliance' (Outhwaite 1994:64). This is a universal policing issue, not specific to British policing or the current time, but one that is manifest in the political and social conditions and, particularly, the mass mediated environment, of contemporary Britain.

One response of the police service has been to pay greater attention to non-operational communication. The police service has sought to communicate its key messages, to refute what it perceives as misguided media coverage, to correct inaccurate reportage. As noted in Chapter 2, since the late 1980s, the service and particular forces have embarked on a number of initiatives, strategies and organisational changes which have all had implications for the police image, from the specific image consultancies provided to the Met. by Wolff Olins to the more general development of professional media and public relations offices across the service as a whole (Mawby 1997a, 1997b, 2001). The service has communicated and constructed images that reach out to different audiences – to generate general support, to signal to the government that it is meeting requirements, or, alternatively, to mobilise support against what it perceives as threats to 'traditional British policing'. Image work has arguably become one mechanism by which the police seek to foster and maintain legitimacy. This raises questions concerning the substance of the police image and, more importantly, of the relationship between image work and the legitimation process.

On an immediate level the police image seems straightforward. In general people have an idea of 'the police', even if it is different to different people's. Surveys and studies which ask people about their impressions of the police (Belson 1975, Skogan 1990, 1994, Bradley 1998: 7) and others which ask people to rate the popularity of the police in comparison to professions or other public sector organisations pre-suppose that there is this entity called the 'police image.' Police officers, politicians and media commentators talk about the police image and how it will be affected by legislation, events, and changes in uniform and equipment, as though the image is clearly defined and accepted as a given. Probing a little deeper questions the logic of talking of a coherent image for this multi-functional emergency law enforcement service.

There is a functional diversity within the police service which raises the question of how or if a unifying image can be constructed. Different departments undertake very different activities, have very different 'customers,' and create different impressions. CID and uniform patrol officers, for example, have different, if complementary functions, and relations between the two can be antagonistic. What image do they have in common? CID and crime prevention officers both focus on crime and yet they have very different images. Internally too, perceptions matter – the status of CID is high whilst crime prevention is low. The internal culture has its own images of functions, often based around what is perceived as 'real policing' (Holdaway 1983, Young 1991, Fielding 1994, Waddington 1999b, Reiner 2000a: Ch. 3). Clearly then there are internal tensions about the essence of the police image. This is not confined to functional determinants as image also deserves consideration both as a policy decision made by chief constables and their executive teams and also as image created from the bottom upwards by the activities and attitudes of police personnel going about their diverse routine duties. There are a number of images – at least two are projected in the constant debate concerning whether the police are a force or service – and managing multiple images can mean that the 'police need to use many rhetorics to persuade many audiences' (Manning 1971: 153). Yet it is also evident that the received image is not necessarily the image purposefully defined internally and projected. Whilst this may be the intention, the extent of influence is not possible to control. Many images of policing appear in the media, some of which the police directly influence, others are outside their control. The police can control their own output in terms of image communication and they can cooperate with the media to influence their portrayal in the media, though the amount of control differs. But what the police, or policing film-makers, cannot control is the outcomes of the communication process. There are intended and unintended consequences of communication.

In short the police image is complex and, given the centrality of the police service as the state institution responsible for law and order, the construction and communication of its image deserves consideration in relation to legitimate, democratic and accountable policing. One reason for this has been identified by Garland, who when writing about the institutions of punishment, but in a manner applicable to policing, observes that these institutions are 'habitual' and 'have created a sense of their own inevitability and of the necessary rightness of the status quo' (Garland 1990: 3). Beetham has also noted that 'within any settled or established power relations, self-confirming processes are at work to reproduce and consolidate their legitimacy' (Beetham 1991: 99). This implies the existence of different dimensions of legitimacy, or, at least, different moments in the legitimation process. There is legitimacy which develops passively through the habitual, the taken-for-granted and all that 'goes without saying because it comes without saying' (Bourdieu 1977: 167). Institutional legitimacy in this form might comprise part of society's 'structure of feeling' (Williams 1961: 64), the 'routine and taken-for-granted "social practices" which characterised the social formation' (Taylor *et al.* 1996: 5).

There is also legitimacy which is actively sought and fostered through an institution's processes and activities. The police service, through its institutional position and through 'self-confirming' mechanisms, including image work, seeks to achieve and maintain legitimacy. At times, as discussed later in this chapter, this involves drawing upon and tapping into the 'structure of feeling' and also motivating feelings at a paleosymbolic level (Gouldner 1976). Policing, through its institutional authority, its enforcement of the law, and through its routine practices, creates an official police view of the world (Loader 1997a). At times this is challenged if the police service fails in performance or does not fulfil expectations and in turn this can threaten its legitimacy. This can be considered in terms of the 'impossible mandate' (Manning 1971: 157). Manning pointed out that the police were perpetuating an impossible mandate in promoting their image as crime fighters, when it was demonstrably the case that this was not their core nor most successful role (*ibid* 1971: 158–9, 1997: 26–7, 31–2). The implication is that the police service can face a legitimation crisis if it does not successfully perform its (perceived) core role, popularly regarded as 'fighting crime'.[1]

The police may also be compromised by the difficulties of reconciling multiple images of policing, for example, forces practising a zero tolerance approach will project different images of policing to forces pursuing a restorative justice approach. These contradictions of (and within) the 'official verities' (Garland 1990: 265) can have a destabilising effect and accordingly organisations learn to 'finesse failures' (*ibid*: 5). As Manning observed this can be achieved through presentational strategies (Manning 1997: 44) and a relevant question concerns where the police world-view and its supporting mechanisms sit *vis-à-vis* democratic and accountable policing. Does image construction and communication work against democratic policing or conversely does it work to make the police as an institution more accountable, transparent and open? Having made many references to the legitimacy of policing, and to communication, the following sections address the concepts of legitimacy, communication and the public sphere.

Legitimacy: power and its need of legitimation

Legitimacy is regarded generally as a good, something that governments and political systems should possess. It is also preferable for state institutions to be regarded as legitimate, especially those involved with coercive force, such as the police and prison services (Bittner 1990, Sparks and Bottoms 1995, Sparks *et al.* 1996: 84). The police service has to address the issue of actively seeking legitimacy and being seen to be conducting police work in a manner regarded as legitimate. But what does it mean to say that an institution has legitimacy? What does legitimacy comprise, how is it achieved and maintained, what undermines it?

Legitimacy is bound up with the related concepts of power, authority and force. *Power* as a concept is much debated (Lukes 1986 provides an overview), but here can be considered in the general sense of the ability or capacity to bring about the 'production of intended effects' (Russell 1938: 25). Power is unequally distributed in society and defines subordinate and dominant status in relations between individuals and organisations. Because the seeking and exercise of power is often conflictual and problematic 'societies will seek to subject it to justifiable rules, and the powerful themselves will seek to secure consent to their power from at least the most important among their subordinates' (Beetham 1991: 3). *Authority* is an attribute of social organisation and can be vested in persons, offices or organisations. Its 'hallmark is unquestioning recognition by those who are asked to obey; neither coercion nor persuasion is needed' (Arendt 1970: 45). *Force* can be used in support of authority and to exercise power. *Legitimacy* adds a further dimension to these relationships, being associated with the rightful exercise of authority or use of power. For this reason those in authority, including the British police, have valued the importance of legitimating their power, in the sense of being accepted, of being considered rightful.

Debate concerning what entitles leaders to rule, and their rule to be accepted as rightful, has occupied philosophers at least as far back as Plato and has implied the problem of legitimacy. History suggests that the entitlement to rule and acknowledgement of the rightfulness of that rule has derived from varying sources. Traditional notions of legitimacy derived from appeals to the will of god and blood relationships were challenged by Locke in his *Two Treatises of Government* published in 1688 (Locke 1960) and by Rousseau who explicitly addressed the question of what makes a given relationship legitimate in his *Social Contract* published in 1762 (Rousseau 1946: 3). Both Locke and Rousseau argued that an essential characteristic of legitimacy was the consent of the parties involved and this remains an essential element of legitimacy.

Contemporary political and social theory, in considering legitimacy often draws on the work of Max Weber and his typology of 'traditional', 'legal' and 'charismatic' legitimacy (Gerth and Wright Mills 1948: 78–9).

Weber argued that legitimacy derived from these three sources, the pure types of which were rarely found. In the realm of 'modern associations' he argued that legitimacy invariably was of the legal type resting upon 'rules that are rationally established by enactment, by agreement, or by imposition' (*ibid*: 294). Weber's typology has attractive applications for examining the legitimation of state agencies, particularly those, such as the police, that possess coercive power. However, in an important contribution to the debate on the legitimation of power, Beetham has criticised Weber's typology arguing that his definition of legitimacy as 'power is legitimate where those involved in it believe it to be so' is fundamentally flawed (Beetham 1991: 8). First, Beetham argues, it misrepresents the relationship between beliefs and legitimacy, a 'given power relationship is not legitimate because people believe in its legitimacy, but because it can be *justified in terms of* their beliefs' (*ibid*: 11, original emphasis). Second, Weber's definition does not account for aspects of legitimacy that are not related to beliefs, for example legality and active consent. From this critique of Weber, Beetham develops his own criteria for the legitimation of power. To Beetham, legitimacy is entwined with power, which when 'acquired and exercised according to justifiable rules and with evidence of consent' is called 'rightful or legitimate' (*ibid*: 3). His criteria for legitimacy are legal validity, shared values and expressed consent.

Legal validity is concerned with rules. Here power is legitimate if it is acquired and exercised in accordance with established rules, which may be traditional and unwritten or formalised in law. The non-legitimate form of this dimension of power is illegitimacy, for example when power is achieved through breaking the rules such as in cases of ballot box rigging. The second element is the dimension of justifying the rules by reference to beliefs shared by those in the power relationship, both dominant and subordinate. For this element to operate, there must be a minimum commonality of appropriate beliefs shared by those in the power relationship, for example, concerning the rightful source of authority and what constitutes the common good. Where these conditions are threatened or no longer hold, a legitimacy deficit of varying degrees exists. Thirdly, the final element is evidence of consent on the part of the subordinate party in the power relationship. This is expressed in various ways, from taking part in elections to participating in ceremonial activities which have a public and symbolic dimension. If there is no evidence of consent or if there are actions of dissent (civil unrest or disobedience) legitimacy is eroded and delegitimation occurs.

Beetham argues then that legitimacy is necessarily multi-dimensional, with the three qualitatively different criteria or levels operating to different degrees in particular circumstances. Each criteria can be said to operate on a continuum, with its own form of non-legitimate power. These three elements comprise 'a set of general criteria for legitimacy' (*ibid*: 21), each representing a necessary, but not sufficient, component of

Figure 3.1: Beetham's legitimacy framework (derived from Beetham 1991)

Criteria of legitimacy	Level of operation	Non-legitimate form
Conformity to established rules	Rules	Illegitimacy – rule-breaking
Shared beliefs	Justification by shared beliefs	Legitimacy deficit – absence of shared values
Expressed consent	Actions	Delegitimation – civil disobedience

legitimacy. Figure 3.1 below summarises the three dimensions, their level of operation and their non-legitimate form.

The criteria, organised in the above framework, project a flexible resource for analysing degrees of legitimacy present in given circumstances. It is a model which is capable of capturing the complexity of different circumstances and changing conditions. This is helpful for conceptualising police legitimacy, which is not a fixed entity.

Before discussing the legitimation of public policing, it is pertinent to address the question of why the police require legitimacy. The answer to this lies in the fact that the police exercise power over others, the state delegates to them the 'monopoly of the legitimate use of physical force' (Gerth and Wright Mills 1948: 78). As Hunt and Magenau observe: 'Governments, after all, are monopolists of force: the ultimate legitimizers of conduct and enforcers of norms. The police embody and actualise this regulative power, holding as they do, a special charter for its exercise' (Hunt and Magenau 1993: 9). This power is significant in its consequences for citizens who can be deprived of liberty and reputation. In liberal democracies such power requires justification. It also requires, to be effective, a measure of consent and the legitimacy of the British police has traditionally been justified by claims of 'policing by consent' which was developed through the 'policy choices' of the founders of the modern police from 1829 (Reiner 2000a: 50), but has antecedents in earlier forms of Saxon policing based on the self-policing of communities (Reith 1952: 25–7, Emsley 1996: 9). Additionally the police also play a 'potentially enabling role in the mediation of social conflict' (Loader 1996: 37) which inheres in them a political role in that policing decisions and actions are 'concerned with the allocation of a significant public good' (*ibid*: 37). In a democratic society, an institution fulfilling such roles must justify the trust placed and the powers delegated; it requires legitimation.

There is also a more prosaic reason why it benefits the police to seek legitimacy, namely that if police power is legitimated, it facilitates the task of discharging policing functions. A police service which is accepted by the policed as just and rightful is more likely to have positive relations with communities and more likely to secure the cooperation and consent of citizens – this in itself can contribute to the effectiveness of policing. As Beetham observes, whilst 'legitimacy makes a difference to the effectiveness of a system of power, through the quality of performance it secures from those subordinate to it', the performance of the power-holder 'makes a significant contribution to, and forms a necessary component of, its legitimacy' (Beetham 1991: 137). Whilst it is clearly simplistic to reduce legitimacy to effectiveness, Beetham is surely correct that there is a reciprocal connection between the two.

Commentators have engaged with legitimacy in relation to policing and have addressed one or more aspects of legitimate policing, for example the legal and political arrangements for police accountability (Jefferson and Grimshaw 1984, McLaughlin 1994, Reiner 1995b, Oliver 1997), police accountability under managerialist policies (Reiner and Spencer 1993) and policing and democracy (Alderson 1984, Jones *et al.* 1994, 1996, Loader 1996). They have approached police legitimacy from particular perspectives with particular aims. More general discussions of police legitimacy have tended to draw on Weberian influences of 'legal' legitimacy and a belief in the need for consent. One contribution, from Robert Reiner, posits that for policing to be accepted as legitimate, 'the broad mass of the population, and possibly even some of those who are policed against, accept the authority, the lawful right, of the police to act as they do, even if disagreeing with or regretting some specific actions' (Reiner 2000a: 9). This is fine as a starting point, but in examining how police image work relates to police legitimacy, a framework such as Beetham's provides a substantive framework capable of capturing complexity and change. It can be applied to the police service in the following manner.

Legal validity

In terms of policing, the legal validity element of Beetham's framework is the most straightforward in its application and exercise. Theoretically the police operate within the law to enforce the law, and to reinforce legitimacy they must also act within a regulatory framework which has the force of law (the Police and Criminal Evidence Act 1984 (PACE)), 'regarded as a model of operational accountability in much of the rest of the world' (Cassels 1996: 3 s. 1.2).

The role of policing has been closely related to enforcing conformity to rules (for the greater good of communal living or in the interests of the dominant groups in society, depending on interpretation). Although British police officers are not formally called law enforcement officers as in the USA, it has always been a core role of the public police to uphold the law and the police service's *Statement of Common Purpose* recognises this: 'The purpose of the police service is to uphold the law fairly and firmly; to prevent crime; to pursue and bring to justice those who break the law; to keep the Queen's peace...' (ACPO 1990).

In principle the role of the police to enforce and uphold the law is recognised by large sections of the community, even if at times the law is enforced against them personally. The police are the institution within which the state vests authority to perform this role and this source of police legitimacy is generally acknowledged. This is a relatively concrete and visible element of legitimacy which is capable of being practically measured and evaluated by all members of the community. In recent years it has been in this very area that police legitimacy has been threatened by the failure of the police service to apply the law fairly or to work within it. The regular coming to light of incidences in which police misconduct has led to miscarriages of justice (the Birmingham Six, the Guildford Four, the Carl Bridgewater case) has eroded police legitimacy. It has been eroded further by the apparent inability of the police to effectively and whole-heartedly investigate crimes equally irrespective of the ethnic origin of the victim (Macpherson 1999). At another level the spiralling of awards for damages against the police in civil litigation cases (for example, in respect of wrongful arrest and assault) further under-mines police legitimacy. In this respect Beetham makes the important point that institutions must observe their own legitimacy rules. This is extremely relevant to the police in terms of police deviance (for example, see Ericson *et al.* 1989: 118 on the particular newsworthiness of police deviance). Police legitimacy is questioned when the police themselves disregard or break the law, when they operate illegitimately or when they choose to enforce the law differently in respect of different sections of the community. There is no greater illegitimating factor than an institution that breaks its trust, committing the sins which it has been appointed to prosecute. This is precisely why allegations of police corruption, and the uncovering of miscarriages of justice, are so damaging to the police image and police legitimacy.

A conundrum exists in situations where the police might indulge in what has been described (by Sir Paul Condon, Metropolitan Police Commissioner 1993–2000) as 'noble cause corruption'. Such an action might be in sympathy with shared values, for example, planting drugs on a known drug dealer. The ends of these actions might attune with the values of a community, but the illegitimate means irrevocably taint the legitimacy of the police officers concerned. In a similar way, vigilantism may enforce some aspect of shared values, but is illegitimate in that it operates outside the legal framework and has no legal validity. Quite clearly these different types of challenge to the legal validity of the police project differing images of policing and police officers. When they arise, the service in general, and forces in particular cases, have to consider the issues involved and then determine what type of messages they wish to communicate. Image management comes into play and media and public relations options need to be considered. Possible general communications strategies are outlined later in this chapter.

A qualitatively different situation to police misconduct and noble cause corruption arises when the police uphold the law (legitimate action), but the law is popularly perceived as unjust (for example, allowing the free passage of live animal exports or policing the Poll Tax demonstrations). This raises particularly difficult issues of image management as in these cases the police are accused of enforcing the moral wrong and their legitimacy is questioned not in terms of legal validity, but in terms of the justification of the rules they are enforcing. This invokes the second element of Beetham's framework.

Shared values

Beetham's second criterion for legitimacy is the justification of the rules by reference to beliefs shared by those in the power relationship. This requires a minimum commonality of appropriate beliefs shared by those in the power relationship, for example, concerning the rightful source of authority and what constitutes the common good. In a society which is increasingly diverse, multi-cultural and economically unequal, there are naturally a variety of attitudes towards public policing, its meanings and implications. How does policing attempt to bind in these different groups and attitudes to acknowledge some element of shared values? What is the appeal of policing to different and diverse groups in society? There are several ways to approach the unravelling of this complex area. First, the multi-faceted image of the police service and their multi-functional role may motivate and contribute to an appeal to shared values, in that different aspects of policing may appeal to different sections of society. Secondly, the police themselves can develop ways of appealing to the values held by sections of society and one way of doing this is through using appropriate communication strategies which communicate particular images of policing (see, for example, Bradley 1998). These aspects are explored in greater detail in the chapters which follow. However, in the following sections I wish to consider whether police legitimacy based on shared values involves, first, the motivation of, and an appeal to, ideas and emotions within communities and, second, the use of history and tradition as agents of legitimation.

'Structure of feeling', doxa and paleosymbolism

In developing the concept of a 'structure of feeling', Raymond Williams argued that meanings and values held by particular societies are kept alive by social inheritance and by embodiment, and that although each generation may 'train' its successor, each new generation will develop its own 'structure of feeling' (Williams 1961: 61–70). In this way the police do not start with a clean sheet when they communicate with, and project their image onto, the public through the media or approach a member of the public on the street. People have preconceived ideas concerning the role and value of the police. These may originate as part of a socialisation process, influenced by parents, peers' attitudes to the police, by jobs, by area of residence, and by ethnic origin. This is an experiential factor, dependent upon personal and group everyday experiences of the police which aggregate to form a consciousness of the role and attitude of the police. It constructs *doxa* – 'opinions, beliefs and understandings which are held and shared by individuals who share the social world' (Thompson 1990: 279).

In this way, each generation inherits an image of the police and subsequently will add to, adjust or reject that image based on experience and mediated images to construct that generation's structure of feeling. This inherited level of interpretation of institutions is something that Gouldner addresses in his description of a 'paleosymbolic' system that operates at a paradigmatic level, below the level of publicly acknowledged ideological systems. The paleosymbolic 'constitutes a set of beliefs and symbols of restricted communicability' (Gouldner 1976: 224). It is 'part of the shared, ordinary (and hence "restricted") languages of everyday life learned during primary socialisation as children' (*ibid*: 225). As paleosymbolism refers to symbol systems older than ideological influences that later come to bear, these underlying values interact with subsequent experience to produce, in Williams' words, a structure of feeling.

Although the construction and transmission of police imagery can be interpreted in the context of *doxa* and paleosymbolic systems, a distinction should be made. The notion of *doxa* and the paleosymbolic both refer to ideas and feelings that are pre-reflexive and below the level of articulation, but the paleosymbolic is distinguished by an emotionally compelling character, by a connection which can elicit a favourable response to the idea of policing (Loader 1997a: 4). This might arise, for example, through a perceived connection between policing and protection and security. Such a connection could also explain the 'feel good factor' surrounding the craving for the return of community police officers and 'more bobbies on the beat'. It is also instrumental in motivating consent by appealing to shared values through rhetoric which speaks of police officers as citizen constables, the idea of police constables being ordinary members of the public, only in uniform (Royal Commission 1929).

History and tradition

Giddens has observed that one view of tradition is as 'an orientation to the past, such that the past has a heavy influence, or, more accurately put, is made to have a heavy influence, over the present' (Giddens 1994: 62). In this sense policing imagery references historical antecedents as a means of establishing legitimacy and maintaining credibility in the present (*cf.* McLaughlin and Murji 1998). Reiner (1995c), for example, has argued that a number of characteristics of 'traditional' British policing (including 'high on accountability', 'public consent', and 'close to the community'), though still embedded in official documentation such as the OPR of 1990, did not in fact apply to British policing in the 1990s. An appreciation of the history and traditions of British policing is fundamental to an analysis of policing imagery and an understanding of how the police communicate enlisting resources from the past. The use of history and tradition enables the police to appeal to values which exist at the paleosymbolic level. The perceived virtues of the past are bestowed on present police officers by mobilising references to: the 'unarmed British Bobby'; the 'Bobby on the beat'; the 'thin blue line'; the symbolism of the uniform; and compelling icons such as Dixon. These retain symbolic relevance today and are used as reference points during periods of change and difficulty. In crisis solace is often sought from the past, for example, in his report on the Brixton riots, Lord Scarman referred back to Mayne's original instructions and advocated due observance (Scarman 1981: 62, s. 4.55–8). More recently the perceived threat of the Sheehy Report motivated a skilful rearguard action by the police staff associations to project images onto the public through the media. These communications emphasised the threat which Sheehy's recommendations posed to the traditions of policing.

Within the history that is drawn upon, the police have developed rituals and myths, which inform the culture of contemporary policing and help to secure the position of the police as a British institution. Arguably there is no stronger symbol than a police officer's funeral. Manning's description of one such funeral (Manning 1997: 19–25) emphasises these events as occasions when the police–public bond is sanctioned and renewed, drawing on all that is heroic and public serving about policing, appealing to the paleosymbolic. Manning's commentary was echoed in the front page newspaper coverage afforded to the murder and funeral of PC Nina McKay in November 1997 ('Her death was needless' *Police Review* 31/10/97, '"Police family" funeral for stabbed woman officer' *Guardian* 6/11/97). The ongoing project, supported by all the police staff associations, to complete a 'National Police Officers' Roll of Honour' detailing each police officer who has been killed on duty also fulfils a symbolic role, sending messages of officers dying for others and defending common values.

Whilst the role of history and tradition are culturally important, both Hobsbawm (1983) and Olins (1989), have observed that tradition can be invented and still be effective. Nostalgic television drama series such as *Heartbeat* which depict idealised 'Golden Age' policing almost ache for bygone days and simple values, and they are received enthusiastically by the public on the basis of viewing figures. Whilst these heart-warming images are dismissed by some senior officers as not only inaccurate, but also irrelevant to a modern technological organisation dealing with twenty-first century issues, the use of history can invest a symbolic power in contemporary policing (*cf.* Mulcahy 2000). As Beetham has noted 'historical accounts are significant and contentious precisely because of their relationship to the legitimacy of power *in the present*' (Beetham 1991: 103, original emphasis).

Having discussed how shared values can be motivated enlisting the resources of history and tradition, there are of course times when the law enforcement role of the police will conflict with the 'mood of the nation', and the 'spirit of the times' and the police find themselves in the position of enforcing the law and also keeping the peace to allow activities which are legal, but against the wishes of substantial numbers of the public, or less numerous but more powerful groups within the community. This can occur in situations where the police are seen to be facilitating business practices which offend public sensibilities as in the case of transportation of veal calves during 1995. It also arises when the police protect the democratic right of groups generally regarded as noxious, such as the British National Party, to hold public marches in sensitive areas. It has arisen in the case of unpopular law with the poll tax protests and more subtlely it occurs when the police charge so-called soft drug users in a social climate in which the use of such drugs is seen less and less as a criminal matter. In these instances, using Beetham's terminology, the police face a legitimation deficit as the rules they are seeking to enforce are not always justified by shared beliefs. In such cases the police have at times developed communication policies which seek, first, to isolate them from the substantive issue by emphasising that they are fulfilling their mandate to enforce the law and, second, to identify some common ground with the opposing forces and with neutrals who observe through the media. Where public order has been a feature, often the motivation of shared beliefs and symbolism has occurred through injuries to unarmed officers, which generates support for the police and renews the image of the unarmed British Bobbies doing their duty, maintaining the peace against the odds. These images have been less easy to invoke as the police have donned paramilitary protective clothing.

Expressed consent

Beetham's third criterion of legitimacy is that of legitimation through expressed consent, existing at the level of actions. Policing by consent was a founding principle of the modern police in 1829 and remains a touchstone, especially of police official communications in times of pressure on the police–public relationship. Reiner has argued that legitimation of the new police was pursued by constructing consent utilising a number of organisational policies. A vital component of this was the incorporation of the 'working class ... into the political institutions of British society' (Reiner 2000a: 58). This analysis is of consent in terms of general passive acceptance of the police by the broad mass of society (Reiner 2000a: 48–59). However, to satisfy Beetham's criterion of expressed consent, it is necessary to consider more concrete and participative measures – at the level of actions.

If we look to the institutional and constitutional arrangements for police governance, it can be argued that policing by consent is maintained by the tripartite arrangement which separates power and provides for democratic supervision of policing. The local police authority includes elected members and the Home Secretary is an elected member, suggesting that there is an auditable trail of consent, albeit a bureaucratic indirect trail. A more direct mechanism for expressing or withdrawing consent is the Police Community Consultative Groups (PCCGs) established under s. 106 of PACE following the recommendations of the Scarman Report of 1981. These committees formed part of Lord Scarman's vision to increase accountability through greater transparency and to build confidence in policing. Research and experience shows that these committees are forums for the police to explain their actions and that they tend to be poorly attended and non-adversarial. They have also been criticised for being unrepresentative of the community and police-led (Morgan and Maggs 1985, Morgan 1989, Fielding 1991: 191–4, Morgan 1992: 165–83, Morgan 1995, Newburn and Jones 1996: 123–4, Harfield 1997). Whilst the committees have been called 'toothless and invisible' (Northamptonshire Police Authority chairwoman quoted in Baker 1996) they do provide a safety valve which can be used to raise major concerns about policing if the need arises.

The 1996 Police Act placed a statutory requirement on police forces to consult with their local communities to seek their views on policing and crime prevention (s. 96, Police Act 1996). This is undertaken in several ways. Many forces now use the mechanism of a questionnaire survey (Skogan 1996). The survey results are published and this is an opportunity for members of the public to make their voices heard. Other methods include police surgeries and road shows. The information collected is then used in corporate planning to construct force and area policing plans. In addition to these force-level measures, under the 1998 Crime and Disorder Act there is a statutory duty on the 'responsible authorities' (which include the police) to consult local agencies and communities and to conduct community safety audits with the objective of producing local community safety plans. Consultation and partnership is emphasised throughout the implementation guidance. In addition to these statutory requirements for the police to consult the public and to take account of their views in subsequent planning, periodically the government commissions the British Crime Survey (BCS). This includes questions on citizens' experiences of the police in terms of their performance, their attitude and their impartiality (Home Office 1997). The results of these surveys receive considerable attention in the local and national media.

Therefore, although formal mechanisms for the expression of consent (and dissent) exist, critics have suggested that these are inadequate, flawed and overly police-centric for the operation of democratic policing. Consequently some voices are simply not heard through the formal mechanisms. These might have other outlets. The media provide a forum which regularly focuses on policing subjects and whether representing the genuine concerns of the community or specific interest groups, they are a means of expressing both consent and dissent with general police performance or specific police operations or actions. Media attention has been significant in bringing to public attention serious miscarriages of justice. Non-governmental organisations (NGOs) also are a vehicle for expressing consent/dissent. Groups and bodies such as Liberty, Justice and Victim Support apply direct pressure and also act as lobbyists, utilising the media and consulting elected members. If all else fails, there is direct action in the form of petitions, marches, protests and even the besieging and attacking of police stations.

Applying Beetham's three criteria of legitimacy to policing suggests that the legitimacy of an institution is interlinked with its role and position in its particular society. It follows that the legitimacy of the police service is linked to the meanings of policing for that society. In this respect Garland, writing about punishment and society, provides insights into the links between institutions and the societies they exist within. Social institutions are society's way of dealing with certain needs and conflicts (Garland 1990: 282) and are shaped by broad cultural patterns. Nevertheless, they generate their own local meanings and values which contribute to the dominant culture. Just as punishment signifies for Garland, policing is also a cultural text which communicates with a variety of social audiences and conveys an extended range of meanings (*ibid*: 253).

So, what contribution can police image work make to legitimacy? Through open and honest communication, will the criteria of legitimacy be satisfied and will policing be transparent in the sense of being democratically accountable? If this is the case then image work has a genuine and significant contribution to make to democratic policing. Alternatively, is image work a symptom or product of a legitimacy deficit, in which the police are projecting images and public relations communications as a sticking plaster solution to wounds in the police–public relationship? If this is the case, then image work can in itself be a delegitimating factor. At the heart of this is the substance of what the police are communicating, their motives for communicating and their conduct in the communications process. To develop this further requires discussion of the public sphere in which policing exists and consideration of the nature of communication.

The police, the public sphere and communication

Beetham discusses the issue of defining legitimacy in 'an age of propaganda and public relations, when the public sphere is dominated by an emphasis on presentation over reality' and the powerful attempt to convince the people that they are legitimate (Beetham 1991: 9). This raises questions of both the nature and motivation of police communications and the nature of the public sphere in which the police operate – 'the public sphere of political debate, popular adjudication and opinion-formation' (Taylor 1997: 61).

The idea of a public sphere requires discussion as it is relevant to both the nature of the environment in which the police work and also to the nature of communication. A key resource to draw on here is Habermas, who in his *Structural Transformation of the Public Sphere* (published originally in Germany in 1962, but not in English until 1989), described the establishment of a public sphere during the late seventeenth century and its subsequent transformation into a stage for rhetoric and gestures without substance. The public sphere described by Habermas is a:

> bourgeois public sphere which consisted of private individuals who came together to debate among themselves the regulation of civil society and the conduct of the state. This new public sphere was not part of the state but was, on the contrary, a sphere in which the activities of the state could be confronted and subjected to criticism. The medium of this confrontation was itself significant: it was the public use of reason, as articulated by private individuals engaged in argument that was *in principle* open and unconstrained. (Thompson 1995: 70, original emphasis)

In the ideal situation, all parties engaged in the argument have equal access to present and defend their views. These views will satisfy four validity claims: they must be comprehensible, truthful, correct in context and sincere (Outhwaite 1994: 40, Loader 1996: 34). If these conditions hold, the best argument will win out and an 'ideal speech' situation exists.[2] The transformation of the public sphere relates to the position where the separation between the state and civil society diminished as states became more interventionist. At the same time the salons and coffee houses providing forums for debate went into decline and the media became dominated by commercial interests, losing their critical edge. The features of this transformed public sphere include the domination of sectional interests; the mass media having a negative effect, being used for the manipulation of public opinion rather than as a forum for critical debate; the reduction of the public sphere to an arena for advertising and staged displays – parliament, for example, becomes organised theatre, not a true debating chamber (Habermas 1989). Under these conditions, the public sphere becomes a setting for developing legitimacy by motivating conformity rather than rational debate – 'public opinion ceases to be a source of critical judgement and checks, and becomes a social-psychological variable to be manipulated' (Outhwaite 1994: 9). We are left with the modern world of politics and media 'spin' instead of honest and open debate.

The weaknesses in Habermas's arguments regarding the public sphere are well documented (Calhoun 1992, Thompson 1993, 1995: 74–5, Outhwaite 1994), and are most critical concerning the transformed public sphere. Despite the flaws, Habermas was moving towards an attempt, developed further in later publications (Habermas 1984, 1987, 1996) to work 'out an intellectual and practical basis for public discussion and effective control of public policy' (Outhwaite 1994: 10). Habermas's public sphere with its rational basis forms a regulative ideal. In terms of explanation, his analysis provides insight into how the (ideal and transformed) public sphere operates and the context in which discourses operate. His public sphere also provides critical purchase, it can be used as a measure of participatory democracy by holding up situations against the idealised public sphere and seeing how they compare. Habermas's public sphere, then, has relevance for the police and image. As a state institution and as an organisation, the police service is one of the actors within the public sphere interacting with different groups, seeking to influence public opinion and to develop legitimacy.

Whether or not we accept Habermas's notion of a transformed public sphere, there is no doubt that the society in which the police operate, and of which they are part, has become increasingly mediated. It is also evident that whilst Habermas, influenced by the work of Horkheimer and Adorno, overestimated the passive and sponge-like character of media consumers (see, for example, Adorno 1991), he was correct to identify the possibility that interest groups and organisations would attempt to use the emerging media to communicate to their advantage – 'the more their [the mass media's] effectiveness in terms of publicity [*Öffentlichkeit*[3]] increased, the more they became accessible to the pressure of certain private interests, whether individual or collective' (Habermas 1989: 188). Such influences and the rise of public relations practices, in Habermas's view, can distort communication and aspire to 'opinion management' (*ibid*: 193). This potential for distortion cannot be over-looked in our increasingly media aware society.

Mediated communication has become more dominant due to changes in society which have increased the importance of mediated relations between people (Thompson 1995: 5, Giddens 1994: 52). These changes include technological advances and organisational restructuring in the media industry which have contributed to larger globalisation processes. Wright has argued that communication is *the* key concept for police forces to address in the new millennium (Wright 2000) and a body of research and theory has emerged which contextualises the public police in these processes as arguably taking on new characteristics. They have joined professional broadcasters to become mediators themselves (Schlesinger and Tumber 1994: ch. 4, Fairclough 1995), and are knowledge and technical specialists providing information to criminal justice agencies and other institutions such as insurance companies (Ericson and Haggerty 1997).

As introduced in Chapter 2, a highly mediated society raises issues of the 'management of visibility' which concerns how those 'who exercise political power seek to manage their visibility before others... to construct their self images and to control their self-presentation' (Thompson 1995: 135). Thompson accepts this is nothing new, but crucially the development of communication media and the accompanying 'transformation of visibility... have changed the rules by which this art is practised' (*ibid*: 135). Visibility management, however, is not omnipowerful, its effectiveness is restricted by gaffes, backfires, leaks and scandals (*ibid*: 140–6). These concepts can be applied usefully to the police service and its management of visibility. However, to get beyond the conception of the management of visibility or image as 'spin doctoring' and nothing more, it has to be considered in conjunction with the concept of 'publicness'. Thompson describes the 'publicness of co-presence' as being linked to the sharing of a common locale, based on face-to-face interaction and involving sound and vision – dialogical events where interaction is possible. Media developments have changed the nature of publicness, which can no longer be linked to the sharing of a common locale – actors can be detached temporally and spatially through mediated publicness. In these circumstances the management of visibility also needs to take into account transparency, by which I mean an openness on the part of institutions such as the police to explain how their organisation works; a willingness to undergo independent examination; to explain their structures and their decision-making processes; to allow public knowledge of complaints and their investigation.

The conditions identified by Thompson are key to image and its management. Quite simply in this highly mediated world there is an organisational need for the police to communicate effectively and to construct and communicate an image appropriate to their role, as one aspect of the legitimation process. It is also crucial for legitimacy that there is a concern not simply with appearance or with the 'strategic manipulation of impressions' (Goffman 1959: 90), but with substance, aligning image management with transparency and accountability. In considering how to manage this dilemma of communication and its implications for image and legitimacy, it is useful to reflect on the spheres of policing activity in which image work takes place and also the broad communication approaches which are theoretically open to the police.

Image work: spheres of activity, types of interaction and communication approaches

The spheres of activity in which police image work takes place include: a) operational policing; b) news management which comprises (i) reactive media relations, and (ii) proactive media relations; and c) public relations and marketing communications. Police forces engage in these activities to a greater or lesser extent and the personnel involved include not only the designated image managers and professional communicators usually deployed in the press office, but also police officers of all ranks and duties. ACPO officers, for example, are often involved in formal public relations ceremonies including the opening of new police buildings and the announcing of new initiatives. At the other end of the rank spectrum police constables who have won awards or are involved in successful community initiatives form part of the 'bread and butter' content of numerous local newspapers (and internal force newspapers). In addition to this intentional image work, there are also activities where the image work is unconscious, unintentional or secondary to other dimensions of police work. This is the case in the arena of operational policing as, for example, making an arrest is not an exercise in image-management but it has implications for image. Similarly public order operations normally are not primarily about image work, but the police are concerned about their image on such occasions and may incorporate image considerations within their planning.

In each of these spheres of activity, communication is based on interaction. As discussed above, Thompson has argued that the development of communications media has created new forms of interaction beyond face-to-face social interactions. These developments have separated social interaction from physical locale – individuals can communicate even though they do not share a common 'spatial-temporal setting' (Thompson 1995: 82). Thompson develops a conceptual framework for analysing 'action and interaction' (*ibid*: 82) which comprises three types of interaction. *Face-to-face* interaction involves the actors being present in the same place at the same time. *Mediated* interaction introduces a technical medium such as the telephone, e-mail, or letter and the actors can be divided by space and/or time. These two types involve two-way communication and are oriented towards specific others, whilst the third, *mediated quasi-interaction*, is one-directional, monological and 'oriented toward an indefinite range of potential

Figure 3.2: Thompson's types of interaction applied to policing

Interaction type	Police example
Face-to face-interactions – *actors present at the same time and in the same place*	Everyday police/public encounters – responding to emergency and other calls, investigation of crimes, crime prevention advice, traffic stops, public order confrontations
Mediated interactions – *technical medium divides actors, possibly in space and time*	Police/public phone conversation e.g. reporting a crime; police/media phone conversation e.g. news gathering for radio, print or TV bulletin; police press office fax to media agencies; police letters to individuals concerning prosecutions, investigation progress, etc.
Mediated quasi-interactions – *one-directional communication aimed at a wide audience*	i) Police generated – annual reports, newsletters, advisory documentation (e.g. home security), contributions to TV, radio programmes and newspaper and magazine features; ii) generated by others – TV programmes, radio and print features

participants' (*ibid*: 84–5). It is the type of interaction which involves watching television, listening to the radio and reading books and newspapers. Thompson's types of interaction apply to police image work as demonstrated in figure 3.2.

Within the spheres of activity outlined and through the types of interaction noted above, the police conduct image work. How they approach the communication of their intended messages and the projection of their preferred images can range across a number of styles. Although not exhaustive, the communication approaches evident or theoretically possible include types which can be termed *managerial, misrepresentative, missionary,* and *dialogical.* These different types form an analytical framework which acts as a sensitising device through which image work can be filtered and made sense of.

The managerial approach

The managerial approach is the least easily defined, in many ways the default type into which much of police communication will fall. It encompasses communication at all levels of the organisation and takes in the mundane, routine, organisational, bureaucratic processing of information and workloads. It includes the type of communication required to 'get the job done'. As such it comprises communication as diverse as: responding to telephone calls from members of the public and from organisations; providing information on the progress of incidents to victims, witnesses and suspects; and answering basic queries from media representatives. This type of interaction might appear to be 'neutral' in terms of image work, but police employees, like employees of all organisations, will communicate in a way that reflects the nature of their organisation, their own position within it and how the organisation 'define[s] the reality of the external world' (Manning 1988: 34). As such this managerial approach is characterised by its objective to manage communications and present information in a way that attunes with the objectives, functions and ethos of the police organisation and the individuals within it (*cf.* Manning 2001). It aims to present the organisation, and its employees, to best effect. In this sense it is managed communication whether practised by professional communicators or professional police officers. This approach can be seen in what Manning defined as presentational strategies – 'the most common modes of the public presentation of the mandate and mission of the organisation' including 'the use of the professionalism rhetoric by police departments' (Manning 1997: 44). Traces of this approach are also apparent in Grunig and Grunig's 'public information' model of 'public relations behaviour' which promotes the dissemination of truthful and accurate information, but discourages the volunteering of negative information (Grunig and Grunig 1989: 30–1).

Whilst commonly police communication falls under the umbrella of the managerial approach, as it is the least substantive style, it is also lends itself to be transformed into other types, or other types contain traces of it. In this respect it can be seen as the default or 'holding' style, communication may remain managerial or it can transform into another style. For example, the one-off publication of 'selective' statistics to support an initiative might be described as managerial, however if this became a routine and systematic manipulation, it would transform from a managerial to a misrepresentative style. Similarly, drawing on an example already alluded to in Chapter 1, Robert Mark in his 1973 Dimbleby Lecture rejected any connection between Met. corruption and pornography. He later admitted that this was a tactical denial. He had adopted a managerial approach for instrumental purposes. Had he continued to reject the connection in the face of mounting evidence to the contrary, his approach would have developed into the misrepresentative.

The misrepresentative approach

In the misrepresentative approach there is a concern with control and manipulation rather than open and honest communication. However, there is a qualitative difference between a managerialist-based approach and one that is based on systematic misrepresentation. A managerialist approach attempts to control the tone and 'spin' of messages that are communicated into the public sphere and the content is selectively substantive – it is, one might say, the truth, but not always or necessarily the whole truth. The purpose is not so much to set an agenda as to influence the arguments. In contrast a systematic misrepresentative approach is characterised by a high control factor in terms of the substance of what is communicated and how it is communicated. At the same time there is often a low information content. There is a low level of transparency, communication is one-directional and there is a manipulative objective. One police example would be the systematic and planned publication of highly selective performance data for reasons of organisational advantage. However, at its extreme this approach may not only be used for such bureaucratic motives, it may also be used for political advantage, to mask wrong-doing, to abdicate or deflect responsibility or to avoid accusations of criminality. An example would be a police force whose communications denied the existence of racist and ineffective policing when there was overwhelming evidence to the contrary.

The missionary approach

The missionary approach to communication involves the police using their institutional position to pronounce as professionals on what a given situation is and how it should be dealt with. Essentially this approach communicates how the police see the given situation, it seeks to promulgate a police-centric way of seeing things with the objective of building (the police vision of) a safe, ordered and law-abiding society.

In using this approach, at times the police will be seeking to persuade, to convert public opinion and at other times they will be harnessing existing public opinion, articulating the beliefs of the 'silent majority'. For instance, the police will utilise this approach to attempt to educate (or to re-educate) public opinion in circumstances where they are communicating unpopular realities – that they alone cannot control crime and cannot provide the numbers of 'bobbies on the beat' that popular sentiment demands. As such this approach includes what Loader describes as 'pedagogic policing' – communication not based on 'mutual dialogue' but on a 'one way process of instruction' (Loader 1996: 88, 120). On other occasions when the police use this approach they are not attempting to educate and convert opinion to the police view (although they might of course also succeed in doing this), but will be tapping into existing public opinion to harness its support. In doing so they will appeal to emotions and feelings which already exist within different communities and sections of the public. This communications approach might accompany the promotion of policing initiatives which target under-age drinkers, persistent offenders, drug dealers and drunk drivers.

The dialogical approach

A communications approach based on a high level of control of both communications processes and the substance of communication is unlikely to enhance legitimacy, particularly if there is a low level of transparency and integrity. In contrast the dialogical is an inclusive approach taking due account of the opinions, values and concerns of all parties – those involved in the communication process and also those close to the subject matter of the communication. In a dialogical communications strategy, communication is a two-way dialogue, there is a high level of transparency, the content is substantive and verifiable if necessary by an external monitor. It is a discursive approach in that it is rational, open to change and flexible. It is a deliberative approach in the sense of taking account of all opinions and being well considered. This approach can be likened to Habermas's discourse ethics and a possible police example would be an open meeting attended by community members and police officers to discuss without hidden agendas and resolve a specific issue. All attendees would have an opportunity to put forward a view and the best argument or means of resolution would win out. In this way the dialogical approach to communication can contribute to the legitimacy and accountability of policing. The dialogical approach, therefore, is the regulative ideal, the model that provides a critical resource for the analysis of instances of police communication.

In practice these approaches can co-exist, traces of each approach may be evident in any one force at any given time and one approach might come to the fore at a particular time in certain circumstances. The same police force might adopt contrasting approaches on different occasions. There may also be differences in approach at the force and the national (for example, ACPO, PSA or Police Federation) levels. Whichever approach is in evidence, there will be particular implications both for the role and work of police personnel directly involved in communications work, for example, media and public relations offices, and also for the processes and content of communication. There are a number of issues which might determine the approach to be adopted and from an analytical perspective these can assist in differentiating the degree to which communications strategies are underpinning or undermining democratic principles. The issues which require consideration include: police motives and objectives; the degree of control that the police have over the processes of communication, the facts of the matter and the messages; the high or low information content; who is included and excluded in the communication processes; and the range of influence and power of the addressees. In adopting an approach, therefore, a force will take into account its relationship with its environment and at the same time may be attempting to control its external environment.

In putting forward these communication approaches that might be evident in police image work, or that the police may consciously adopt, I am not arguing that police image work can be reduced to a simple linear categorisation of this nature. Rather the purpose of suggesting these different approaches to communication is to provide a sensitising device which can be brought to bear on empirical data as a means of understanding and explaining police image work.

The research design

In order to map out empirically the range of image work existing across the police service and then to explore its complexities, I combined the quantitative method of a questionnaire survey with the qualitative methods of interviews, observation and documentary analysis. The aim was to generate data on police image work through complementary methods of data collection utilising what Layder (1993: 108) has described as a 'multistrategy' approach. This enabled in-depth study of image construction and communication from the perspective of the police service.[4] The detailed fieldwork activities were planned over three stages which integrated the selected methods of data collection.

The first stage of the research was concerned with image work at a national level and served a role in laying the foundations of the research. Its objectives were to map out the terrain of police image making, to identify and interview key players in police forces, both leaders and policy makers, namely ACPO officers, and also practitioners, the heads of the media and public relations departments. Other individuals were targeted for their functional position, for example, the press officers of the three staff associations. In order to negotiate access I approached the ACPO General Purposes Committee, which agreed to support coopera- tion with the research without imposing conditions or restraints. The committee provided a letter of support to ease access to forces during the fieldwork. During the stage one research between July 1996 and March 1997 I visited six police forces and the three staff associations, conducting 17 focused interviews. Interviewees included four ACPO officers, two of whom were members of ACPO MAG, force senior press and public relations officers and staff association press officers.

The second research stage ran between November 1996 and February 1997. This comprised a questionnaire survey of the media and public relations functions in all 43 Home Office police forces, together with the RUC, the Isle of Man Constabulary, Jersey Police, Guernsey Police and the British Transport Police; a total of 48 forces, 46 of which responded, (the only two forces not to return questionnaires were Cheshire and Greater Manchester Police). This second stage overlapped with the first stage and complemented it in that it was also concerned with generating data on the range and depth of police image work. However, whilst stage one collected detailed data in a sample of forces, the survey was seeking to establish the scope of image work throughout the police service. This national survey was repeated between November 2000 and February 2001, targeting the original number of forces and also *an Garda Siochana* and the Ministry of Defence Police, a total of 50 forces. This second survey achieved a 100 per cent response rate.

The third stage of the research comprised a detailed case study of how the image of one police force, South Yorkshire Police, is constructed, communicated and managed – a study of image work in one force. The case study combined three methods – observation, interview and documentary analysis – to capture the richness and complexity of image work. The fieldwork was undertaken between April and July 1997 and during this period observation became the central research method. The observation was usually overt and negotiated. It included visits to force departments and officers to observe processes. It involved attending internal meetings and briefings and participating in the behind the scenes activities, for example, those leading up to press conferences and public order events. It included accompanying officers during their shifts visiting schools, patrolling beats, policing public order events and cruising motorways. It involved sitting in police canteens and talking and watching. I attended staged events such as the launch of force initiatives. On occasions I simply turned up and watched public events and meetings in which the police were involved, for example, PCCG meetings and single issue meetings. By attending numbers of different events and activities in which the police image was projected, I was able to observe not only the formal and intended management of the force image through its official communications channels, but also the image work that is bound up in everyday police work, through diverse functions and everyday encounters.

The observational research was complemented by focused interviews with officers and civilians of differing ranks and grades, who discharged various functions including full and part-time media liaison, marketing, public order policing, traffic policing, crime prevention and schools liaison. These interviews, some with individuals whom I had observed discharging their official duties, were opportunities to seek clarification and explication of what I had observed and to explore how these individuals related their duties and conduct to the image of the force. With the press office staff it was a chance to discuss the intricacies of their strategies and tactics in managing the force image and to learn about the nuances of their relationship with their force and the force's relationship with media organisations. In contrast, interviews with operational officers provided the opportunity to reflect whether image work permeated their routine duties. Such occasions were sometimes chances to seek the views of 'the late turn van driver' on image work.

The third research method employed during the case study was documentary analysis. Throughout the research stages I collected documentation produced by the police for internal and external audiences. On my visits to forces I collected copies of force newspapers and leaflets which were displayed in police station receptions. The practitioners I visited supplied copies of annual reports, departmental aims and objectives and good practice guides. Whilst conducting the national press office surveys I invited respondents to forward documentation such as job descriptions and media strategies. During the case study I gathered an array of documents. These included internal documents such as district policing plans, operational policing briefing notes and minutes from internal meetings. I also collected documents in the public domain, from press releases and the minutes of the PCCGs to the glossy information leaflets and packs which were distributed at initiative launches. Scott has argued that in interpreting texts three aspects of meaning should be recognised, 'three "moments" in the movement of the text from author to audience' (Scott 1990: 34). This requires consideration of 'intended content', 'received content' and 'internal meaning'. For the purposes of this research I was primarily interested in 'intended content'. Therefore the documents I collected were scrutinised to examine and understand the environment of construction, the underlying assumptions and the intended meanings. In particular I drew on documents produced by South Yorkshire Police to analyse and understand the image that the force was promoting at the time that the research was undertaken.

In summary the three stage research design combined the methods of interviews, survey, observation and documentary analysis. The activities generated substantial amounts of data, which are presented and discussed in the chapters which follow.

Notes

1 In this respect, the flirting by some English police forces with the raft of initiatives named 'zero tolerance' can be seen as an attempt to deliver the impossible mandate, especially in terms of the gung-ho images portrayed in media coverage of Superintendent Ray Mallon (686 media interviews in 1997) and Middlesbrough police. However, this approach has had an adverse effect on other aspects of the police image, not only by ignoring, or at least marginalising, other policing functions, but also through the linking by the media of the zero tolerance approach to the suspension of Middlesbrough officers in Autumn 1997 for alleged misconduct. (For analyses of zero tolerance

policing, see Johnson 2000: 63–7, Manning 2001, Wright 2002, Ch. 5).

2 Habermas subsequently expressed regret with this phrase as 'it conjures up a vision of a concrete form of life, rather than a set of critical procedures' (Loader 1996: 178, n. 2). He confirmed that his concept of the public sphere was meant as 'an analytical tool for ordering certain phenomena and placing them in a particular context as part of a categorical frame' (Habermas 1992: 462).

3 Habermas refers to publicity or publicness (*Öffentlichkeit*) as the idea that the personal opinions of private individuals could evolve into public opinion through a process of rational critical debate (Thompson 1995: 240).

4 Substantial bodies of literature address images of policing arising through the media (including Chibnall 1977, 1979, Hurd 1979, Ericson *et al.* 1989, 1991, Laing 1991, Clarke 1992, Schlesinger and Tumber 1992, 1994, Sparks 1990, 1992, Reiner 1994a, 1997b, 2000a, 2000b Cashmore, 1994, Perlmutter 2000) and images arising through observational studies of the police organisation (including Skolnick 1996, Punch 1979b, Ericson 1982, Holdaway 1983, Norris 1993, Manning 1997). Whilst this literature is voluminous, few studies primarily address image work from the perspective of the police service and its specialist communicators (Motshall 1995 is one exception). Indeed Schlesinger and Tumber (1992: 186) noted that apart from their own work, only Ericson *et al.* (1989) had studied how police news sources interacted with the media.

Chapter 4

The national picture: systems of police image work

'The image of this force has got bugger all to do with me.' (Serving chief constable, 1996)

'The press office is not concerned with "image" but in conveying important messages to the public, usually concerning community safety...press officers are not employed to put a gloss on a force image, but to reflect the work of the force on behalf of the community it serves.' (Police Press Office manager, Northern England, 1997)

In the previous chapters I have suggested that developments in police image work historically have been localised and piecemeal. At the same time I have argued that since the late 1980s the police service has recognised the need for better communication. In this and the following three chapters I map out the contours of contemporary police image work.

The aim of the current chapter is to explore and unravel image work from a national perspective. The first section of the chapter provides a systemic perspective on police image work at the national level. It examines who is communicating and how they do it. This perspective encompasses chief constables, in their role as force leaders, some with national profiles, and also in their ACPO role representing and speaking for the leadership of the police service. It also encompasses the three main nationally focused staff associations – the Association of Chief Police Officers (ACPO), the Police Superintendents' Association (PSA) and the Police Federation. These bodies also provide a national image of policing and are active in communicating messages through the national media. The second part of the chapter provides a complementary perspective, that of how individual police forces organise for media and public relations.[1] It examines the routine nature of police communications by surveying what is happening in force media and public relations departments. These departments, often referred to anachronistically as 'press' offices, have specific responsibility for communication within police organisations. They, and the strategies and policies they implement, have a direct influence in communicating the work and role of the police.

By focusing on the police service leadership, the national staff associations and force media and public relations departments, this chapter constructs an aggregated picture of how the police image is constructed and communicated from the police perspective.

Breaking down the police voice

The police service occupies a privileged position in terms of being in demand by the media and other agencies to give views and positions on criminal justice matters – 'as a body possessing an aura of authority and knowledgeability, the police are well-placed to "name" contemporary problems and diagnose their solutions' (Loader 1997a: 10). This manifests itself in the police 'voice'. The Police Federation's magazine, POLICE, claims to be the 'voice of the police,' and on his retirement as PSA president, Brian Mackenzie claimed that the PSA represented 'the voice of the service' ('The life of Brian', Police Review 20/3/98). This voice, however, is not monolithic, it has a number of forms which at times overlap, sometimes complementing and supplementing, and at other times in a state of tension or contradiction.[2] Chief constables and the staff associations – ACPO, PSA, the Police Federation – represent such forms, competing to be the police voice, the embodiment of policing. Recently more diverse voices have emerged through the establishment of the Black Police Association, the Lesbian and Gay Police Association and the British Association of Women Police.

What are the components of the police voice at this national level? The senior voice is that of the police leaders, officers of the rank of assistant chief constable (ACC) and above. These highest ranking police officers, collectively known as the ACPO ranks, appear in the media as representatives of the police commenting on operational matters, policing policy and on occasions the state of society. They occupy a position in which they can represent different constituencies when communicating publicly. Whether they represent their local force, the service nationally or a faction within the service depends on the circumstances. They might be representing the leadership of their home force, speaking about force policy or operational or disciplinary matters. Alternatively senior officers might be representing ACPO, which has a themed structure of 'ACPO Business Areas' and the head of each area becomes a focus for the media as a spokesperson on specific subjects such as crime, race and community relations, and traffic. The ACPO Head of Information, a civilian based at ACPO headquarters in London, coordinates the 'party line' and monitors what ACPO officers are communicating. On other occasions ACPO officers might comment on national issues, whilst not speaking formally on behalf of ACPO. If such pronouncements do not comply with ACPO policy, then officers can incur the corporate displeasure of ACPO.

In this respect it has become increasingly less likely for chief constables to court public attention by speaking out in the manner of earlier chief constables, for example, John Alderson, Robert Mark and James Anderton (Reiner 1991: 216–19, 2000a: 71–4, McLaughlin 1994: 35, Loader and Mulcahy 2001b: 254–6). The instances of rogue elephant chief constables willing to comment on all and any subjects are fewer, at least partly due to greater ACPO coordination and control (Savage and Charman 1996a, Savage et al. 2000). Amongst the ACPO ranks, individuals hold different views on whether ACPO should continue its consolidating role 'strengthen its internal organisation and perhaps become the body which provides the vision for the police service as a whole' (Savage et al. 1998: 40). Whilst greater ACPO discipline limits the numbers of officers willing to speak out, those that are willing to do so can become branded as mavericks. Nevertheless recent research shows that although many ACPO officers support ACPO's greater cohesion for the united front it provides, they believe their first responsibility is to their force rather than to 'toeing some party line' (Savage et al. 1998: 40; see also Savage et al. 1999). This was reinforced by the senior officers I interviewed. In terms of whose images chief officers present and promote, the informants were unanimous that they were representing first and foremost their force, rather than ACPO or the police service in general. One informant, for example, advised that they had been appointed with the task of putting their new force 'on the map'.

In contrast to the communication activities of chief constables as force leaders, the staff associations, including ACPO, provide an alternative voice located in the sectional interests of the ranks represented. Each of the staff associations has its unique features which characterise its contribution to the police voice, each brings a facet to the police image.

ACPO is distanced from the other staff associations in that it communicates on behalf of the service leadership and with the responsibility of command, in contrast to the PSA (middle managers) and the Federation (rank and file). PSA past President Brian Mackenzie has referred to the PSA as being in the best position to wield influence as it is made up of 'managers in the field ... the Federation can't speak with authority about management and the managers at the top have little knowledge about what's happening on the ground' ('The life of Brian', *Police Review* 20/3/98). At the time of the fieldwork the PSA National Press Officer believed that the Association had a role to play in communicating 'the police view'. This regards the view of the police service as a whole and the PSA view as one and the same. At the same time the PSA provides a non-force perspective in that officers speaking on behalf of the PSA express a national, not a force, view. The Federation unequivocally speaks for the workforce, the rank and file. The main functions of the Federation are legal representation of its members and the negotiation of pay and conditions, ostensibly backstage, low profile roles. At the same time, however, the Federation has developed a high public profile, with prepared positions on policing issues and its officers frequently quoted in the media. A few, particularly the national chair and the chair of the Met. branch of the Federation, have a national media profile. They are much sought after as media sounding boards to provide comment on policing issues. Rooted in the rank and file and established as a policing stakeholder, the Federation conducts itself with the air of being the authentic police voice, promoting the common sense position.

The staff associations represent different policing interests. At times these interests will overlap and at other times they will be in a state of tension. The balance of these interests can ebb and flow impacting on the likelihood of coordinating the different police voices to provide one coherent police world-view. Whilst any tensions might have their roots in the different ranks which the associations represent, part of this tension lies in establishing the prime police voice. An element of professional competition exists. Nevertheless recent history has shown that the associations can put aside professional rivalry and combine effectively if the police service as a whole is perceived to be under threat, evidenced by the Operational Policing Review of 1990 and the organised opposition to the Conservative government's 1990s police reform programme. The three staff associations united to target a general audience and project positive messages about the police service. They produced, for example, a series of promotional policing factsheets prepared by ACPO with the support of the PSA and the Police Federation (ACPO 1993,1994,1996).

This is arguably the most obvious public example that a united police voice exists and that they have overlapping interests around which they can and do coalesce.

Promoting the police: the means of communication

Having discussed the different components of the police voice, I now wish to consider how the police image is communicated at this national level. Again this is considered as the view from the top of ACPO officers and the national view of the staff associations. In terms of means these two groups occupy different positions. ACPO officers are figure-heads and policy makers. They can determine how the image of their force will be managed with respect to policing styles, policies on media and public relations and the resources committed. The staff associations, particularly the PSA and Federation, do not occupy such a position. This is not to say that they have no power, indeed they have, through their ability to coordinate media forays and PR campaigns (McLaughlin and Murji 1998). They are also accomplished lobbyists. The approaches of these groups are now explored.

The view from the top

ACPO officers as force leaders can seek to influence the police image through three principle means: a) implementing and supporting a professional media and public relations department, b) sponsoring internal policies which build the force image, and c) personal activities – maintaining direct relations with executives in media organisations and personal appearances through the media as force leaders and ACPO spokespersons.

A professional media and public relations department

The ACPO officers interviewed during the research, without exception, stressed belief in the importance of an 'open' and accessible police organisation and two-way communications. To achieve and promote this, most favoured a proactive media and PR office. One informant spoke of his belief in a proactive press office, 'pushing out good news'. Another spoke of the need for these offices to be constantly scanning, anticipating issues and events and planning for them in terms of media and PR communications. A third spoke of his dependence on his head of media and PR, they met most days to discuss media issues. The evidence gathered through the national surveys (discussed below) would seem to contradict one informant who suggested that in their experience press and PR offices generally had not moved beyond their original purpose of press liaison.

Within the sample of ACPO officers, interviewees differed in the extent of responsibility they were prepared to allow their force media and PR specialists. For example, in one of the forces the head of media was a full-voting member of the senior management team and treated as a senior management equal. In another force, the chief officer restricted the head of media and PR to a support role: they did not participate in policy meetings but were brought in when necessary to give advice on communication matters. The advice proffered was not always taken. Other informants took the middle route of including the head of media in senior management meetings, but not in a key role.

Building image in

The second category is the sponsoring of strategies and policies which are concerned with image building. These include the obvious examples of developing media, communications and marketing polices which have an obvious external focus. As discussed later in this chapter it became increasingly common in the 1990s for forces to develop communications strategies. The will to implement these must come from the top. One of the interviewed ACPO officers with a keen interest in the media had written a media policy for his force, which in turn was updated once a professional communicator was appointed as force head of media and PR.

In addition to media and PR policies, image is built in through other policies aimed at building the corporate identity of organisations. These policies have internal as well as external dimensions. They include work aimed at improving internal conditions as highlighted by the Wolff Olins consultancy's work with the Met. (Wolff Olins 1988). In one of the forces visited during this research, the chief constable had previously played a central role in developing the Met.'s PLUS programme, which arose from Wolff Olins' recommendations. On his appointment to chief constable in his current force he implemented similar policies to those advocated by Wolff Olins.

Operational policies too, have an image perspective. This was alluded to by the ACPO officers interviewed, one of whom promoted the building-in of media awareness to operational work as a matter of course. This officer encouraged middle management officers to use force media departments as an integral part of operational policing and not as an optional extra. In this respect some forces will develop media policies for specific operations.

Direct relations with the media

The third area in which ACPO officers can have a direct influence on image work is that of their direct dealings with the media, both frontstage and backstage. This includes their work as performers and as lobbyists. In terms of the former, ACPO officers are able to groom their public appearances through specialist media courses and some have become competent media performers, conducting radio and television interviews representing their forces and/or ACPO. A small number of chief constables feature on the circuit of radio and television programmes sometimes representing ACPO as a Business Area spokesperson and at other times appearing as an individual. However, the backstage activities of ACPO officers are just as important in terms of the police image in the arena of news management. The practice of cultivating relations with newspaper editors has been maintained by chief constables from Trenchard and Scott in the 1930s and 1940s through Mark in the 1970s to the present day. Chief officers have consistently remarked on the need for maintaining good relations with their equivalent heads of organisations in the media industry whilst at the same time expressing surprise that these relations were not more common.

The media and the police occupy very different roles in public life, roles that will bring then into conflict at times. They have different agendas, the police to prevent and detect crime and to maintain order, and the media traditionally to fulfil the role of the fourth estate, challenging state institutions on behalf of the public, but also to maximise their audiences and revenues. One of the interviewees acknowledged the inherent conflict between the police and the media, setting out the situation as they saw it from the perspective of a chief constable:

'... the media want everything and the police are not able to give them everything. Perennial conflict results. The police want to be open, the media want information, the public want privacy – squaring this and maintaining an open policy is a dilemma.'

Nevertheless this officer felt that relations with the media had changed for the better over the years, in his opinion mainly due to ACPO's improvement as lobbyists. Another interviewee reiterated this belief commenting that the police had become more comfortable in general with the media (see also Loader and Mulcahy 2001b: 254–5).

Staff associations

Whilst ACPO officers can influence and project policing images through the means identified above, the staff associations operate under different conditions which affect the way they organise their communication operations. Senior officers generally speak as the voice of their force, which has a defined organisational structure, policies and channels of communication. In contrast staff associations straddle forces and need to rise above local issues in order to represent their nationally defined membership. This presents cohesion and cooperation issues.

The greater organisation and cohesion of ACPO has already been alluded to and has been the subject of recent research (Savage and Charman 1996a, Savage *et al.* 1999, 2000). This cohesion has carried through into the way ACPO communicates. In the 1990s ACPO took steps to appoint a full-time professional press officer (1990) and to establish a Media Advisory Group (MAG) in 1993. The first appointee as press officer, returned as 'information officer' in 1996 (the post was subsequently developed into 'Head of Information'). For a media relations manager the greatest difference between working for structured organisations (for example, individual forces) and for a disparate group of individuals such as ACPO is the difficulty of monitoring what individual ACPO officers in 43 forces are projecting into the media and also the task of coordinating a consistent ACPO 'voice'. However, cohesion increased coinciding with the strengthening of the ACPO secretariat and the committee structure becoming more effective during the 1990s. It also became evident that if chief constables intended to pronounce on controversial or sensitive issues, then it was more likely than hitherto that they would fore-warn the centre.

The issue of cohesion is relevant also to the Police Federation, which employs one civilian Press Manager at its headquarters in Surbiton. The Federation has a committee structure comprising a Joint Central Committee and individual constables', sergeants' and inspectors' committees. This is compounded by another organisational feature: the force-based Federation representatives and groupings. The Federation does form official views from the centre and in most forces the Federation representatives will liaise with the centre and the party line will hold. But due to the disparate structure there are opportunities for mixed messages – for example, the chair of the Met. Federation branch is regularly contacted by the media and their opinion may be at odds with the official line. During the summer of 1998 the specialist police press featured a running story about the Met. branch threatening to break away from the national Federation on the grounds that it had failed to adequately represent them (see, for example, 'Met. talks of breakaway viability', *Police Review* 3/7/98). Whilst this development made little impact on the mainstream media, it indicates the tensions that exist in projecting a cohesive image.

The Federation, through cultivating the media over a number of years (Judge 1994: 316, 325), is capable of getting issues and comment into the news through its media contacts. It can also act proactively. On specific issues media approaches can be planned and implemented. Some issues are foreseeable, including the perennial issues of arming the police and the fight for resources. The Federation was at the forefront of campaigns in favour of the side-handled baton and a self-defence spray and is proud of its ability to drive these agendas. In addition the Federation has prepared a number of one page flyers headed *'Where we stand on...'* which then set out concisely its position on 'firearms and the police', 'protecting the public', identity cards, 'the nation's drug problem', 'community involvement', etc. (Police Federation 1996). It has also produced short glossy brochures such as *The Policing Agenda* in which it sets out its view on law and order (Police Federation, undated).

The PSA differed from ACPO and the Federation at the time of the fieldwork in that it did not employ a full-time or professional press officer. The National Press Officer for the PSA was a serving superintendent, based in his home force, who acted as a media filter and coordinator in addition to his 'day job'. This officer maintained a register of superintendents in each force who were willing to speak on behalf of the PSA. On receiving requests from the media for a spokesperson, the press officer would arrange for the most appropriate officer to deal with the matter. Since the mid-1990s the PSA has made concerted efforts to build its media activities, for example, developing the national conference as an important vehicle for profile raising, at which particular efforts were made to accommodate the media. The PSA became more organised in its media liaison. This was taken a step further in April 2000 when it appointed for the first time a civilian Communications Manager based at its Pangbourne headquarters. This signalled the professionalisation of the PSA's media function and the postholder is responsible for not only media relations, but also for undertaking research and maintaining the Association's website.

Just as chief constables have an interest in maintaining working relations with newspaper editors, the staff associations must also develop and cultivate similar relationships. The associations differ from force media offices (where local media are serviced daily) in that they are dealing with national agendas, national policy issues and single issues which have been elevated to national prominence. Consequently the level of media liaison is primarily national and local media have little contact with the associations operating at national level.

This examination of the systemic perspective reveals a blend of organised and *ad hoc* image work. However, the underlying trend indicates that policy makers and the three staff associations have recognised that 'buffing the image' is not enough, that there is a need to plan and organise external (and internal) communication. To this end the actors at this level are involved to a greater or lesser extent, as policy makers and practitioners, in projecting the language of 'openness', in establishing and maintaining channels of communication, and in engaging in news management and promotional activities which communicate meanings of policing.

Force level organisation of media and public relations

Having examined the national systemic perspective, in this section I turn to image work at the level of force media and public relations departments. In doing so I examine how forces have responded to the pressures which have compelled them to address image work through media relations, public relations, marketing and corporate identity activities.

Despite documenting above some indications of a movement towards more centralised control of communications at the systemic level, forces operate as individual organisations which have each had to respond to the pressure to manage their image. No forces have been insulated from this though the pressure manifests itself differently in the varying force contexts. Each force has its own perceived organisational requirements. In recent years there has been periodic discussion and debate, inside and outside policing circles, concerning the police service's increased image work activities, but little empirical evidence has been generated to judge the extent of police media and public relations, how this is organised and how individual force activities compare.[3] This section uses original data gathered across forces to discuss and explain what is actually happening in terms of image work and to identify convergence and divergence in intentions and practices. The data was generated through a national survey of 46 police force media and public relations offices in 1996–97 (Mawby 1997a) which was repeated and expanded (to 50 forces) in 2000–01 (Mawby 2001), and through site visits to police forces to interview press officers and examine how their forces organised for media and public relations. The data generated, and its analysis, provides an overview of how police media and public relations is structured across the police service.

Police 'Press Offices' – origins and context

The first press office to be established was at Scotland Yard in 1919. It was to plough a lone furrow for a number of years as the next recorded press offices were not established until the late 1960s (when Derbyshire Constabulary, Lincolnshire Police and the RUC set up press offices). During the 1970s more press offices appeared, but it wasn't until the 1980s that they were established in greater numbers, this growth corresponding with technological advances in mass communications and the growth of the media. By the late 1990s press offices were an established component within the structure of the police organisation, but at the same time the 1990s were a period in which forces set about reorganising their media and PR functions. At the time of the 1996–97 survey, one-third of the responding forces were undergoing some form of reorganisation and the 2000–01 survey confirmed that press offices had mostly been established under their current structure in the 1990s (45 since 1990 and 35 since 1995).

Despite the growth in media forms and increasing technological sophistication, these departments are still commonly referred to as 'press offices'. In 1997 the two most common titles were 'Press Office' and 'Press and Public Relations Office', a legacy of the departments' origins, initially bureaux servicing the press rather than television or radio. By 2001 'Press and Public Relations Office' had become the most common name, and the titles 'Media and Public Relations' and 'Corporate Communications' had become more popular, informing on their expected role.

In terms of the place of the press office in the force organisational structure, most often they operate as independent departments with the manager regarded as senior management in 64 per cent of forces and reporting to one or more of the force's executive team. Physical location of the offices is predominantly at headquarters though in recent years there has been a trend for increasing numbers of forces to place a proportion of press office staff in divisional locations (between 1997 and 2001 the percentage of forces doing this increased from 20 per cent to 32 per cent). This ranges from forces with satellite press offices in one or more locations (West Mercia, West Midlands, West Yorkshire), to one force, Thames Valley, which had appointed 'Area Communications Managers' in each of its areas. Of the forces which located all press office staff at headquarters, a number (for example, South Yorkshire) had set up a network of divisional media liaison officers, who were territorial divisional officers with part-time responsibility for coordinating and facilitating media liaison within their area and between the division and headquarters.

This latter arrangement reflects the situation that media relations is no longer regarded as the sole preserve of designated press officers. Prior to Robert Mark's memorandum of May 1973 it was a disciplinary offence for rank and file officers to divulge information to the media. The results of the 1996–97 survey suggested that forces were involving as many officers in media liaison as possible, though providing officers with support from press officers, if required. Advisory documentation provided practical tips to officers when liaising with the media, had a rhetoric of openness, and actively encouraged personnel to release information and to use the media positively.[4] By 2001 60 per cent of surveyed forces were tasking non-press office staff with media and PR duties, this being more often in addition to, rather than part of, their core activity, and in 86 per cent of forces it was policy to allow all officers to liaise with the media. This authorisation was often conditional and based on the position that officers should liaise with the media only within their area of operation and responsibility.

Staffing Profiles

Although the first press officer was a civilian, most commonly press offices were established and staffed by officers. Research undertaken in the early 1990s suggested that press offices were then a blend of civilians and officers but that there was a trend towards civilianisation (Schlesinger and Tumber 1994: 130–5). This trend continues. My surveys confirmed increasing professionalisation and civilianisation of this section of the work force. Press offices are increasingly staffed and managed by civilian professionals rather than career police officers. By 2001 it was practice in 82 per cent of forces to recruit trained journalists and marketing and public relations specialists. Whilst the largest professional grouping is that of journalists (121 employed across the forces surveyed in 2001), followed by public relations specialists (45 in 2001), the broad range of expertise and support which press offices were able to provide to forces was indicated by the number of different specialisms employed. These included media studies graduates, graphic artists, designers, photographers and audio-visual technicians.

The trend towards civilianisation is evidenced by the fact that of 515 staff employed across the police service press offices in 2001 (headquarters and staff located in the divisions), 87 per cent were civilians; 88 per cent of press offices had civilian heads of department. In 32 (64 per cent) of the surveyed forces all press office staff were civilians (compared with 52 per cent in 1996–97). This evidence of forces recruiting civilians for the specific skills that they can offer is not an isolated example, but part of a wider civilianisation movement. This has been encouraged through Home Office circulars (Home Office 1983, 1988), and is also evidence that civilians are breaking through into senior management and policy-making positions. This data supports Highmore's research which traced four phases of civilianisation:

- Phase 1: Manual functions, for example, cleaning and catering (pre-1939).
- Phase 2: Administrative/clerical support functions (1939 onwards).
- Phase 3: Administrative and specialist (SOCO, fingerprinting) functions (1966 onwards).
- Phase 4: Professional functions – financial/accounting, IT, personnel specialists (1988 onwards).

(Derived from Highmore 1993: 3–13; see also Loveday 1993.)

Highmore observed that in Phase four a new class of civilian employee emerged, 'a body of men and women with the necessary managerial and specialist skills to ensure a professional civilian support function for the police service of the twenty-first century' (1993: 6). Elsewhere I have argued that in the mid-1990s civilians were on the threshold of a fifth phase in which they would be consistently appointed to senior management positions (Berry *et al.* 1998: 233). There were already isolated examples of civilians being appointed to senior management teams as forces' corporate arrangements became increasingly complex. It was likely that similar appointments would follow, leading to the appointment of civilians with financial, corporate or strategic management skills to executive positions. The primary characteristic of this fifth phase of civilianisation is the move from support to senior managerial policy-making roles. These two surveys of press offices support this argument in that a number of forces have appointed civilians with specific communication skills to senior management posts.

If the civilianisation and professionalisation trends are points of convergence then the staffing level of press offices is a point of divergence. The range of staff resources allocated stretches from single person operations in two non-Home Office forces (Guernsey and Jersey) to the RUC, which had a staff of 25 and the Met. with a staff of 62. It could of course be argued that both these forces are special cases in terms of the media demands they routinely encounter. The most frequent number of personnel allocated by forces to work in press offices is four, but almost as many forces allocate two people and five people. As figure 4.1 shows, in 2001 74 per cent of forces (37 respondents) allocated 10 or less staff to the press office and 46 per cent of forces allocated five people or less. The figure also shows that between 1996–97 and 2000–01, there was a shift towards press offices with larger numbers of staff.

Figure 4.1: Press Office staffing levels 1996–97 and 2000-01

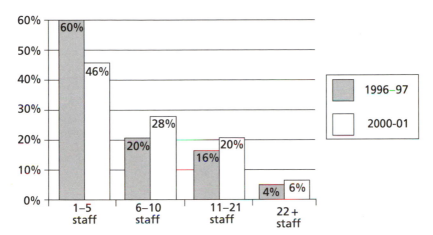

Whilst the most common number of staff allocated to a press office was four, staffing levels do not necessarily reflect the media demands on individual forces. During 1996 I spent several weeks with a force that employed two press officers. An activity analysis exercise indicated that their work was mainly reactive due to their considerable workloads. This lead to frustration that they could not develop the proactive and strategic side of their work. An additional member of staff in such departments can mean the difference between 'fire-fighting' and a planned approach.

Terms of reference and departmental responsibilities

Thus far I have discussed how press offices are organised and structured. What though of press offices' roles and responsibilities? Analysis of returned questionnaires, departmental strategies, job descriptions and presentational documentation, shows that press offices have many and varied responsibilities. Core responsibilities cited by most forces included:

1. Promoting and projecting the reputation and work of the force by clearly informing the public of its activities.
2. Maintaining relationships between the force and the community, through the media where appropriate.

3. Maintaining and developing police-media relations.
4. Responding to media enquiries.
5. Proactively issuing stories and information to the media.
6. Coordinating media and public relations activities across the force.
7. Providing quality control on internal and external force publications.
8. Producing videos and other promotional materials.
9. Organising open days.
10. Developing and maintaining internal communications.
11. Providing support/consultancy to force personnel on media relations.
12. Providing in-force training on media handling.
13. Providing in-force advisory documentation.
14. Monitoring the media for police-related stories.
15. Supporting force initiatives and campaigns.
16. Responding to major incidents.
17. Arranging and coordinating press conferences.
18. Producing the force newspaper.
19. Maintaining the force internet website.
20. Producing the force annual report.

Other responsibilities, cited less frequently, included:

21. The communication of key messages.
22. Advising the local police authority on corporate issues (*ad-hoc*).
23. Providing media and PR support for the local police authority.
24. Providing media and PR support for local community safety partnerships.
25. Providing external training on media handling.
26. Development and maintenance of corporate identity.
27. A role in the force sponsorship activities.
28. Maintaining the force museum.

As this data was provided by forces in the form of a list of functions or through the provision of some form of documentation, the information was not structured in such a way that it was possible to grade these responsibilities in terms of the importance placed on them by individual forces. However, it is interesting to note that the activities listed include higher level strategic work and lower level tactical work (discussed in the *Media Strategies* section below). The activities also divide into those which have an external and those which have an internal focus. The externally-focused activities are those where the target of the activity is outside the force, such as the general public or a segmented group. An example of this would be a press office proactively issuing information to the media. For the internally-focused activities, the target group is within the force and an example of this is where the press office coordinates media and public relations activities across the force. Many of these internal activities have external outcomes. The production of the force newspaper, for example, is an internal activity, but has the purpose of not only informing force personnel, but also families of staff, retired staff and the wider community. It is a mechanism of pushing force information, messages and news into the public sphere.

Whilst common sense might suggest that press offices will be predominantly externally-focused, it is interesting to note the documented emphasis on internal aspects. For example, one force submitted extracts of their 'Business Plan' which contained three aims, the first being to 'Maintain awareness *within the force* of the services provided by the Press and Public Relations Department' and the second being to 'Provide information about the force externally to the media and the public and *internally* to staff' (emphasis added). Another force did not have specific terms of reference, but submitted the job description of the Press Officer Manager, which, *inter alia*, required the incumbent to 'manage the media' and to 'provide a resource of expertise in order to give guidance and assistance to all officers regarding media relations and the release of information to the media'. For those forces that chose to list their terms of reference rather than supply documentation, it is clear that significant importance is placed on internal activities, though this is not to infer that these forces place greater importance on internally-focused activities. One press office, for example, described its terms of reference as 'to provide a media-related service to the force and a force-related service to the media'.

It is also notable that the activities listed place the press office in different parts of the communication process, that is, for some activities the press office is the active agent communicating messages to a targeted audience, for example, promoting initiatives internally and externally. For other activities, the press office is a support agent enabling other members of the force to communicate in planned ways or to project the force in appropriate ways. An example of this is where the press office will provide advice to officers concerning the promotion of an initiative and the officer will then communicate to the media and public. In other circumstances the press office provides a support service at major incidents, both in advising the senior investigating officer (SIO) and his/her team on media handling and also in acting as a buffer between the media and the investigating team by communicating with the media in place of the investigating officers. This allows the investigation to progress without delay whilst the media are informed of events and developments.

These external/internal and primary/supporting dimensions of the press office activities interact. In some circumstances the press office will provide advice to officers to make external communication more effective. Here the target of the message is external to the force, but the work of the press office is internal, the provision of advice. In other circumstances the press office will communicate messages as the main agent both internally and externally. Across these different dimensions the press office will work at both tactical and strategic levels.

This collected information on terms of reference and departmental responsibilities can be operationalised and applied to image work's spheres of activity which were introduced in Chapter 3. Press office staff undertake image work in the spheres as follows:

A. Operational policing – press offices working in real time on operational matters, either as a main agent communicating with the media or as a support agent, for example, assisting the SIO during a major incident. In undertaking this work press office staff are likely to work at the site of incidents, although this will not always be the case. This sphere of activity includes an important role in preparing and supporting officers in media handling in order to equip them to deal with the media during operational police work.

B. News management
(i) Reactive media relations – press offices responding to inquiries from the media. Within this sphere of activity press office staff work from force press offices, typically based within force headquarters.

(ii) Proactive media relations – press offices taking the initiative and contacting media outlets with police related stories. These activities tend to be conducted predominantly from within force press offices.

C. PR and marketing communications – press offices promoting their forces through a broad range of PR activities including the planning and implementing of PR campaigns and the production of promotional materials. This goes beyond pure press and media liaison (spheres B(i) and B(ii)) and is more about promoting open days and specific initiatives than about operational policing (sphere A).

The activities generated through the surveys sit within these spheres of activity as detailed in figure 4.2.

Figure 4.2: Image work's spheres of activity and press office activities

Image work's spheres of activity	Press office activities
A. Operational	1. Developing internal communications. 2. Providing media consultancy/support to the force. 3. Providing in-force media training. 4. Responding to major incidents. 5. Arranging and coordinating press conferences. 6. Providing external training on media handling.
B(i). News management: reactive media relations	1. Maintaining and developing police–media relations. 2. Responding to media enquiries.
B(ii). News management: proactive media relations	1. Maintaining and developing police–media relations. 2. Proactively issuing stories and information to the media. 3. Monitoring the media for police-related stories. 4. The communication of key messages.
C. PR and marketing communication	1. Promoting and projecting the reputation and work of the force by clearly informing the public of the force's activities. 2. Maintaining relationships between the force and the community, through the media where appropriate. 3. Maintaining and developing police–media relations. 4. Coordinating media and public relations activities across the force. 5. Providing quality control on internal and external force publications. 6. Producing videos and other promotional materials. 7. Organising open days. 8. Providing in-force advisory documentation. 9. Supporting force initiatives and campaigns. 10. Producing the force newspaper. 11. Maintaining the force website. 12. Producing the force annual report. 13. The communication of key messages. 14. Advising the local police authority on corporate issues. 15. Providing media and PR support for the local police authority. 16. Providing media and PR support for local community safety partnerships. 17. Development and maintenance of corporate identity. 18. A role in the force sponsorship activities. 19. Maintaining the force museum.

A number of activities operate across spheres. For example, the activity of *maintaining and developing police–media relations*, operates in both news management spheres, B(i) reactive and B(ii) proactive media relations, and also in the PR and marketing sphere, depending on the particular circumstances. Working within these spheres of activity is not a discrete activity, press office staff do not consciously compartmentalise their daily tasks. Activities and spheres overlap; proactive press relations is an opportunity to market the force and engage in positive public relations work. Operational work can involve both proactive and reactive media relations. The same people may be moving in and out of these areas or operating simultaneously across activities and spheres.

The above figure gives an impression of which activities fall into each sphere of activity and to some extent this reflects the staffing of press offices in that in the larger departments there is often a demarcation, splitting sections into *press* officers and *public relations* officers. The press officers' duties would fall into the operational and reactive/proactive media relations spheres and the PR officers' duties would fall into the PR and marketing communications sphere. In offices with less staff, demarcation is obviously not possible.

Although only two activities are listed in the reactive media relations sphere and 19 in the PR and marketing sphere, this does not necessarily mean that more resources (people, effort and time) are devoted to one sphere than another. The amount of effort put into individual activities and relating to each sphere depends on the amount of staff available, their skills and interests, and force priorities. It also depends on external circumstances which will dictate that certain activities are required. How forces' resources are deployed across these spheres will therefore fluctuate. Nevertheless, as one example, consider an illustration from one force, in which I conducted an activity analysis of the press office over a two-week period in 1996. Initially 51 separate activities were identified and coded. Then for each 15 minutes of every hour the two press officers coded their primary activity over that 15 minute period. Analysis over the two-week period showed that the press officers had spent 71 per cent of their time on reactive activities and that the single most performed activity was 'reactive day-to-day press enquiries – hot news' which occupied 58 per cent of all available time. Whilst the force executive expected their press office to be proactive and the senior press officer aspired to be so, this exercise showed that the nature of the workload and the resource levels determined that the press office was primarily reactive. The site visits I undertook also suggested that forces in general had a desire to be proactive in their media relations, but workloads commonly dictated that there was more reaction than proaction. This contrasts with earlier work carried out by Crandon and Dunne with Avon and Somerset Police. Analysing police/media interactions during 1993 they found that 92.56 per cent were initiated by the police and 7.44 per cent by the media (Crandon and Dunne 1997: 84–5). This finding is quite different from my own research findings and is possibly evidence of the unevenness and divergence that exists in police–media relations across forces.

Media strategies

There is a great deal of variety in the way forces approach and present media and PR strategy. I regarded a strategy as a long-term plan which gave direction to the activities of a department. The documentation collected through the national surveys and site visits in evidence of strategies varied from brief statements of purpose and broad aims to detailed business documents containing five-year plans with aims, objectives, performance measures and targets. The range included forces which used business planning methods, such as environmental scanning and SWOT (Strengths, Weaknesses, Opportunities, Threats) analysis, to forces which stated their broad aim and then provided practical advice.

It is also significant that this documentation and the descriptions of offices' responsibilities on the returned questionnaires embraced both high-level aspirations and lower level, on-the-ground, processes (which might be described as strategic and tactical levels). Most forces which chose to list terms of reference detailed very practical level functions, for example, one force detailed 'press, publications, internal communication, Force museum' and another listed 'Press liaison (pro/reactive), displays, corporate identity, exhibitions, tours, publications, museum, daily electronic news service, media monitoring, media training'. These types of replies indicated that the departments had a practical process-driven role as their focus rather than higher-level objectives.

In contrast, a number of forces provided their higher-level aims, some linking their terms of reference to the force relationship with the public. One press office, for example, described themselves, as 'responsible for relationship between force and media and through the media, the public'. Similarly, another press office described their responsibility 'to promote the correct image of the force to the public it serves by making planned efforts to establish understanding between the police and the public'. Yet another press office provided a more technical response, with their responsibility to 'act as facilitators for the transfer of information/facilities between the force and the public, usually via the media'. Whilst these forces couched their language in technical, neutral styles, a number used promotional terms setting out declared intentions to project the image of the force. These included:

- *Example 1:*
  Aim – *to maximise opportunities to promote the force through the media.*

- *Example 2:*
  Aim – *to protect and promote the good name and reputation of the force.*

- *Example 3:*
  Long-term objective – *to project a positive and caring image of the force to the community we serve.*

- *Example 4:*
  Aim – *to promote a positive image of the force.*

These four examples above differ from the previous ones in that they are overtly projecting and promoting positive images rather than using the language of service and response which others utilise. Two forces in particular highlight this characteristic, one illustrating the negative work of a press office and the other the positive work. First, one press office provided a document detailing the responsibilities of the Head of the Press Office including 'implement damage limitation strategies when required, in order to protect the Force's image'. It is open to interpretation whether this advocates a *managerial* or *misrepresentative* approach to communication and its veracity is likely to be dependent on the situation and the personnel involved. Secondly, one force's annual plan for its press office stated in its introduction (emphasis added):

> This PR strategy is geared to promoting the Force in the *most positive manner* through the news media and other publicity mechanisms ... presenting police topics in the *most constructive light* ... influencing opinion formers ...

> Primary Mission: To provide PR support ... *by generating positive publicity* thereby *influencing public opinion in favour of force objectives.* The prime mover in this endeavour is effective use of the news media as a conduit into the public consciousness.

This last example is the most blatant declaration by any force of an intention to construct actively and manage a positive image. It is not mitigated in subsequent paragraphs by commitments to openness and honesty in media relations.

These strategies then are presented in different ways, the language varying from the technical to the promotional. The language and content of these documents imply how the force concerned intends to approach image work and this can be considered in relation to the communication types suggested in Chapter 3. At a theoretical level, for example, the documents using neutral or technical type language and which talk of building relationships with the community and using media relations to foster mutual understanding might reflect a dialogical (substantive negotiable content, two-way communication) or a missionary approach. The documents which pick up on promotion and projection (examples 1– 4 above) might reflect a managerial approach involving communication which is selectively substantive, and content which is selected and idealised, showing forces in the best light. The language of the final two examples, arguably, crosses the line into a misrepresentative approach, where communication is essentially one-way and based on high control and low information to manage image. In the case of the final example above the language appears to express a willingness to manipulate public opinion to support force objectives.

The evidence suggests that there is little consistency between forces as to what constitutes a strategy. Notwithstanding this, the surveys indicated that over two-thirds of forces had what they regarded as a media strategy. These are something of a recent development, the majority dating from 1995 and after. This upsurge reflects the increasing demands that the media are making on the police service and the recognition by senior managers that there is a need to respond in a planned way, for example, by putting in place a media strategy. This flurry of activity over a relatively short period was matched by the high number of responding forces in 1997 that were in the midst of change, including departmental restructuring and the (re)drafting of media strategies. Despite unevenness and the state of change, the data indicated that a significant number of forces were developing overarching corporate communication strategies. This suggested an endeavour to move towards a more strategic approach, integrating the most obvious function of media liaison with others such as internal communications and corporate identity.

Analysis of the work of police press offices has provided an insight into the image work that goes on nationally in individual police forces. It has identified instances of divergence, but also common trends of professionalisation and civilianisation of the workforce. It also suggests that image work is no longer conducted only from headquarters by specialist communicators, but is permeating outlying divisions and the responsibilities of greater numbers of police personnel. This analysis has provided a complementary perspective to the systemic analysis offered earlier in this chapter, although several common themes are evident. Policing stakeholders, for example, aware of the changing mass mediated environment and its demands, have reacted by greater involvement in image work, by trying to improve coordination and cohesion, and by drawing on the expertise of professional communicators. They have also embraced the rhetoric of 'openness' and are actively cultivating mutually beneficial relationships with media organisations.

In this chapter I have argued that the police service in general, despite patterns of unevenness and difference, is aspiring to a more concerted, proactive approach to image work. This increasingly draws on communication specialists but also, in the name of both transparency and promotionalism, encourages all staff to engage in image work. The research evidence also throws light on the relationship between image work and police legitimacy. Police forces appear to be engaged in image work for a number of reasons, including as a means of justifying their organisation and institutional position, as a means of explaining their actions, promoting their interests and also to build and maintain relationships with the organisations and public(s) they interact with. In the following chapters these concerns and emerging trends are explored further by focusing on image work within one police force.

Notes

1 Defining public relations is contentious. In the professional literature at its narrowest public relations is regarded as synonymous with press relations. In contrast van Riel argues it is 'concerned with disseminating knowledge in order to create understanding of an organisation and its products and services. It is not about creating favourable images or persuading people to buy. It deals with the real world where things are not always favourable' (1995: 33). According to the Institute of Public Relations it is 'the planned and sustained effort to establish and maintain goodwill and mutual understanding between an organisation and its public' (Michie 1998).

2 For example, in May 1999 the *Guardian* reported that after the Met. issued statistics on 'stop and search', there were 'angry exchanges' between a Met. ACPO officer (Assistant Commissioner Denis O'Connor), the Met. Federation chairman (Glen Smyth) and the Black Police Association chairman (Inspector Paul Wilson). For good measure, a Home Office minister (Paul Boateng) also contributed a view ('Police fall out over search-robberies link' *Guardian* 15/5/99).

3 A number of studies emerged in the late 1990s which examine how the police manage the media to assist operational work, but these do not focus on, or

examine in any detail, the activities of press offices (Boyle 1999, Feist 1999, Innes 1999).

4   However, it was interesting to note amongst these documents that one force's *Media Guide* stated the need to 'foster and cultivate increased openness, awareness and plain speaking in dealing with the media' yet goes on to set out the force policy as 'the chief constable has decreed officers of the rank of sergeant and above can supply factual information to the media, although there are circumstances when constables would give interviews'. Openness indeed.

Chapter 5

One force and its image

'And lastly, fish and chips, Mr. Chairman, you can have them open or wrapped. We prefer them open and that is our purpose here today...We hope to encourage the very opposite of that old Yorkshire adage, hear all, see all and say nowt, and to get people to have the confidence to hear all, see all and say sommat.' (Chief Inspector Pratt addressing the South Yorkshire Police Committee, March 1979.)

Chief Inspector Pratt was part of a senior delegation from South Yorkshire Police (SYP hereafter) responding to the report of a council working party set up to address concerns over police–public relations. It is significant, looking back, that the force (senior management, PSA and Federation) had declined to contribute to, or participate in, the working party's programme of activities. Instead senior officers including the chief constable, J.H. Brownlow, prepared and presented their response to the working party's draft report. Brownlow claimed to be incensed on first reading the report due to its 'subtle bias against the police' (Moores 1979: 26). This was a reflection of tensions that had emerged nationally in the relationship between the police and local politicians in the 1970s. However, the significance of this 1979 inquiry also lies in it being a catalyst for the development of image work within SYP. This chapter discusses the image of SYP in the context of its history, the force's 1990s trajectory and its press and public relations approach. In doing so the chapter examines one force which experienced problems of legitimacy and in the 1990s sought to rebuild its identity. It traces the development of image work in the force. The case study is developed further in Chapters 6 and 7, in which I analyse the practice of image work in South Yorkshire. In this chapter, I first explain how and why SYP was selected as the case study. A short history of policing South Yorkshire is then presented, following which I analyse and discuss recent official documentation which seeks to construct and communicate the 'official' image of SYP. Finally, I consider the formal means by which SYP promotes and presents its image.

In reviewing suitable locations for a case study I was seeking a police force in which specific conditions existed that made image considerations particularly pertinent. South Yorkshire Police was selected, for a number of reasons. First, it has a varied policing area, despite being relatively geographically compact (385,605 hectares). The policing area has a population of approximately 1.3 million living in one city (Sheffield), towns (Barnsley, Doncaster and Rotherham) and large areas of countryside (the Howden and Hallam moors), some of which are isolated. The contrasting landscapes of the area, taking in both industrial urban districts and the hills and moors of the Peak District National Park were captured memorably in verse by John Betjeman's *An Edwardian Sunday, Broomhill, Sheffield*. However, as an area South Yorkshire has a reputation for being economically deprived. This was confirmed in European terms in March 1998 when the European Commission named South Yorkshire, along with Sicily and the former East Germany, as amongst the most deprived areas in Europe, qualifying for EU 'Objective One' status by virtue of the area's GDP being less than 75 per cent of the EU average – South Yorkshire's was 70.7 per cent of the average. The industrial wealth of Sheffield, 'steel city,' and the Yorkshire coal fields had provided steady employment until the industrial decline and strife of the 1970s and 1980s, which saw the loss of 60,000 jobs in the steel industry alone. In the 1990s the picture was one of coping rather than prospering and of an area coming to terms with industrial decline and social change (Taylor *et al.* 1996). This was captured in two 1990s films, *The Full Monty* and *Brassed Off*, both of which encapsulated the issues of how industrial decline impacts on areas and how communities seek to cope and adjust.

Secondly, SYP is a metropolitan force, though one of the smaller ones. At the time of the fieldwork in 1997 the force had 3,554 sworn officers and 1,453 civilian staff. Thirdly, it has a traumatic history and a problematic public image arising from incidents including the 1984–85 Miners' Strike and the 1989 Hillsborough disaster. Fourth, and finally, it had, between June 1990 and July 1998, a chief constable with a national profile, who had extensive experience of police–media relations. At the time of the research he was chair of the ACPO Media Advisory Group (MAG), of which he was a founder member.

All this made SYP an intriguing research subject. The area policed was diverse, the force had a legacy of problems in terms of its image and it had, during the period of the fieldwork, a chief constable who, acutely aware of image and media relations, had attempted to rebuild public confidence in the force. The force agreed to cooperate with the research following an interview with the chief constable and the head of media and public relations became the liaison officer for the project. She set up initial visits and acted as an enabler. Access never proved a problem in four months' observation of the force and its work.

A short history of South Yorkshire Police

The South Yorkshire Police came into being in 1974 when the number of police forces was reduced to the current 43 in conjunction with the Conservative's local government reorganisations. This followed on from a series of amalgamations made possible by the 1964 Police Act which gave the Home Secretary the power to amalgamate (Emsley 1996: 174). The Sheffield and Rotherham police forces had merged in 1967 and the 1974 changes brought Barnsley and Doncaster police into the SYP. Following a force reorganisation in April 1995, the five divisions and 14 sub-divisions were restructured into 11 operational districts.

Figure 5.1: The South Yorkshire policing area

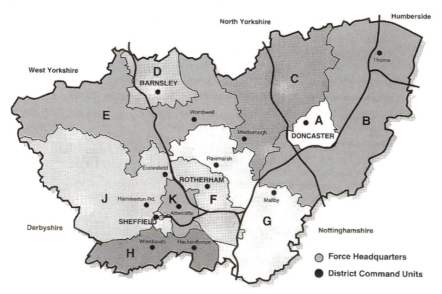

Sheffield is the only city in the force area and has a colourful policing history. The first hint of organised policing in the area was in 1818 when, under the Local Improvements Act, Colonel Francis Fenton had been appointed Superintendent of Police in Sheffield.[1] In 1825 Fenton's resources consisted of five constables. Some six years after the creation of the Metropolitan Police in London, a force of 20 'day policemen' was formed in Sheffield in 1836, despite local objections by those concerned about the cost. Advertisements were placed for 'officials who will be required to work after the cleansing, lighting and watching of the public streets.'[2] Following recruitment, wearing a uniform of blue coats with buttons bearing the Sheffield coat of arms, the officers patrolled from noon until the night watchmen came out after dark (Bean 1987: 47). By 1843, when Sheffield was incorporated as a borough, the responsibility for maintaining a police force was placed on the Town Council, who vested control over the police in the Watch Committee. At this point Thomas Raynor (who succeeded Fenton in 1836) became the first chief constable.

The Watch Committee issued its *rules, orders and regulations for the guidance of the officers and constables of the police* (Sheffield Borough Watch Committee 1844). These are similar to, but less detailed than, the original instructions to the Metropolitan Police, which as detailed in Chapter 1 have specific image and communication implications. The Sheffield regulations are not as comprehensive in terms of image building, but the conditions of appointment address image in terms of the requirement of officers to 'always appear neat and clean ... dressed in complete Uniform' (*ibid*: para. 4). There are many references to conduct that is appropriate, to effect a particular impression, e.g. instructions not to take drink or money from charged persons (*ibid*: para. 10), not to alter police clothing in any way or conceal police numbers (*ibid*: para. 12). Officers were not allowed to carry a stick or umbrella, or smoke or drink on duty (*ibid*: para. 12). In terms of the role of the police, prevention of crime was the prime emphasis of the police function, with other 'objects of the Police Establishment' being the traditional founding principles of 'the security of person and property, the preservation of the public tranquility and of good order' (*ibid*: iv).

Histories of policing Sheffield through the nineteenth and early twentieth centuries depict a tough, often violent, city policed by robust officers. Nineteenth century records suggest the local police were not popular. Bean recounts one instance when a convicted murderer slipped the police with the assistance of the gathered crowd and the local papers record a 'well-grounded dislike of the police' (Bean 1987: 48). There were frequent complaints against the police, few of which were upheld, e.g. in

1834 sergeant Crookes was accused of repeatedly twisting a suspect's nose between his knuckles. He was acquitted. Crookes was again accused of assault the following year and was again acquitted (*ibid*: 48). Violence was an accepted part of everyday life in Victorian Sheffield, usually revolving around brawls fuelled by drinking, many of which turned into affrays and then free-for-alls in which the combatants would combine to fight the police as they arrived to break up the disturbance (*ibid*: 50–1). During the 1860s trade unionists fuelled industrial violence through widespread 'rattening', the theft of tools and grinders' wheelbands, which developed into explosions and murders. These incidents became known as the 'Sheffield Outrages' and were instrumental in the establishment of the first Royal Commission on Trades Unions (Baldwin and Bottoms 1976: 50).

Robust policing continued into the twentieth century and the 1920s gang wars over betting rackets and the breaking of the gangs has passed into national policing folklore (Sillitoe 1955: 77–84, Cockerill 1975: 87–94, Baldwin and Bottoms 1976: 50, Bean 1981). Under the leadership of Chief Constable Percy Sillitoe (1926–31) the taming of the Garvin and Mooney razor gangs was achieved by a squad of officers who would target the gangs and fight 'gun, razor and cosh with fist, boot and truncheon' (Bean 1987: 92). Christened the 'flying squad' this team was an early exponent of targeting known criminals and was given a relatively free hand (Sillitoe 1955: 79–82). The tactics were successful if not always strictly within the law (Bean 1981: 109–15). Sillitoe was an adept image-builder, aware of the reputational value of his association with taming the Sheffield gangs. In his autobiography he neglected to mention that the flying squad had been established in May 1925 by his predecessor and had achieved considerable success prior to his appointment (Bean 1981: 126). He took steps to improve the image of the Sheffield force by introducing steam presses for the upkeep of uniforms and by organising elocution lessons for constables. To maintain the 'prestige and morale' of the force he also arranged for the discreet treatment of cases of venereal disease, to spare his officers the indignity of attending the public VD clinic (Sillitoe 1955: 100).

Whilst the success in defeating the razor gangs has become part of policing folklore, it is ironic that police officers using similar methods to Sillitoe's officers brought the force into disrepute in 1963 in the notorious 'rhino whip' affair. Two detectives from the force's recently formed crime squad, assaulted three suspects with a 'rhino tail' a confiscated offensive weapon, eight inches long, made of a gut-like material and with a plaited loop at one end. The assaults came into the open once the men's injuries were revealed in court and set in train inquiries which resulted in the dismissal of the responsible officers, the early retirements of the head and deputy of CID and finally the resignation of the chief constable. The tactics used by the 'rhino whip' officers were reminiscent of Sillitoe's flying squad, hence Robert Mark's comment that in the 1930s Sillitoe was rewarded with a knighthood, whilst in the 1960s 'he would have got the sack' (Mark 1978: 262). At variance with this tough, sometimes tarnished image, Sheffield Police in the 1970s showed their willingness to collaborate with academics at a time when the police service nationally was suspicious of letting sociologists loose in their areas. They cooperated with the Sheffield Study on Urban Social Structure and Crime (Baldwin and Bottoms 1976, Mawby 1979) in the development of what became the 'Sheffield school' initially concerned with spatial approaches to crime and later with the 'residential community crime career' (Evans 1995: 4–5). In this respect Sheffield featured in the wave of original policing research which was emerging in Britain in the 1970s.

During the 1980s policing in South Yorkshire was again brought to national prominence through two events. The first was the 1984–85 Miners' Strike which, although a national strike, featured prominently in the South Yorkshire area. The second incident was the Hillsborough football ground disaster of April 1989. I will now consider each in turn.

The 1984–85 Miners' Strike

> ...the largest peacetime police operation in British history. (Waddington [1999a: 82])

The 1984–85 Miners' Strike lasted from March 1984 to March 1985 and has become a political, industrial and policing landmark (Fine and Millar 1985, Wilsher *et al.* 1985, McCabe and Wallington 1988, Waddington *et al.* 1989, Green 1990, Alderson 1998). During the course of the strike, as Alderson has noted:

> the public image of the British police was to undergo a transformation...millions of television viewers daily watched scenes of violence between the police and picketing miners. The 'people's police' seemed more and more to be the 'government's police' (Alderson 1998: 143).

At the time of the strike the coal industry was in public ownership and the employers were seen as synonymous with the government such that any industrial dispute was automatically also a political issue. The policing of such a strike accordingly had political connotations with the police cast as the coercive arm of the government (Alderson 1998: 143–4). The policing of the Miners' Strike included the operation of the National Reporting Centre (NRC) which was seen as sinister harbinger of a national police force (Kettle 1985). Critics in parliament, the media and academia raised concerns for civil liberties in the face of police forces providing mutual aid and setting up roadblocks to prevent the movement of pickets around the country. The use of riot gear on picket lines and the saturation policing of mining communities alienated the police who were derided as 'Maggie's Army'.

South Yorkshire proved to be a key battle-ground – 'the cockpit of violence' (Waddington 1998: 134) – during the course of the strike. On 19 April 1984 approximately 7,000 people attended a National Union of Mineworkers conference at Sheffield City Hall and outside the hall scenes of disorder followed. Later the same day 69 arrests were made at an incident outside the Sheffield Trades and Labour Club. Of a more serious nature, Orgreave Coking Plant became the location of the strike's fiercest confrontations between police and miners. Images of pitched battles at Orgreave remain an enduring legacy, symbolising the breakdown of order and the relationship between police and miners during the strike. The most violent day was 18 June 1984 when 10,000 pickets faced 4,000 police officers drawn from across England and Wales and 93 arrests were made. The exchanges which occurred have been described vividly:

> squadrons of visored figures, reins in one hand and wooden batons in the other, cantering across a vast cornfield, scattering pickets by the thousand...a picture without modern precedent in Britain (Wilsher et al. 1985: 88).

At the height of the battle television cameras filmed a police officer repeatedly aiming blows with his truncheon at a cowering picket. The officer, from Northumbria Constabulary, was traced and a file sent to the Director of Public Prosecutions (DPP hereafter), who determined not to prosecute. Nevertheless, Peter Wright, chief constable of SYP, was quoted as believing 'that incident very nearly lost us Orgreave in the eyes of the public. It gave credibility to all the other statements of police misbehaviour which were rife' (Wilsher et al. 1985: 102; see also Graef 1989: 72–4). Violent incidents also occurred at the Cortonwood colliery, where the police were blamed for inflaming the situation.

The policing of the strike 'fundamentally reoriented the attitudes of the policed' (Green 1990: 45) and undoubtedly caused tension between

SYP and the mining communities of South Yorkshire. Many police officers were from mining families and faced the dilemma of divided loyalties. Nevertheless, Waddington records that after the strike, within mining communities generally, relations between former strikers and the police returned to normality, achieved by 'local people and their police conspiring to blame confrontation on those officers drafted in from elsewhere' (Waddington 1994: 15). As in other areas, the Met. were demonised in South Yorkshire, but the Met. could not be held solely responsible. In the villages of Grimethorpe (near Barnsley) and Maltby (near Rotherham), for example, there were minor incidents between local people and police officers, including those from SYP, that acted as triggers for larger scale disorder. In Maltby the police station was stoned on 15 June 1984 and running street fights occurred as police reinforcements arrived. In Grimethorpe on 15 October 1984 the police station was besieged by miners and their wives in protest over the police preventing the acquisition of fuel by locals 'coal picking' from the colliery wastage tip. Later in the day the police had sealed off the village and in the evening after the pubs closed further trouble occurred involving the police and local youths. At a public meeting in Grimethorpe organised on 17 October by the South Yorkshire Police Committee, the chair of the committee accused police officers of behaving like 'Nazi stormtroopers' (Wilsher et al. 1985: 186, Waddington et al. 1989: 133).

Analysing the circumstances surrounding the events in Maltby and Grimethorpe, Waddington et al. believe they represent 'acts of community resistance' exacerbated, not caused by, the presence of 'outside' police forces, with potentially long-term consequences for police-community relations (Waddington et al. 1989: 137–8). Locally published literature in the wake of the strike would appear to support the case that the strike and its policing harnessed a community spirit within South Yorkshire that excluded the local police (Coulter et al. 1984, Worsborough Community Group 1985, Jackson 1986, Samuel et al. 1986, Keating 1991). This distancing of South Yorkshire communities from their local police was also evident at a decision-making level. The chief constable had set out his policy to assist anyone who wanted to work, but local MPs lobbied the chief constable, and the Police Committee attempted to curb his policy by restricting his expenditure. To counter this he obtained Home Office support and High Court rulings which allowed him to police the dispute as he saw fit. In doing so, Peter Wright was accused of policing without the consent of the community and declared resignedly 'the only way I could have satisfied the local politicians was by not policing the dispute' (Wilsher et al. 1985: 100–1).

At the conclusion of the strike, over 300 SYP officers had been injured, hundreds of miners and residents were charged with offences relating to the dispute and the cost of policing the disorder in the county exceeded £18 million. Police–public relations had been set back and the credibility of SYP was further damaged when 15 men charged with riot at Orgreave were acquitted at Sheffield Crown Court after a trial lasting 48 days. Proceedings against a further 220 pickets were subsequently halted and the sum total of successful prosecutions brought in South Yorkshire was 67 men bound over to keep the peace (Bean 1987: 138). In summary the strike had caused a rift between SYP and the mining communities that would take years to bridge. Whilst nationally the strike is regarded as a key stage in the politicisation of the police service, at a local level in South Yorkshire its lasting effect was on the relationship between local people and local police. Within four years of the strike, an event occurred which has kept SYP in the national spotlight to this day.

The 1989 Hillsborough Disaster

> South Yorkshire Police will never stop 'paying' for the Hillsborough tragedy. The 'debt' is of Third World proportions and the creditors are either dead or scarred for life. ('Hillsborough's open wound', *Police Review* editorial, 27/2/98.)

The Hillsborough tragedy has proved to be an axial event for SYP and its impact on the force endures. As the disaster looms so large over the force, to understand how it still influences the image of SYP, it is necessary to consider the events of the day and the subsequent developments.

On 15 April 1989, Sheffield Wednesday's Hillsborough football stadium was the venue for the FA cup semi-final between Liverpool and Nottingham Forest. Liverpool supporters had been allocated the Leppings Lane end of the ground and ten minutes before the 3.00 p.m. kick-off, a considerable number of Liverpool supporters were still outside the ground. The numbers waiting led the senior police officer outside the ground to become concerned about the pressure building up at the entrance. To relieve this pressure he requested the opening of a gate (a 15 feet wide metal barrier) to let the supporters into the ground. As the gate opened approximately 2,000 people streamed into the stadium and many headed through a tunnel leading onto the terraces. This influx added to the crowding in this area of the ground and in the crush which ensued 96 people received injuries from which they died and hundreds were injured. This outline of the events leading to the Hillsborough tragedy is largely accepted as fact. However, the apportionment of blame and responsibility was played out in the media and two versions emerged in opposition. The first version blamed the crush on the sudden, late arrival of drunken Liverpool supporters, some without tickets, who put such pressure on the turnstiles that the police had no option but to open the additional gate leading to the fatal crush. The second version cited inadequate crowd control arrangements at Leppings Lane and when the gate was opened, the police and stewards failed to direct supporters into the less crowded areas of the terraces. Different newspapers supported each version (Taylor 1989, Scraton 1999).

A judicial inquiry into the tragedy was conducted by Lord Justice Taylor, who issued an interim report on 4 August 1989, which placed blame on different organisations including Sheffield Wednesday Football Club and the County Council. Senior officers of SYP were also blamed and the principal cause of the disaster was cited as the failure of police control. In addition the officer in charge, Chief Superintendent David Duckenfield, was accused of 'freezing' and also of lying in telling Graham Kelly (the Football Association Secretary, who ran to the police control room as the disaster unfolded) that fans had forced a gate. On the day the report was issued, Duckenfield was suspended, Chief Constable Peter Wright apologised for the role of his force in the tragedy and offered his own resignation, which was not accepted. In placing the blame primarily on the police, the Taylor Inquiry raised expectations, particularly amongst families of the victims that action would be taken against those responsible. They were to be disappointed as the DPP ruled in August 1990 that there was insufficient evidence to bring criminal prosecutions against any police officer. Further disappointment resulted from the Coroner's inquest which in 1991 returned a verdict of accidental death rather than unlawful killing. This disappointment was compounded when David Duckenfield retired on ill-health grounds in November 1991 and thus never faced the disciplinary charges which the Police Complaints Authority had directed should be brought against him. As Duckenfield was retired, the disciplinary charge against his deputy, Superintendent Bernard Murray, was not pursued as the PCA considered it unjust that a joint charge should be prosecuted against the junior officer in the absence of the senior officer.

These developments frustrated those who believed that the police should be held accountable and their campaign for action was given impetus by the television drama-documentary *Hillsborough*, written by Jimmy McGovern, which was screened by ITV on 5 December 1996. SYP had decided not to cooperate with the programme makers and the programme contained suggestions that police officers had lied, suppressed evidence and pressured witnesses. The disaster was again a national issue and in June 1997 the new Home Secretary, Jack Straw, announced that he had requested the Appeal Court judge, Lord Justice Stuart-Smith, to scrutinise whether new, relevant evidence had become available which would justify a fresh inquiry. In February 1998 the Home Secretary announced that on the basis of the scrutiny (a 120,000 word report from Stuart-Smith LJ) there were no grounds for a further inquiry. The Hillsborough Family Support Group (HFSG) called for the Home Secretary's resignation amongst cries of 'New Labour, new cover-up' (Trevor Hicks of HFSG, Radio 4, 18 February 1998). Six of the victims' families then took out private prosecutions against Duckenfield and Murray. In July 2000 Murray was cleared of manslaughter, but the jury failed to reach a verdict on Duckenfield, and despite an application from the families, the trial judge ruled that there would be no retrial.

The impact of the Hillsborough disaster on SYP cannot be under-estimated. Since it occurred in April 1989, the name of SYP has been inextricably linked with the disaster and for being partly responsible for the tragedy of the day. Whilst the police are often at the heart of disasters, and perform a service role which brings them respect and honour, the key difference with Hillsborough has been that the police are perceived as being part of the problem, not only through incompetence and mismanagement on the day, but in their subsequent conduct during the inquiry which followed, including suspicion of cover ups and the withholding of information (Scraton 1999: 294–5). Although SYP has accepted it was at fault and has apologised repeatedly, the impression remains that not only were members of the force incompetent on the day, but that diversionary tactics were utilised to deflect blame. It also clearly rankles that no-one from SYP was punished for their actions on the day and that a number of officers sought and obtained financial compensation for injuries sustained, whilst numbers of victims and their families had yet to be compensated. No amount of declarations of the known facts by senior police officers and government ministers can remove this stigma whilst members of the victims' families remain convinced that justice has not been done. It is unlikely that there can ever be a satisfactory outcome for SYP. The families' long-running campaign means the connotations of police malpractice remain and SYP will always bear the negative connection with the tragedy – in admitting its part in the disaster, incompetence is accepted and SYP must live with this.

From Wright to Wells

In the wake of Hillsborough, the image of SYP was tarnished and the force turned its gaze inwards, battening down the hatches and treating outsiders such as the media with great suspicion. The force had arguably reached its nadir. A turning point was the retirement of Peter Wright in May 1990 and the appointment of a very different successor, Richard Wells, an Oxford-educated, Bramshill-trained, deputy assistant commissioner from the Metropolitan Police. Wells had served 28 years with the Met. and had experience in operational command, community relations, media relations and training. The chairman of the South Yorkshire Police Authority, the late Sir John Layden, explained that in seeking a new chief constable in the wake of the Miners' Strike and Hillsborough, the prime concern was to 'win back public support and to restore confidence in the police'. The Police Authority required an individual who combined 'police experience and political and public relations skills' (Harvey-Jones 1992: 184). Richard Wells was appointed chief constable on 1 June 1990.

Wells took over a force which was beleaguered and dispirited. The force was demoralised as a result of a series of events which had damaged its reputation, confidence and integrity. First, the Miners' Strike of 1984–85 had placed the police and the mining communities on opposite sides. In its aftermath the morale of SYP had declined as criminal cases against pickets collapsed and were followed by civil cases against SYP by the pickets. Second, there was the Hillsborough disaster and the subsequent Taylor Report which criticised the force. Third, after the Hillsborough disaster, morale was further damaged when the force's senior officers became concerned over leakages of information to the local media. In a climate of suspicion the CID undertook internal enquiries and subsequently three press officers were charged with disciplinary offences. The senior press officer was dismissed from her post, but became a *cause célèbre* championed by the media, forcing SYP to offer reinstatement, which she refused. Fourth, a probationer's initiation ceremony, a night-shift prank, came to public attention when a staged robbery was mistaken for a real incident. This led to the disciplining of several officers and headlines in the local newspapers lampooning SYP as the 'Keystone Kops', a label which was subsequently re-used by the local media. As a result of these factors Wells inherited an embattled force with awful media relations. Sir John Harvey-Jones, who 'trouble-shot' SYP in 1992, provides a corroborating view, describing SYP as having 'major problems' and 'feeling pretty sorry for itself' at the time Wells was appointed (Harvey-Jones 1992: 155–6).

From this low point Wells identified the major task of developing a strategy to take the force forward. He was concerned with rebuilding the identity of the organisation and changing the prevailing culture. Such ambition would be challenging to many organisations; to an embattled hierarchical police force, it was particularly challenging. To achieve these aims Wells utilised prescription and consultation. In terms of prescription he set out a '10 Point Plan' together with a vision for the force termed the *'Six Hill Horizon.'* These are reproduced below and encapsulate the approach which Wells maintained throughout his term of office.

Chief Constable's '10 Point Plan'

1. Emphasis on public service.
2. Staff care for customer care.
3. Human face.
4. Reasonableness of action.
5. Communication of doubt upwards.
6. Catching people doing right.
7. Regular meetings to establish common ground.
8. Do not waste any energy fighting each other.
9. Honesty with courtesy.
10. Allow individuality.

The South Yorkshire Police Six Hill Horizon
Within five years, or as soon as practicable, to have a South Yorkshire Police Service which:

a) is more open, relaxed and honest with ourselves and the public;
b) is more aware of our environment, sensitive to change and positioning ourselves to respond to change;
c) is more clear about our role and our identity and is obviously and justifiably proud of itself;
d) is more closely in touch with our customers, puts them first and delivers what they want quickly, effectively and courteously;
e) makes its decisions at the appropriate levels;
f) is the envy of all other forces.

The themes introduced in these 'prescriptions', including 'openness', 'honesty', 'sensitivity', 'trust', 'service' and 'humanity', recur in the force documentation produced during Wells' term of office. The language and messages of these 'mission' type statements were novel to the police service of 1990. They not only utilised management sound-bites such as 'catching people doing right' and 'staff care for customer care' but also, through the use of language encouraging officers to be relaxed, sensitive and thoughtful, they challenged the more traditional police notion of compliance with hierarchical command and control systems.

So much for prescription. In terms of consultation Wells initiated a consultation process which took in over 250 community groups and each member of SYP, all of whom received a personally signed letter from Wells concerning core values. This process generated what was to become the *Statement of Force Purpose and Values,* comprising the policing 'purpose', the 'values' of SYP and its 'way of working'. The *Statement* concerns what the force will do and how it will conduct itself in the discharge of its duties. It exhorts staff to strive to act with 'integrity' to be 'honest, courteous and tactful' and to 'use persuasion, common sense and good humour'. It emphasises also that staff should display honesty, humanity and compassion, be willing to listen, to try new ways of working and to admit failings. It is, in sum, a statement which both provides guidance to members of SYP and also gives people expectations concerning how they will be treated in their dealings with the force. The language and tone is similar to that of the prescriptive documents, the core values from these being embedded in the *Statement* providing a clear indication of the type of force and image that is being projected and aspired to.

In forming this strategy to take the force forward, the notions of humanity, rationality and even fallibility presented challenges to the workforce based on their recent experiences. Sir John Harvey-Jones visiting the force in 1992 captured the mood of a force which was not quite trusting of the new approach. He describes Wells as a chief constable 'faced with massive problems of changing entrenched attitudes and ways of organisation and operation' (Harvey-Jones 1992: 163). During his visit Harvey-Jones met officers who accepted the need for change, but who variously thought change was too quick, too slow, some who welcomed the new environment and others who remained suspicious.

Although the approach adopted by Wells should rightly be examined in the light of the recent history and the particular circumstances of SYP, we should not forget that at the same time on the national stage there were pressures on the service as a whole to embrace new management ideas and reform. As detailed in chapter 2, at the time of Wells' appointment to chief constable in 1990, ACPO had launched a 'quality of service' crusade which included the development of the ACPO Strategic Policy Document (1990) incorporating the *Statement of Common Purpose and Values* (Waters 1996). Whilst the ACPO and SYP 'statements' are not identical, the ACPO *Statement* also includes references to acting with fairness and courtesy. It advocates restraint and calmness and emphasises the need to listen to and respond to 'well founded criticism with a willingness to change' (ACPO 1990). Accordingly the way forward for SYP was both a reaction to its predicament in 1990 and also a reflection of the managerialist and social pressures on all police forces (McLaughlin and Muncie 1994; McLaughlin and Murji 1997).

South Yorkshire Police in the late 1990s

Having laid out the chief constable's mission and strategy to lift the force and take it forward, what documentation was available seven years on at the time of the fieldwork to paint a picture of the force? The original *Six Hill Horizon* had specified a five-year period in which to make progress. By 1997 five years had elapsed and the *Horizon* was reviewed as part of the strategic planning process. The first *Strategic Plan 1996–2001* had been published in April 1996 (SYP 1996a). The review of this by the senior command team resulted in slight amendments to the *Six Hill Horizon*. The newly-worded 'horizon' retained the original subject areas and carried through the promotion of the core values of openness, honesty, sensitivity to the external environment, self-confidence and acceptance of change. It also added the quality of 'acknowledging occasional mistakes and learning from them' (SYP 1997a: 5). It appeared to signal a force that had grown in confidence.

The *Six Hill Horizon* and the *Statement of Purpose and Values* provide the mission of SYP and give an indication of the identity and image that the force aspired to and wished to present. These provided an overarching framework, within which SYP undertook its strategic planning, incorporating long-term planning and annual planning at force and district/department level and also taking into account, since the 1994 PMCA, the externally formulated national policing objectives set by the Home Secretary, which in turn became 'Ministerial Priorities' from August 1998. Figure 5.2 summarises these different levels. The combination of these processes and the documentation which results form a picture of SYP as a police force. The annual report of the chief constable is another document which brings these different levels together and reports on progress over the year. In the following sections these documents are examined with the purpose of analysing the type of police force the official formal documentation promotes.

Figure 5.2: South Yorkshire Police: official representations

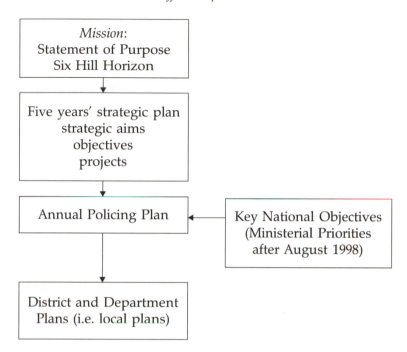

The Strategic Plan

The aims specified in the force's 1997-2002 strategic plan are:

- Valuing the people we serve.
- Crime and community safety.
- Valuing our own people.
- Effective structures.
(SYP 1997a: 9–17).

These high level aims and their associated objectives project a force that intends to work with and for the community of South Yorkshire, utilising partnerships, communicating well, fighting crime and making the county safe for its residents. At the same time it aims to recruit and retain good people and manage its resources and organisational structure to provide effective service to the public. Under each strategic aim are a number of objectives and attached to each are projects through which it is planned the objective can be achieved. There is only one area in which image work is specifically addressed. Under the first aim is the objective 1.1:

To improve the service we provide by developing how we communicate with the public and respond to requests for assistance, and tell them how their enquiries are being progressed (*ibid*: 9).

Project 1.1.2 is *improve and develop media relations and information services*. The lead department for the project is Press and Public Relations. This is the only project within the strategic plan which the press office has ownership of. Although this is the sole reference in the strategy to non-operational communication and the press office, it is a key responsibility in terms of projecting and managing the image of the force.

The Annual Report of the chief constable

The annual report of the chief constable was originally a mechanism of accountability, produced in compliance with the 1964 Police Act. It now fulfils this and also a promotional role. A brief examination of three annual reports captures a flavour of the official representation of SYP in the late 1990s. Each report follows the same format, comprising the chief constable's foreword, a tour of the districts and the support departments and finally a statistical section.

The chief constable's 1995–96 annual report provides a review of the 11 newly-formed operational districts claiming in the introduction that the reorganisation 'meant considerable improvement in community policing and a better relationship with the public throughout South Yorkshire' (SYP 1996b: 11). The tour of the new districts projects a force that fights and prevents crime, engages in multi-agency community-based projects and gave considerable attention to public consultation over the year. The following years' reports follow a similar pattern and tour the districts citing examples of successful crime detection initiatives, working with the community in partnership variously to prevent crime, to encourage good citizenship in the young and to help the old and infirm. Good works by individual officers and by members of the public, usually youngsters, are captured and celebrated by photographs. Following this round of the districts, the work of the force-wide support and operational units is reviewed. The reports end with a supplement providing a statistical breakdown of the force including facts and figures about finance and personnel, together with performance indicator statistics. This format, combining promotional images with statistical performance details, is a template common to police forces.

The chief constable's foreword is an opportunity to review the work of the force over the operational year and to comment on the wider context of policing. The foreword of the 1996–97 report is notable for Wells' comments on image building. In the late 1990s policing context of central targets, tight budgets and raised public expectations of performance, Wells cites the difficulties of balancing the supply of, and the demand for, policing. He forecasts 'ultimate disappointment [as] almost a self-fulfilling prophecy' (SYP 1997b: 5) and recognises that:

the pressures of apparently declining public popularity (despite our increased integrity and professionalism) are consciously or sub-consciously driving police forces to maintain services which are non-confrontational and image-building. Greater emphasis on an open and consultative style of policing means we have to employ people solely to help us to improve our external communication (*ibid*: 6).

The theme of image work continues as he goes on to confirm the need to shape public expectations of service levels by advertising policing standards and communicating repeated reminders to the public that calls to the police outnumber the officers who deal with them. In highlighting these difficulties of managing expectations and being pulled in different directions by Home Office policy and budgetary constraints Wells, in this section of the report, appears to advocate image work as one means of maintaining legitimacy.

The 1997–98 annual report was Wells' final report. He marked this in his foreword by reflecting on the financial difficulties facing SYP, the legacy of Hillsborough, technological progress and partnership. Four main beliefs about partnership working, the self-proclaimed hallmark of SYP, are espoused. These, in character with the *Six Hill Horizon* and the *Statement of Purpose and Values*, embody themes promoted by Richard Wells during his time as chief constable. The beliefs are: transparency of personal and corporate conduct; active listening in an attempt to understand others' view points; flexibility demonstrated in the will to try new ways of working; and a 'can-do' approach to even the most intractable problems (SYP 1998: 9).

Having reviewed briefly the official documents of SYP and referenced the types of messages which are being promoted, thereby building an official image of SYP, what does this documentation say about the character of SYP and the image it is striving to promote? First, the initial prescriptive documents project a force that is rebuilding and as part of this is setting out a number of key values, which it will aspire to embody. These values prominently feature transparency, honesty and openness.

The same can be said for the *Statement of Purpose and Values* which is aimed at both internal and external audiences. The other documentation – the strategic plan and the annual reports – is also relevant to internal and external audiences, but the annual reports are the most obviously promotional. The three reviewed reports project a force which has crime detection and prevention as its core activity, which promotes consultation and partnership and believes in local, community-focused policing. The combination of this documentation provides the official version, how SYP would like to see itself and how it hopes to be seen. This version is, of course, open to question and the benign official image of the force is also obviously at odds with the images of incompetence and deceit projected through television programmes such as *Hillsborough*. In Chapters 6 and 7 as a counterpoint to the official documentation I examine, drawing on fieldwork, how the force had developed its image work since the mistakes of Hillsborough and the confrontations of the Miners' Strike.

Promoting South Yorkshire Police

The department with explicit responsibility for image work is the Press and Public Relations Department. The following sections trace the emergence of the press office as an independent department and the struggle of the press officers to be recognised by their uniformed colleagues as civilian specialists. The work of the press office is then considered.

Press office history

At the beginning of this chapter, reference was made to South Yorkshire County Council's 1979 *Report on Relationships between the Police and the Public in South Yorkshire* (Moores 1979). The report made a number of points under the heading 'Publicity' suggesting that SYP should make better use of it and boost its public relations activities to increase 'public awareness of the police and their services' (*ibid*: 38). In response senior officers from SYP detailed, somewhat defensively, how the force had been addressing such issues through the establishment of a 'Community Relations Department' in 1974. They gave assurances that 'consideration is given to promoting the police image at every opportunity' (*ibid*: 36) exemplified through press liaison, talks to organisations, publications, advertising, displays and exhibitions, and open days.

Like many press offices across the police service, the SYP press office had originated as a section within the community relations department. This department was based at force headquarters and initially included an inspector in charge of press relations. Between 1974 and 1978 the staffing levels were increased and a civilian public relations officer was appointed to release the inspector from his work in the press office. In the divisions journalists were invited to liaise with station inspectors on a daily basis to collect local police news. In September 1979 the community relations department was reorganised, within which there were plans for the press office to be upgraded, resourced by an inspector and a sergeant to provide service over longer hours. In addition, a public relations officer was to be appointed with responsibility:

a)   To relate press information of a non-operational matter.
b)   To advise the Community Liaison, Crime Prevention and Recruiting Departments on the displays and exhibitions that are such a vital link with all sectors of the community.
c)   To edit the house magazine SYNEWS at two monthly intervals – which is more frequent than at present – initiating a supplement entitled 'LIAISON' that will both in picture and writing inform all of the community work undertaken in the Force. (Moores 1979: 35).

The reorganisation also established 'Community Liaison' personnel in each division, comprising one inspector, one sergeant and between four and six constables. Each officer was to liaise with the press, thereby providing an additional press facility.

This attention to image work in late 1979 reflected the council's inquiry and criticisms at a time of national concern about the politicisation and accountability of policing. The response of the force illustrates how they were being compelled to re-assess their community involvement and the promotion of their activities. It shows how SYP were tentatively addressing image work through press and public relations activities and how they were restructuring for the 1980s. In this nascent media and PR framework, the origins of the current organisational structure for image work are visible.

Despite the new organisational arrangements for media relations, the service remained patchy. A serving officer, interviewed for this research, recalled working in the press office between 1985 and 1987. At the time the press office, still situated within community relations, was resourced by an inspector, a sergeant and a constable. In each of the divisions the community relations inspector had a responsibility for press liaison. The officer remembered that the service provided was variable with the press often having to speak both to the divisions and then to the headquarters press office to obtain the required information.

Three civilians were appointed to the press office in 1988. These civilians, working under a superintendent, were brought in as communication professionals to deal with the media. One of these press officers immediately felt the constraints of working for the police organisation. As a newcomer they felt that the organisation was very closed and that 'the senior ranks were paranoid about the media, we were told what to do rather than being asked for our specialist advice'. They were not allowed to exercise their professionalism and as civilians found that they lacked credibility within the organisation. The senior ranks' obsession with the negative influence of the media arose from a series of leaks from within the force to the local paper, *The Star*. These infuriated them to such an extent that to trace the leaks they ordered internal investigations. Subsequently all three civilian press officers had disciplinary charges placed against them. The senior press officer was dismissed and the deputy received a final written warning. Both went to industrial tribunals which found the charges unsubstantiated. The senior press officer refused the offer of reinstatement but the deputy returned to work in the press office.

A sea change occurred in June 1990 with the appointment of Richard Wells, and the reorganisation of the press office within the force structure. In 1991 he civilianised the department appointing a journalist as 'Head of Press and PR' in place of the uniformed head, a superintendent. The department was re-established as an independent department reporting directly to the chief constable and the head of the department was invited to join the regular meetings of the senior command team.

The press office and force media relations in the late 1990s

At the time of the case study fieldwork in 1997 the SYP press office, in the context of the national surveys (Chapter 4), was unexceptional in terms of its staffing levels, hours of opening and its responsibilities. The press office had five members of staff (the most common number in the surveys was four). It existed as an independent department with the departmental head reporting direct to the chief constable. The head was a civilian of 'Principal Officer' grade who sat as a voting member on the force policy group. All the staff of the press office were civilians – two trained as journalists and had worked previously for newspapers. One member of staff was a public relations professional. The department opened for business between 0700 to 1600 hours Monday to Friday and operated a 24-hours call-out procedure.

The responsibilities of the press office were:

- to advise officers/staff at all levels about the best way to get across the force's information and key messages; and

- to act as facilitators for the transfer of information/facilities between the force and the public, usually via the media.

This included responsibility for media and public relations, corporate image and the full range of in-force activities incorporating the provision of in-house media training, the preparation of advisory documentation for force members, the provision of media consultancy services to members of the force, production of the force newspaper and chief constable's annual report, production of promotional materials and the monitoring of media coverage. Although the force was not typical in providing an elevated role and authority to the head of the department, the press office was fairly typical in terms of its numbers of staff and professional civilian profile. Its responsibilities were also comparable with most forces. This typicality was surprising given the chief constable's known championing of the importance of media relations. Despite this, the press office resided in cramped accommodation with limited equipment, and the repeated submission of plans to improve the service provided had been refused due to more pressing operational priorities.

At the time of the fieldwork the priorities for the press office were set out within the 1997-98 'Policing Plan Summary' as:

1.   To assist the force in the formulation of a range of corporate key messages.
2.   To maximise opportunities to communicate those messages to the public.
3.   To evaluate the presence of the corporate key messages in news coverage about the force.
4.   To help district commanders to develop local strategies for communicating with their communities.
5.   To raise the publicity profile of patrolling officers and their operational colleagues.
6.   To improve the systems for circulating digests of news coverage promptly and comprehensively to police staff.
7.   To increase the satisfaction of local and regional media contacts with the information services provided by SYP.

(SYP Policing Plan Summary – Press and Public Relations 1997–98.)

The core element of these responsibilities is communication, both direct communication between the press office and media agencies and also the provision of support to force members to enable them to communicate more effectively through the media. There is also a responsibility to maintain and improve processes for effective communication both internally and externally. Clearly the press office had a central role in the image work of the force. However, media relations was not the exclusive responsibility of the press office. Each district had a 'District Press Officer' (DPO), a role which designated officers fulfilled in addition to their day-to-day responsibilities. These officers were inspectors and in most districts there was a deputy of sergeant rank. These individuals were district image managers and had the opportunity to build and maintain the force image locally through feeding stories to the media and responding to the media's local needs.

In addition to the full-time media and PR professionals in the press office and the part-time DPOs in the districts, all members of SYP were actively encouraged to cooperate with the media to the limit of their knowledge on routine matters. For sensitive issues such as policy matters, serious crime, complaints and criticisms, officers below the rank of inspector were advised not to discuss such issues with the media without permission. To help prepare and reassure officers in their dealings with the media the press office embarked on an in-house training programme which provided officers with basic media skills. These courses were targeted at specific priority groups of officers, such as those in operational command and those ranks where it was considered 'media blockages' occurred, principally at inspector level. At the time of the fieldwork, 300 officers had been through the three-day course.

There were a number of documents which prescribed the work of the press office and guided the whole force on press and public relations. In 1991 for the first time a media strategy was prepared, entitled *Into the Light*. The title of this document signified the intention of the new chief constable to adopt a different approach to his predecessor and one that would be uncomfortable. Indeed the introduction warns that opening the force 'doors' will throw a bright painful light on the force as its 1.3 million 'customers' across the county take a closer look at how the force operates. The document urges force members not to 'slam the door and retreat' but 'instead of running from the light...have confidence in what it will reveal' (SYP 1991: 2). The first word of the first paragraph is 'openness' and this theme threads through the whole document. The introduction explains that SYP have set their sights on 'new standards of openness and honesty in our dealings with the public' and its concluding paragraph explains that 'by being more open with journalists – on behalf of the greater community – we can attain a new level of trust and understanding which can only enhance any efforts towards the other important goals of the service' (*ibid*: 2).

The 1991 *Into the Light* media strategy was not sophisticated and has the feeling of a foundational document, setting a vision and covering the basics. It had sections on 'improving media liaison', 'gathering our news', 'marketing our news', 'dealing with criticism', 'managing a crisis', and 'monitoring success'. However, it did specify key components as essential to a media strategy and these are significant as they encapsulate the vision of SYP at that time to throw off the past and to start anew, emphasising 'honesty' and 'openness'. The factors are:

- *honesty* – the media and the public must feel able to trust us; lies and dishonesty are not acceptable;
- *openness* – holding back only what we must and explaining the reasons wherever possible;
- *a pro-active approach* – seeking opportunities to market our excellence and being at the forefront in publicising our points of view rather than simply reacting to inevitable pressure later;
- *media awareness* and commitment at all ranks and among civilian staff;
- recognising *media relations as a resource* and support service for policing in South Yorkshire.

(Extracted from *Into the Light* 1991 [p. 3, original emphasis].)

The 1991 strategy was updated in 1996 and entitled 'South Yorkshire Police Media and Public Relations Strategy – *Reality and Reputation*' (SYP 1996c). This document had the same sections as the earlier strategy and was updated to recognise organisational and technological changes. Importantly it retained *verbatim* the key factors listed in the previous document as the essential foundation of a media strategy. However, the introduction was changed reflecting that in 1991 SYP were embarking on a new uncharted direction and this had to be explained and justified. In 1996 the need to promote the core elements of honesty and openness continued to run through the different sections, but the introduction was less explanatory and visionary and was more instrumental. The following paragraphs are quoted in full as they underpin the overall approach of the SYP policy makers to managing the image of the force. They project a force aspiring to communicate in the interests of accountability and transparency:

> ... The most powerful public relations tool in trying to improve the force's reputation is the direct service – both in its actual content and in its style of delivery – given by those front-line police staff who have contact with the public, whether they are operational officers, counter assistants or people who answer telephones or written enquiries.
>
> However, there will always be many people who have no direct experience of the force and form their opinions entirely on the picture presented to them by others, usually by the media. South Yorkshire Police is moving beyond trying to build a good reputation by either presenting its own flawless 'too good to be true' cameo for the public gaze or by standing back and letting others paint an unflattering caricature.
>
> The current aim is to allow the public as full and unclouded a view of the force's activities as possible, if not directly then through the mirror of the media.
>
> Sometimes the image will be distorted, but the more often and more fully the force is revealed, the more accurate an impression the public are likely to gain. Sometimes it will reveal unsightly flaws, but these are more likely to be treated if the force may face their painful or embarrassing exposure. It is healthy to be scrutinised by others, for often they see the good and bad features that we fail to recognise in ourselves.

(Extracted from *Reality and Reputation* 1996 (p. 1).)

Notes

1   *The Sheffield Telegraph*, 9 February 1922, refers to an '1819 Police Act' which led to the appointment of approximately 60 'watchmen'. Authority to 'work the Act consisted of the Town Trustees, the Master Cutler and Wardens of the Cutlers' company and about 100 other Gentlemen'. At this time there also existed an association for *Opposing Insolvent Debtors* and since 1804 an *Association for the Prosecution of Felons* which put up rewards for the prosecution of offenders.
2   *Sheffield Telegraph*, 1933, unspecified date.

Chapter 6

Press and public relations officers at work

The police have become proactive in making their public image. The police now accept that in relation to a particular incident or activity, a proactive approach to the news media is useful in controlling the version of reality that is transmitted, sustained, and accepted publicly. (Ericson, Baranek and Chan 1989: 93)

We live with the media and by the media. (Castells 1996: 334)

The previous chapter reviewed the recent history of South Yorkshire Police (SYP) and considered the image that the force was aspiring to project during the late 1990s. This and the following chapter, in contrast, are based on observation of the police at work. They examine how the image is constructed and communicated in practice, both through promotional channels and through routine police work. They explore the image work of SYP. The approach that this and the next chapter take is to analyse four areas of policing and for each to draw on fieldwork to analyse the meanings of policing that SYP are endeavouring to communicate. In this chapter the area addressed is media and public relations, whilst the following chapter examines public order policing, operational policing (including urban and rural patrol and traffic) and community involvement.

This chapter focuses on the civilian communications professionals from the headquarters press office – the members of the Press and Public Relations department – and also on the police officers in the districts who on top of their routine duties were designated 'District Press Officers' (DPOs). Examining the activities of these district-based image workers revealed that there was diversity in the way each approached the role. There was unevenness in practice reflecting local, on the ground conditions and the attitude of the postholder. It was also notable, as this chapter will demonstrate, that there was clear divergence between district media relations and headquarters media relations.

Media relations: the view from headquarters

Media and public relations is the prime responsibility of SYP's Press and PR Department. At the time of the research this department had five full-time staff, namely the force head and deputy head of press and public relations, an assistant press officer, a public relations officer and a media clerk typist. These staff occupied three small offices on the ground floor of the force headquarters. Although based at headquarters, the press office provided support to all of the districts and departments within the force.

News management

The day-to-day routine work of the press officers within the head-quarters department focused on news management, incorporating both proactive and reactive processes. Proactively the department fed police stories to the media through daily press releases and used the media to request information from the public to help solve crimes, provide evidence and to seek missing persons. Reactively the department responded to media requests for information. These processes involved a press officer arriving for work before 07:30, checking incoming faxes from departments and districts, and checking with the headquarters control room (and its log) what overnight incidents had occurred. This enabled the press officer to determine the stories of media interest, the stories which the police wanted to get into the news and those incidents where a request for information to the public could be routed through the media. The press officer then researched the selected stories by contacting the officers involved or by interrogating the force computer system. This enabled the press officer to prepare appropriate press releases and to be prepared when the media made contact requesting information. The press officer also scanned the daily papers for (national) policing stories which might generate local media interest.

The department dealt with local, regional and national media including newspapers, press agencies, radio and television. A survey undertaken by SYP showed that of the Press and PR Department's external customers, 20 contacted the department several times daily (SYP

1996d). The news organisations surveyed were local newspapers, regional television stations, radio stations and news agencies serving South Yorkshire. Locally-based national journalists were also included. The survey suggested that relations between the police press office and the media were good and that their service was valued. The press office staff confirmed this was the case, the adversarial relationship having eroded. Relationships had been built with both the local and national outlets, who operated quite differently. The nationals were held in higher esteem by the press office staff, although relations with them were more ephemeral. Relations with the local media were different, partly due to the regular contacts and partly due to the historical attitudes of police and media organisations and episodes of antagonism in the past, for example the lampooning of SYP as the 'Keystone Kops' by *The Star*. *The Star* was still perceived as being negative in its treatment of the force, whilst *The Yorkshire Post* was thought to be more balanced.

Although the headquarters press officers talked of the improved state of police-media relations, observation of the press office at work suggested that there remained internal organisational difficulties. In one instance I arrived at 07:25 and found a press officer cursing the force control room for not notifying the press office of three incidents: a serious traffic accident, the stabbing of three men and the beating of a young woman. The last had occurred the previous afternoon and had the information been passed to the press officers, they would have mobilised the media to include bulletins in the evening news programmes. The force control room, it seemed, was a consistent communications bottle-neck as far as the press office were concerned. The press officers outlined ongoing difficulties concerning the readiness of officers in general to pass information to the press office and to liaise with the media generally. This was despite attempts by the press office to raise the level of media awareness amongst officers by arranging media training sessions.

These practical examples of flaws were cracks in the corporate gloss. Whilst SYP managers and force documentation were stressing openness and the disclosure of information, it was apparent that on the ground there were still tensions and incomplete understanding and trust. Nevertheless, the press officers believed that there had been significant change during the 1990s. The police-media relationship had developed and there had been subtle changes in the balance of power. One example of this was that the police had become better organised in their relations with the media. One press officer noted the changes since 1990. Prior to then, they had had to utter the immortal 'no comment', which they admitted had been professionally embarrassing. Since 1990 and the appointment of Richard Wells the press officers had determined to carry through the corporate values of 'honesty and openness' into the press office. Whether dealing with local or national media, the press officers were clear on the need to be honest. They believed that a 'no comment' response or worse, lies, would have the effect of encouraging the media to pursue the 'real' story.

Whilst the press officers felt they had greater freedom to practise their skills since 1990, they also noted that their counterparts in the media had become less effective. They confirmed that in their experience journalists no longer had the time to scrutinise and validate information from the force press office by undertaking their own independent enquiries. In these circumstances journalists had come to expect more of the press office and, for routine news, to be less challenging of their versions of reality (Mawby 1999). This meant that the police press officers found it easier to shape the news in that their press releases would be accepted with little or no editing. For example, reports such as the Doncaster CCTV evaluation (as demonstrated below) would be précised to present them in the best light. However, as the analysis of the Doncaster CCTV press conference also shows, although the police might package their good news as they would wish to see it in print, the resulting coverage will reflect the editorial decision of each newspaper.

Media relations: the view from the districts

District Press Officers (or DPOs) are officers who assist:

> ... the Press and PR Department by being a recognised focal point in the district for liaison with the local media on routine matters, dealing with routine media enquiries, preparing news releases and arranging facilities with and for colleagues on matters likely to be of interest within the community (District Press Officer job description, December 1994).

Officers take on this role in addition to their normal duties, without a reduction in their other responsibilities and without force guidance concerning how much time they should dedicate to the role. Most often (but not always) inspectors in the Crime and Community Services Departments were the designated DPOs and they could, and did, inherit the role without previous experience of media liaison. The DPOs and senior members of the press office met on a bimonthly basis to discuss media issues and to share good practice. Observation and interviews at district level revealed that although there were similarities in the processes of media relations at headquarters and districts level, there was also divergence. In addition there were differences between how the districts approached media relations at local level. This unevenness is presented below through a typology in which, in terms of media relations and news management, the headquarters staff are termed 'professionals' and in comparison those at district level are termed 'semi-professionals', 'parks players' and 'spectators'.

This use of a footballing analogy identifies the headquarters staff as full-time professionals who earn their living through media relations. The semi-professionals do not work on media relations as a full-time job, but they commit themselves to spending a proportion of their time on the work and they approach it in a serious and organised manner. The parks players are capable pragmatists, some of whom will have a regular input into media relations, others will perform adequately when the need arises. This type does not regard media relations as a key part of their police role, though they appreciate the need to maintain good media relations. The final type are the spectators – they know the rules of the game, have played in the past, but do not really participate actively in their current position. These types are expanded upon below.

The semi-professionals

The semi-professionals organise themselves most like the headquarters professionals. Although they are police officers and not civilians recruited for journalistic or public relations skills, they have undergone the force's in-house media training course and they have adopted processes for media relations. They operate as a team to provide a media service at district level and they cultivate relationships with the local media representatives.

One district which SYP considered to be a difficult policing area provided a good example of the semi-professionals. In this area relations between the police and the mining community had deteriorated during the 1984 Miners' Strike. There had been attempts to rebuild relationships and the local media relations work of the DPO formed part of this – by requesting information through the media and trying to place positive police stories into the local news.

In this district media liaison was the responsibility of the Support Services department based at the district headquarters. The department comprised an inspector (the DPO), one sergeant (deputy DPO) and three constables. In contrast to the other districts observed, media liaison was accepted as a joint responsibility rather than the job of the nominated officer, though in practice the sergeant dealt with routine media liaison and had been through the in-house training (as had the three PCs). These arrangements were established in 1995: before then media relations depended upon the duty inspector and were person dependent. The deputy DPO emphasised that throughout the force there was still no uniformity and much remained dependent upon the individual in post. In this district the officers prided themselves on the way they had developed media relations.

The role which the DPO and his team had developed included feeding stories to the local media, responding to local media inquiries and facilitating the process of officers talking to the media. The facilitation service included agreeing the type of questions with the journalists, warning them against 'foul play', and briefing the officer. The press officers also provided a cuttings service for all stations and managers in the district. For further assistance to colleagues the department had set up a district press line which officers could leave messages on, concerning requests for help or breaking news. They were also prepared to set up the media facilities at major incidents, assisting the senior investigating officer (SIO) and the headquarters press office.

The processes for news gathering and dissemination were similar to those in place at headquarters. The morning routine involved the DPO examining the overnight crime incident reports as a source of stories and selecting likely 'runners' for further investigation. The computerised incident log was then interrogated to match up the crime reports and to scan for other stories. The 'logs' of the potential runners were printed off. The selected stories were written up on 'Media information' forms, effectively as press releases and then the DPO either rang the media or awaited their calls, coinciding with relevant deadlines. On average this part-time local press officer dealt with between six and twelve media enquiries each day, routinely liaising with the five local and regional newspapers and two local radio stations which cover the general location. The national expansion of media outlets had not impacted on this local level of media relations. The press officer and his colleagues had not noticed that there had been any increase in demand for news or more and tighter deadlines. Nevertheless they had noticed that the workload had increased but felt that they were victims of their own success, by providing a good service, they were generating more custom.

Observation of the above processes revealed that in scanning the crime reports and incident log, this DPO looked for unsolved, often shocking crimes, for which the police wished to appeal for information through the media. One example of this was the case of a man who disturbed juvenile burglars and was attacked with an iron bar. The police fed this story into the media requesting help from the public and the offender's family gave up the responsible youth. This was considered a particular success as the youth was a persistent offender and his family did not normally cooperate with the police. The police saw this as an illustration of the media being used to penetrate communities that were not generally supportive of the police. The DPO was confident that he could place the stories he chose into the local media. He felt that the police had this influence because they were a constant and reliable news source and the journalists wanted to maintain this cooperation. In terms of the police-media balance of power this officer felt the police were the dominant party. The police control access to the information which the journalists need and journalists that 'cross the line' were made aware that cooperation could not be assumed – they received a limited and minimal service until they become more compliant.

Despite the DPO's comments concerning the dominance of the police in their relationship with the local media, from observation of the news selection process, it was evident that in selecting stories the officer was constrained in two ways by the nature of the media industry. These were related to two of the three criteria which the officer set out for his news selection. In considering incidents for their news suitability, he advised that he had to take account of the legal position, the subject matter and the medium concerned. The legal aspect concerns *sub judice* considerations. The subject matter aspect takes into account what the media will be interested in and also the messages that SYP want to promote, together with force requests for information. With this in mind the officer looked for stories involving public safety, human interest, requests for information (crime solving), showing the force in a good light. Assessing the subject matter involved looking for what the officer described as 'newsworthiness', i.e. what he knew the media looked for including road accidents, fires, any incidents or accidents involving children, and also robberies and burglaries involving high value items. From observation of news selection and the interview data it was evident that the officer was looking just as much for what journalists would regard as good stories as for stories that the police would benefit from, although in some instances it was not an easy matter to disentangle the two interests. One example during the observation period concerned a story about badger baiting. This was thoroughly researched and passed on since it was perceived as newsworthy and useful to the local media.[1] The officer's third criterion of news selection was matching stories to suit the different media. For radio items, which he described as 'the bullet points of the industry' he looked for 'the instant, the snappy which fit nicely into hourly round-ups of news'. Newspaper items can be longer, more thoughtful and less dynamic, whilst television companies need a visual impact. In this way the officer's selection of news was constrained by the formats of the industry he was dealing with, namely the technical formats of newsprint, television and radio. This is an example of what Ericson and Haggerty claim is the condition of 'policing the risk society', a central feature of which is the pressure police forces come under from other institutions to 'produce and distribute knowledge' in particular formats or within 'new rule-governed frameworks' (Ericson and Haggerty 1997: 9). These formats are not determined by the police, but shape, from the outside, how and what they communicate.

Therefore whilst this DPO worked happily in the belief that he controlled the relationship with his media contacts, the evidence of the news selection process suggests that he was working in a situation where he was constrained not only by the technical structure of the media industry, but also by the media's own story-line and thematic interests. Whilst the first constraint, that of media formats is relatively fixed, the second constraint concerns the boundaries of subject matter which is more negotiable, allowing the press officer some control in that he exercised his judgement in news selection. The issue of subject matter, negotiation and police and media agendas is addressed in detail later in the chapter through the example of the Doncaster press conference.

It was evident that the officer enjoyed cordial working relations with local newspaper reporters. Local police–media relations prior to establishment of the current media relations protocols (1995), were not as close. When the newly appointed DPO arranged an open day, local journalists were 'amazed' to be invited. The new 'press team' at the station introduced themselves and told the media representatives that in the future they would be the point of contact for media enquiries. This was the beginning of building relationships with individuals and their mediums (and reflects at the district level senior officers' belief (Chapter 4) in the value of cultivating relations at editor level). If the media representatives were initially surprised, the local operational officers also displayed some suspicion of the changed approach. The DPO encouraged local officers to feature in the media as an element of building a rapport with the public. However, officers could still be reluctant to liaise directly with the media, a legacy of the days when speaking to the media was discouraged.

This examination of a localised operation produced evidence of convergence with headquarters operations to an extent which allows the district's media relations to be classed as semi-professional. The officers involved in media relations approached the task in an organised manner with processes for gathering and selecting news similar to headquarters processes. The district also, like headquarters, provided a comprehensive service, including not only the fundamental news gathering and liaison, but also facilitating contacts between local officers and the media, assisting at major incidents, cultivating media contacts and providing a news cuttings service. Similarly to headquarters press officers, the DPOs also had some difficulties in persuading officers to deal routinely with the media.

The parks players

The parks players are the pragmatists of the typology. They have undertaken the in-house media training, are capable of maintaining media relations and they are prepared to do what is necessary to fulfil their terms of reference. They appreciate the benefits of servicing the media and are willing to be involved. At the same time, however, media liaison is not their core function, but is imposed on top of their main responsibilities and the time and effort they devote to their media duties must reflect this. However, within this type there are different levels of activity. Two examples are compared below.

In the first example, the DPO was an inspector based at a district's headquarters and the media liaison role came in addition to responsibility for schools liaison, neighbourhood watch, the special constabulary, victim support, crime prevention and crime analysis. This DPO accepted his role as a local focus for media enquiries but in practice he had little day-to-day contact with journalists or media organisations. On being appointed to the post, he telephoned the reporters on *The Star* and *The Yorkshire Telegraph* to introduce himself. He did the same with the two local radio stations, *Hallam* and *Sheffield*. However, since then there had been few contacts. Accordingly in this district, in contrast to the semi-professionals, there were no formalised daily processes for gathering information and selecting and disseminating news stories. This is not to say that there was no police–media interaction in this district, rather the DPO believed that media enquiries went direct to the relevant officers and there existed a relaxed relationship such that officers were willing to talk to the media. If there were problems in finding the appropriate officer, then reporters liaised with the DPO, who would facilitate the process. On the occasions that this officer had liaised with the media he had recognised that the relationship was symbiotic and if reporters asked him for information, then there was an implicit assumption that they would cooperate in the future if he needed media assistance, for example, to publicise an initiative. However, he was in no doubt that it was the media who controlled the agenda and within that he could only develop a relationship that enabled the free communication of information.

In the second example the DPO was also a pragmatist, but one with a developed and (self-declared) effective system for media relations. This inspector's portfolio included media relations together with responsibility for CCTV, schools liaison, victim support and partnership development. He had been responsible for media relations since 1992 and, similarly to other district press operations observed, the role had developed in character with the postholder. Initially he had held daily press briefings at 08:45, but he later discouraged these unless there was news of special importance. Instead the 'system' had evolved of the DPO arriving in the morning and checking the overnight incident reports and the detective inspector's briefing note. He then telephoned the three local newspapers. This approach he adopted and the processes he used were minimalist versions of the processes utilised by his 'semi-professional' colleagues and by the 'professionals' at headquarters. They were minimalist in that he never wrote out press releases or kept records of stories telephoned to the media. He discharged his media duties as quickly and as efficiently as possible and expected journalists to do a certain amount of research themselves. The combined processes of gathering, selecting and disseminating news and then responding to media enquiries took him approximately one hour each day.

The proactive selection and generating of stories by this DPO was balanced by his reactive responses to media enquiries for information on incidents and the ratio between these elements was estimated to be 70 per cent proactive and 30 per cent reactive. In selecting incidents to feed to the media, the inspector made choices based on his experience of what the media required. He looked for community-based stories, for example, burglaries, but also stories that were slightly unusual and he cited recent news of 'flashers', a theft of pigeons and a case of a rabbit murderer. However, it is again evident that the proactive selection of stories was undertaken within a framework of what this officer believed the media required. In selecting news that he knew would be of interest to the media, he had an understanding that the media would reciprocate by running 'boring' stories through which he needed to communicate corporate messages or launch local initiatives. In this way, at this local level the inspector, like his semi-professional counterparts, believed the police were the dominant party in the police–media relationship due to their position as a regular and reliable source of news. His media work was constrained by the needs of the media, but he did not feel that constraint as he exercised a level of control that worked to the advantage of police media coverage.

Whilst the DPO believed the balance of power lay with the police, he recognised the need to cultivate and maintain relationships with the local media. Since 1995 and the restructuring of the policing districts he had been more active in maintaining relationships with the media, principally the local newspapers. To this end he had made a point of getting to know the editors and lunching with reporters. New editors were invited to meet the police district command team over lunch. The inspector commented that the chief constable's encouragement to force personnel to be 'honest and open' had influenced the more cordial approach to forging relationships with the media. As part of this the inspector encouraged all the district's officers to speak to the media and he often facilitated this. As a result of cultivating the media relationship, the inspector considered that the local police–media relationship was 'wonderful'. Although inevitably he had on occasions to deal with bad news, he advised that in such circumstances, his approach was to be 'open and honest – never defend the indefensible'.

Like his semi-professional colleagues this incumbent had not been troubled by the media explosion of outlets and the increased demand for police news. Although he recognised that this might create issues for the headquarters press officers, it had no impact at his local level. However, the advances in police computerisation had caused him problems. Ironically he had found it easier to gather his news for the media when the data was readily available through hard copies. With computer systems replacing some paperwork systems, he now had to gain access to a computer terminal and use a system to extract his data, a system which was designed for other purposes. Gathering the data now required additional time, computer competence and the availability of a computer terminal.

The spectator

The 'spectator' appreciates the benefits of media liaison and has experience in it. However, the spectator is not a regular active participant. This type was identified in a district where the nominated DPO confessed that he rarely had anything to do with the media and certainly had no regular contacts in terms of news management. He recalled that he had once spoken to *The Star's* crime reporter who was friendly and said he would keep in touch. He had not heard from him since. This officer had no processes in place for media liaison, and was unaware of how local policing stories made the news. He guessed that local journalists dealt direct with the duty inspectors. In making this observation, the inspector was referring to the position in many forces where there are no designated press officers at station or divisional/ district level and it is the practice of local journalists to telephone station duty inspectors for local policing news.

The spectator's approach to his DPO's role, compared to the semi-professionals and the parks players, demonstrates the diversity which existed across the districts of SYP. There was, of course, convergence in that all those dealing with the media were dealing with certain processes and agendas that are associated with the media organisations and whoever in the districts liaised with the media would have to work within these. As demonstrated, these constraints exist both in the fixed technical area of media formats and the negotiable area of subject matter. Yet the documented divergence of approach, from semi-professional to spectator, does raise the question of how this situation arose and whether the force head of press and PR, to continue the football metaphor, could act as a referee and enforce the rules to develop a consistent approach across the districts.

The reasons why the situation was diverse have already been touched on. The DPOs were not appointed as media professionals and they did the job in addition to their core role, not as an integral part of it and their performance in the role was not measured. Accordingly the level of commitment varied and it was difficult to achieve uniformity or consistency throughout all the districts. The force had processes in place which the districts could draw on or ignore. How the districts approached local media relations in practice was person dependent. Although there were terms of reference, observation and interviews suggested that these posts were what the incumbents made of them, from highly organised near-satellite offices of the HQ press office (the semi-professionals) to almost no media involvement (the spectators).

Although this organisational structure and its inherent divergence might have the appearance of being haphazard and disorganised, media relations was comparatively sophisticated in SYP. The framework of a headquarters office supported by DPOs went beyond the structure of media relations in most other forces in the late 1990s, as discussed in the previous chapter. Nevertheless the structure depended on the person appointed as DPO and their responsibility for managing their local media had an element of risk. Effective and active DPOs (semi-professionals) meant that the headquarters press office had less control over the force's news contacts. Less effective DPOs (some parks players and all spectators) may mean less media contacts and less effective local media relations, but ensures the dominant position of the headquarters press office. The force head of press and PR accepted that there was an element of risk management in passing control to the districts and in encouraging the development of local media contacts. However, the force view was that an open organisation was preferable and the risk that more contacts may lead to occasional mistakes was an acceptable one.

Press officers and set-piece promotions

The previous sections have focused on day-to-day (frontstage) news management and the police-media relationship where headquarters press officers and DPOs directly manage the relationship with the media and through this manage the force image. This arena of image work is one in which the main concern is not overt 'PR', but 'hot news', breaking stories on a daily basis. This section considers another facet of the work of press officers, that of their involvement in staged set-piece promotions to which the media are invited. As the section illustrates, these staged events involve the press officers in work which is not dissimilar to that undertaken by the headquarters-based force public relations officer, whose role is examined in the subsequent section.

The headquarters press officers, like the PR officer, are involved periodically in staged media events. These promotional events are distinguishable from day-to-day news management work of the press officers in that they are focused on a single subject and the police are able to determine the agenda in advance and to prepare the messages they wish to communicate (messages which might be included in press kits issued to the media). In these events the press officers have a (backstage) support role as facilitators and mediators rather than direct communicators and the direct communication is between the media and police officers. As examples of these set-pieces, I will now discuss two instances of pro-active public relations that provide an insight into the dynamics of this aspect of image work. These examples are invaluable in that they illustrate the processes of news selection and negotiation. Only by observing the whole process is it possible to understand how one event opens up a wide range of possibilities or interpretations for broadcasting or newspaper reporting. In this respect these events become struggles over meaning – the meaning of policing and its activities as promoted by the police and as interpreted by media representatives. As Ericson *et al.* point out, 'what is at stake in news production is the meaning attributed to events, processes, or states of affairs' and there is perpetual conflict over meanings within news source organisations and between the source organisations and the news organisations (Ericson *et al.* 1989: 377). Analysis of these events also demonstrates not only the negotiation which occurs between police and media to determine the dominant images generated by the event, but also that the production of a 90-second feature on a local television news programme or a few columns in a local newspaper is the result of many hours of preparation (by both the police and the media) and of the sifting and negotiation of masses of information.

The Doncaster CCTV evaluation launch

In June 1997, the SYP press office facilitated a press conference which announced the results of an evaluation of Doncaster's CCTV system. The evaluation was commissioned by the police and local council and was undertaken by a criminologist. The press conference was held in the council buildings in Doncaster and the invited media audience included local and regional press, radio and television representatives.

In preparation for the conference the press officer had prepared a short bound report, *Doncaster CCTV Study: results, comments, examples and background,* containing SYP press release number 57. This comprised a general statement of the evaluation's findings (3 pages), comment by the police commander (2 pages), a councillor (2 paragraphs), three examples of serious crimes which the CCTV system helped to solve (3 pages) and background information (2 pages). Copies of the report were distributed to all attendees. The launch was addressed by the academic, the local police commander and a councillor. Each made a brief statement and then invited questions.

The question and answer session focused on the police officer and the academic and there was a notable contrast in the approach adopted by the academic author and the police commander. The academic opened his statement warning the journalists 'you'll get no sound-bites from me' and proceeded to speak very technically and to qualify everything he said. He accused the media of fuelling fear of crime and at that point the commander tried to lighten the tone by saying the police were not above criticism in this by supplying video tapes to the media. In contrast to the academic, in an interesting juxtaposition of what might normally be expected, the commander took a very different approach. Citing the corporate line, drawing on the words 'honesty and openness', he released full copies of the evaluation report and video tapes (released on limited loan terms) to the assembled journalists, whilst seeking their assurance that selections from the tape would not materialise later on television entertainment programmes.

As he spoke the commander emphasised that the study and the commitment to CCTV were not only about crime, but also 'public tranquillity and the best use of police resources'. He aired the key messages of reassurance and public safety, together with the openness of SYP in sharing the full results of the evaluation with the public through the media. As the commander enthusiastically aired his views and the academic guardedly answered questions, the press conference moved on. The exchanges were civilised as the journalists asked stock questions, taking the replies at face value. This applied to questions about the displacement of crime away from the town centre and into the suburbs. It applied to other predictable questions on CCTV's effect on detection rates and on fear of crime. This understated tone changed during the post-conference 'one-to-ones', when each journalist could develop their angle in more detail. The academic was interviewed by BBC television's *Look North* and maintained his guarded approach. This again contrasted with the commander's interview with the same news team. He was extremely fluent and pitched at an accessible level. The last question he was asked was 'What about the Big Brother criticisms?' and he fired back the response:

> 'If I had a big brother that watched over my car all day whilst I was at work, that ensured I could walk the streets in safety, I'd be more than pleased.'

The watching police press officer was delighted with this knockout finish. During the conference the press officer had observed carefully without intervening and afterwards had set up the one-to-ones and generally ensured that the media representatives had all the information they needed.

Some days after the press conference the outcome of this struggle for meaning emerged in three newspaper reports arising from the launch. It was covered by *The Yorkshire Post* (25/6/97) (12 column inches), *The Doncaster Star* (25/6/97) (9 column inches) and the local *Advertiser* (25/6/97) (4 column inches). Two lead on displacement, 'Crime shifts to suburbs – spy cameras blamed' in *The Star* and 'CCTV not to blame – Town sees 30 per cent increase in reported crime' in the *Advertiser*, which referred to an increase in crime in Mexborough. The third paper led on crime reduction – 'TV cameras cut town-centre crime'. The information in the reports drew on data from the press releases and also on information resulting from the question and answer session. *The Yorkshire Post* provided the greatest detail and reported comments from the police commander which were in the press release but which were not spoken at the conference itself. This would be regarded by SYP as successfully transferring premeditated key messages into the media; at the same time it makes journalists' lives easier to use such material. In this respect there is collusion between the police and media. Theoretically a newspaper could have written a report on the launch using apparently reported speech, without actually attending the event.

Following the press conference, the BBC *Look North* film crew accompanied the police to the CCTV suite to select CCTV footage and to interview police representatives. The object of this exercise was to capture sufficient material for a 60–90-second feature on the local news. A short version would appear on the afternoon news and then a longer version on the main evening news. The processes of gathering 90 seconds of screen time took several hours of negotiation and selection. After a brief tour of the CCTV suite negotiation began over the footage to be used. During the course of these negotiations, the different agendas of the police and the television crew became apparent. The *Look North* reporter negotiated with the local commander and the press officer. Other police officers provided advice on the progress of legal proceedings involving some of the footage and civilian operators offered advice on 'interesting' footage. The police opened negotiations by suggesting suitable footage for the news feature. Their concern was to present a range of scenarios showing different uses of the system – they suggested footage which conveyed safety messages, the potential for quick command and control of emergency services, and which provided material for evidence purposes in criminal prosecutions. Their repeated concern was notable – that the selection should not be voyeuristic, nor pure entertainment, nor titillating. They were also emphatic that faces should not be recognisable and should be pixilated – all the footage that was eventually selected had to be analysed concurrently by the reporter and a designated police officer who specified the faces to conceal.

Three suggestions were initially put forward by the police in the following order:

- A girl being hit by bus. The police commander expressed the message that this would convey, namely that a CCTV operator saw the accident and used the CCTV system for 'command and control' purposes to get an ambulance at the location within 1.5 minutes. The tape was also used for evidential purposes, to absolve the bus driver of blame for the accident. Discussion ensued concerning whether a 'health warning' should be broadcast prior to its showing in case it upset people. The police insisted on a warning whilst the reporter was not too concerned. The police were also concerned that the victim should be consulted before its showing.

- A clip showing smoke emerging from the Littlewoods department store. Several passers-by had used the CCTV 'Help Point' facility (a number of telephones situated in the town centre which are connected direct to the CCTV operators) and reported smelling smoke. The operators scanned the area and spotted smoke emanating from Littlewoods. The fire brigade was directed to the fire and this use of the CCTV system was credited with catching the fire early enough to prevent its spread to adjoining buildings. Again a public safety message.

- The final suggestion showed three youths carrying with great difficulty a quantity of lead. The CCTV operators spotted the youths and directed police officers to the scene who discovered that the lead had just been stolen. This provided a crime detection message and also was an example of CCTV footage being used as evidence.

The public interest agenda of the police selection of material now met the television crew's agenda and also the constraints of producing a 90-second news feature.[2] The *Look North* reporter watched the tapes and was obviously bored by the undramatic nature of the content. He asked 'Have you got any serious crime? Any muggings?' He was disappointed when he was told that there was nothing violent he could use due to pending criminal proceedings. He again emphasised his preference for crime-related film and at this point the operators began to scour the archived tapes to try and accommodate him. Various tapes were recovered and shown to cries of 'here's a good 'un' and 'this one's a beauty'. The operators were referring to notably violent material, in particular a systematic beating and a number of spontaneous attacks.

After viewing a number of the operators' 'classic' selection, the reporter and the police were able to agree on a clip which featured two patrol officers being directed by the operators to a man who was wanted for questioning. The operators had spotted the man queuing to get into a night club. The cameras pictured the officers approaching the man to arrest him. He decided to fight and this was captured on camera as the officers and man struggled on the floor whilst the orderly queue looked on. A successful arrest was finally made with the assistance of the night club's door man. A second clip was agreed as a possibility. This showed an unprovoked street attack as a young man walking in the town centre at night was subjected to a stunning punch around the head followed by a kick to the head. The tape had been used to identify the attacker and subsequently for evidence in the proceedings which resulted.

In this negotiation process the different agendas of the police and media became clear. The reporter had a sensationalist, crime-centred approach, he wanted strong, attention grabbing images. On the other hand, the police wanted to convey public safety and crime fighting messages – these would of course have the added advantage of showing the police in a good light. Inevitably there was negotiation and compromise and both parties appeared to be satisfied with the final selection of material. The police did seek assurances on the context in which the material would be placed and the reporter did agree to check the final content with the press office before screening. He had pushed as far as he could but wanted to stay within the police defined borders. He signed a license before leaving. This license stated that SYP would pre-view the feature prior to transmission, but in practice they were prepared to waive this condition as it was not feasible for a same-day news feature. Whilst this waiving of the pre-viewing right suggests some element of mutual trust, at the same time the existence of such licenses represent an ultimate sanction, held in reserve, that the police can invoke if media organisations break agreements. This negotiating process over the selection of video footage illustrates (again) how the different media and police agendas can converge in that the police recognised the media agenda and selected material which tempered, but used that agenda, whilst still meeting their own objectives.

The annual report launch

The police force annual report has a public relations role in promoting the work of the force over the previous 12 months. For the public it is an opportunity to take stock of its local force. For the media it is an opportunity to cast a critical gaze. On 23 July 1997 SYP held a press launch for its 1996–97 annual report. It was held in a small function room within the force headquarters in the centre of Sheffield. The setting was relaxed – a plush carpet, comfortable chairs and the presentation area in close proximity to the audience. The gathered audience comprised representatives from the media (radio, press and television), a few of the force's 'partners' and members of the police authority. The chief constable appeared early and encouraged informality by sitting chatting with the audience for a few minutes.

At the allotted time, the chief constable began his presentation and for 30 minutes held forth on the previous year supported by a computerised slide show. He highlighted 'a year of mixed fortunes . . . some not so good points, some growth points, some tangible developments, some achievements!'. The delivery included hard statistical data mixed with points of information and to conclude the chief constable emphasised the benefits of SYP working in partnership. Following the presentation there were a few questions – one on crime statistics and one from *The Star* reporter concerning local business support for police initiatives. This concluded the formal part of the conference. Up to this point the whole launch had the appearance of being well-organised and planned. Thus far the chief constable had controlled the communication flow. This impression changed with the 'one-to-one' interviews held with individual reporters.

The one-to-ones were noteworthy because they brought into direct conflict the messages that the chief constable wished to convey with the lines of questioning that the reporters wished to develop. The first tape-recorded interview went well with no controversial points developed. There followed an interview with BBC Radio Sheffield which comprised two parts. Initially, the chief constable was asked to record a sound-bite for a short bulletin on a particular Radio Sheffield initiative. He was happy to comply. Second, the main questions were posed and the reporter asked the chief constable if he had taken to sermonising, a reference to the report's foreword which contained an allegory concerning the chief constable helping youngsters to rescue an eel from a sea-side rock-pool despite the attentions of other, stone-throwing, youngsters, whom the chief constable took to task. The reporter asked whether this was building towards a 'zero tolerance' stance. The chief constable dismissed the sermonising reference and laid out his disagreement with zero tolerance. Whilst the chief constable on air was civil and affable, as soon as the tape stopped he harangued the reporter 'What a question! Sermonising indeed!' After a brief exchange of views the reporter walked away laughing.

The next interview, with a reporter from *Calendar* (the daily news programme of the local independent television channel, *Yorkshire*), also had its distinct frontstage/on-air and backstage/off-air segments. It proceeded as follows:

On air
Reporter: A good year for South Yorkshire Police?
Chief: Yes. *[he sets out the reason he thinks so]*
Reporter: Though good, what about the greater number of road accidents and complaints against your officers?

Chief: Why are you emphasising the negatives when there is
            so much good news? To answer your points [*provides
            explanation*]
Reporter: Thank you.
End of interview.

The camera was switched off and the following exchange took place off
air:

Off air
Chief: You emphasise negatives all the time. If there are eight
            good points and two bad ones, you want to talk about
            the two.
Reporter: We ask, you give a reply and you justify your position.
Chief   [*in exasperation*] But only the bad stuff is concentrated
            on!

These exchanges were quite different to the CCTV police–media
exchanges. In Doncaster there was two-way communication, negotiation
and compromise. In contrast, at this report launch, the formal
presentation was controlled by the chief constable and in the following
one-to-ones, which he was less able to control, on-air he was the
consummate professional, at ease with the camera, knowledgeable of the
media technical aspects and answering questions fluently. The image of
the chief constable conveyed in interview to the listening and watching
public would be fluent and authoritative. However, off-air the chief
constable was determined to take reporters to task on what he perceived
as misguided or negative questions and comments.

   Following the press conference, a review of the coverage in the South
Yorkshire press suggests a mixed reaction. The reporters took stock of the
contents of the presentation (and the handouts replicating the slides
used) and also the question and answer session. The *Sheffield Star* led
with 'Police blast traders on CCTV spy cameras'. This angle had been
developed by *The Star* reporter during the morning of the press launch.
He had arrived early at the press office. The reporter took this
opportunity to take a preview of the report and scanning the chief
constable's foreword he picked up comments that expressed disappointment with local traders' input into the financing of CCTV systems. He
took up this point with the press officers who dismissed it as a matter of
limited significance. At the launch itself the reporter asked the chief
constable whether he was 'sending a shot across the bows of the traders',

to which the chief constable retorted 'Please don't put those words in my mouth – it's more of an exhortation to the traders'. Despite the chief's comments, *The Star* took the very approach that the chief constable had spoken against. A complaint was made by the press office to *The Star* and later editions were less critical. In contrast to *The Star*, the *Barnsley Chronicle* lead on the success of anti-crime initiatives. Coverage in Rotherham was balanced, leading on the reduction in crime, but also mentioning the reduced levels of satisfaction with the presence of 'visible foot patrols'. The press office expected more positive stories to emerge in the days that followed as reporters drew on the body of the report for more material, to fill space. One predicted example was the work of the force helicopter. This was a subject that the press office had targeted to push for positive publicity.

The different agendas of the press and the police emerge from observation of these two set-piece events. The police have their agenda and endeavour to communicate their key messages. The media have their own agenda and sometimes the two will be compatible; at other times there is conflict. The CCTV launch exemplifies how the police tempered and used the media agenda. In contrast there was direct conflict of agendas at the press launch, and although this was managed professionally on-air, recriminations ensued off-air. It is also notable that the police made considerable efforts to meet the media's demands and to adapt to the constraints of media formats; equally the media pressed to the limits but observed them. This reflects the symbiotic nature of the relationship and the need to maintain working relationships. Despite the parties staying within the rules and conventions, the police were not always happy with the resulting coverage, for example in the case of *The Star*'s coverage of the annual report launch. This was a clear example that although the police will construct and communicate their preferred images, these can be transformed through the communication process. On such occasions the force does not accept criticism passively and will make representations to the media organisation concerned.

The examples of these set-piece promotions suggest that, in addition to demonstrating accountability, they are staged for public relations purposes and yet they are orchestrated by press officers rather than the force public relations officer. The following section puts the role of the public relations officer in context.

The public relations officer at work

The role of the press officers within the headquarters department contrasted with that of the public relations officer (PRO). The press officers, like operational officers, had to deal with both negative and positive aspects of policing whilst the public relations officer's role was concerned solely with positive promotion, assisting with initiatives and open days and every kind of promotional event. The incumbent saw her role as one of 'breaking down barriers, showing the human face of policing' through the promotion of, for example, the mounted section and the dog section at county shows and village fairs. She had also recently been involved in assisting the traffic division, which was becoming more interested in public relations as it changed emphasis away from the road-side lecturer and law enforcer and towards the educator (the role of the traffic division in image work is discussed in the next chapter). The public relations officer's focus was not solely external, however, there was an internal dimension, helping communication and morale by promoting the work of different departments. One vehicle for this was *Billboard*, the force newspaper.

The public relations officer believed her work could popularise and show the direction the force was moving in, through initiatives such as *Lifestyle*. This was an annual multi-agency initiative involving SYP as the coordinating agency and supported by almost 150 sponsors including Yorkshire Electricity, *Hallam FM*, Yorkshire Water, most of the major banks and all South Yorkshire's football clubs. The initiative encouraged young people (aged nine to 18) to form teams to undertake projects in the community over the summer months. For such initiatives as *Lifestyle*, the PR officer would be extensively involved in the preliminary work, a member of the project team planning the launch and associated activities such as coordinating the media campaign and the publicity materials.

In 1997 *Lifestyle* was launched to loud music and flashing lights. The event, organised by the police public relations officer, was compered by the local commercial radio station, *Hallam FM*, broadcast live on mid-morning radio. Local dignitaries and sponsors were invited. At the venue the *Lifestyle* project manager (a police inspector) stood on the door personally greeting and shaking the hand of each guest. The formal part of the launch lasted an hour. A video, *Get up and Go with Lifestyle '97*, was shown followed by short statements from the major partners. In these partner segments, the language of partnership and community and youth was prominent. The message was consistently conveyed that most youngsters were 'good' and the 'bad' ones were the exceptions – and these might be diverted if they were reached early enough by such schemes as this. This missionary theme ran through the presentations of the police contributors – the deputy chief constable, the project manager and a community constable. There was also a managerialist twist as two partners (the police and Yorkshire Electricity) referred to their strategic objectives and how the initiative satisfied them. The event management was slick throughout: bright lights, loud music videos, dancing school children, invited dignitaries, best police uniforms. A glossy handout was also provided to all attendees. Heavily involved in the preparation work for the initiative up until this launch point, hereafter the involvement of the PRO diminished as it moved into its operational phase. She would, however, maintain a role in publicising the positive outcomes of the initiative.

Notes

1   This situation is akin to comments made by a press officer (from another force) concerning recognising media agendas and then adapting the police agenda to interact with them (Mawby 1999: 280). He realised this at a strategic level whilst the semi-professionals had developed the approach heuristically as part of their way of working.
2   Although both the police and the media can and will claim to be promoting the 'public interest' this South Yorkshire example shows that their perceptions of the public interest can differ and the police will seek signed undertakings from media representatives as guarantees that the police perception of the public interest is protected.

Chapter 7

Image work in routine policing

Unlike some organisations, the police cannot regard public
relations as something separate from the way they do their
everyday work. The internal efficiency of police departments in the
long run affects public attitudes far more than press reporting or
publicity campaigns. (Banton 1964: 264)

It should not be overlooked that the spoken word in an interface
between police officers and members of the public is the most
impressive of all communication. (Alderson 1979: 104)

The previous chapter examined image work from the perspective of
media and public relations activities. This chapter now examines image
from the perspective of public order policing, routine (urban and rural)
operational patrol and community involvement. These arenas of policing
differ from media and public relations work in that their primary focus is
not, on the face of it, image work. However, for different reasons, each of
these spheres of policing is shot through with image implications and the
following sections explore the images which each creates and analyse the
extent to which image work is permeating police work.

The image of a police force develops not only through active media
and public relations, but also through the routine undertaking of police
work, involving countless police-public encounters which create
impressions of the police. For this reason in addition to examining the
work of individuals whose core role is image work, it is necessary to take
account of the work of officers fulfilling other police tasks, where the
main concern is not with image, but with law enforcement, community
safety and maintaining public order. These functions, ostensibly, do not
have image at their core, but nevertheless they are essential to the image

of the police. How the police perform in these areas creates impressions, both with the members of the public they come into contact with and also through the media to wider audiences.

In the following sections, I consider these different arenas of policing taking public order events first as these tend to be highly mediated. From these publicised and symbolic events I then consider routine operational police work in the form of urban and rural patrol and traffic patrol. Finally, I consider the work of the community services department. These latter arenas are not as highly mediated as public order policing. They are essentially localised, there are less people publicly involved, the encounters between police and public are more personal and the meanings of policing are controlled in different ways.

Public order

The policing of public order events can make or break the police image as South Yorkshire Police (SYP) have come to experience. Public order events influence the police image for a number of reasons. In the first instance public order involves the policing of citizens, not criminals (Waddington 1998: 129) and protesters in recent years have included 'respectable' people, from whom the police traditionally receive support (Reiner 1998: 48). Second, events are often attended and reported on by local and regional media organisations and coverage will become national in the event of dramatic events developing or in those cases where the event is local, but the subject is national, attracting nationwide interest. These events can be contentious and there may be rival factions supporting or denouncing the event. This presents the police with a number of different situations, through which they endeavour to maintain their authority and legitimacy and project an appropriate image. During the 1990s police forces became more conscious of their image during these events, aware that they were not only enforcing the law and keeping the peace but communicating meanings of policing. The media strategies deployed in 1995 during the policing of the live animal exports demonstrations on the south coast of England evidence the care and planning that went into projecting favourable police images whilst at the same time enabling an export trade that many considered repugnant.[1] In the following section I consider how SYP approached the policing of two public order events.

Policing football: Hillsborough — Sheffield Wednesday v Liverpool

The policing of this football match at Hillsborough in May 1997 had symbolic overtones. The opposition were Liverpool and as noted in Chapter 5 the families of the Hillsborough victims have continuously lobbied for the punishment of SYP for its part in the tragedy and in the days preceding this game pressure was mounting on the government to open a new inquiry. At a number of games prior to this Hillsborough match, football supporters had organised 'red card' protests. These involved supporters holding up red cards at matches urging the Home Secretary to open a new inquiry. On the previous Saturday, the Football Supporters' Association had organised a day of support for a new inquiry. At Liverpool's ground, Anfield, red cards were put on all 40,000 seats for the televised match with Spurs and the cards were held up simultaneously for the television cameras. There was some concern that this gesture of support might be repeated at Hillsborough. For other reasons SYP needed to police the event sensitively. On the previous day, Anfield had staged a rock concert in aid of 'Justice for the 96', namely the Hillsborough victims' families. In addition, Jimmy McGovern's television drama, *Hillsborough*, had just won a BAFTA award. For all these reasons the police approached this event with some delicacy and this was reflected in the operational policing notes prepared for the event, in the briefings themselves and in the low-key style of policing implemented during the afternoon.

As it was anticipated that a red card protest might be staged, Sheffield Wednesday officials requested the police to confiscate cards and banners prior to supporters entering the ground. Club officials were reluctant to allow a protest in their own ground. The police took a contrasting approach. From a legal perspective they did not consider that they could prevent supporters from taking banners into the ground and although they realised that any protest would contain an 'anti-South Yorkshire Police' message, they accepted the right to protest. The police maintained this stance, emphasising in the briefings that confiscation of banners was not a police decision and that supporters with banners should be allowed to pass through to the turnstiles, at which point the club stewards would make decisions concerning confiscation.

The sensitivity of the day was reflected in the detailed planning of the police and club roles. The police's operational briefing placed the responsibility for searching fans on club stewards at the turnstiles (with police assistance if required). They also emphasised the stewards' responsibility for ejection and that police officers should only become physically involved in the event of breach of the peace or a criminal offence being committed. The intention of the police policy was to place the police in a low-key support role, minimising the possibilities of physical confrontation between officers and supporters.

The operational arrangements for policing a football match at Hillsborough involve a three-level command structure. The overall 'Gold' commander, two 'Silver' commanders (one inside the ground and one outside), and seven 'Bronze' commanders with responsibilities for specific functions or locations. Each bronze commander (inspector rank) is responsible for serials of sergeants and police constables. In the hours building up to the kick-off, a series of briefings take place. The command team meet initially and then there are cascaded briefings. The gold and silver commanders brief all the officers on duty and then the bronze commanders brief their sergeants and constables.

At the main briefing the gold commander gave a short introduction, emphasising the sensitivity of the game before passing over to the silver commander for the main talk. This highlighted the significance of the game and warned that the officers would face a difficult afternoon:

> ... it's going to be difficult, you're going to get some abuse, but be courteous, be good humoured, remember that you are representing South Yorkshire Police – don't rise to taunts, don't get involved and remember what this means to Liverpool people ... *whatever actions you take today will not change people's minds* (original emphasis retained).

He went on to summarise that the police role was to assist the club stewards in crowd safety, to prevent public disorder and to enforce the criminal law. The tone of this briefing was an acceptance and an expectation that the police would be subjected to verbal abuse but that officers should maintain as much dignity as possible and should police the event unobtrusively. The content of the briefing confirmed that the police had a damage-limitation objective. Realising the poor stead they were held in by football supporters generally and by the people of Liverpool particularly, SYP did not want to attract further bad publicity which inevitably would have attracted the media spotlight. In this way the operation can be seen as an operation not only in the control of crowds but also in the control of meaning – promoting the right image and public order policing could not be separated for this operation. On this day, policing was image work.

One bronze commander had responsibility for meeting and parking visiting supporters and for maintaining public order in the area

immediately outside the ground. Briefing his officers he again emphasised the need to remain calm, to be courteous and not to get involved in
confrontational exchanges with Liverpool supporters. He urged them –
'be professional, be understanding'. In the two hours before kick-off he
walked around outside the ground, directing his officers, helping
supporters with directions and greeting arriving coach-loads. The fans
were well behaved, there was no protest and no anti-police actions or
abuse. This pre-match period passed without incident of note, but several
of the officers on duty expressed apprehension, speaking of the
significance of the day and their resignation that there would be abuse
and 'grief' during the afternoon. Once the supporters were in the ground
and the match had kicked off, the officers relaxed and took turns to have
a tea break. In the refreshment area one of the assistant chief constables
had arrived and was congratulating the officers, encouraging them to
continue in the same vein. On the pitch the game passed uneventfully
and ended in a 1-1 draw and afterwards the crowds filed away in an
orderly fashion. The worst expectations of SYP had not been realised

The key point to emerge from these observations is that SYP
recognised the sensitivity of the day and its implications for the
reputation of the force. Accordingly a prime objective of the operation
was to prevent further damage to the force image. The force conducted
an operation in the *control of meaning* and on the day *operational work and
image work were interwoven*. Hence each briefing emphasised the
importance of officers' good behaviour, made exhortations to be
professional and included pleas to be understanding. The force prepared
for the worst and made every effort to ensure that if problems occurred
they would not exacerbate them.

Policing demonstrations: Reclaiming the Streets

During 1997 a grouping of environmentalist and anarchist groups with a
common belief that streets should be enjoyed by people and not polluted
by cars organised demonstrations in several British cities. These 'Reclaim
the Streets' demonstrations followed a similar pattern. Posters and flyers
would appear in a city giving notice of a forthcoming demonstration
indicating the day and time of the event but not its precise location. The
posters advised people to meet up in a given place and once people had
gathered the organisers gave a signal and the protesters headed towards
a targeted area of the city centre where a major road was blocked and a
party commenced. A traffic jam ensued whilst the protesters partied.

In April 1997 flyers appeared in Sheffield giving notice of a Reclaim the
Streets demonstration to be held on 17 May 1997. Would-be protesters

were invited to assemble at Devonshire Green at 12:30 on the outskirts of Sheffield city centre. The police commander of Sheffield Central District attempted to make contact with the organisers, by letter and also through an appeal in the local newspapers. The language of these appeals was conciliatory, sympathising with their environmental messages, supportive of peaceful protest and inviting discussion with the aim of keeping all parties (protesters, police and public) happy. The tone of the letter is captured by the wording of its last sentence:

> I know you will find this suggestion [*a meeting to reconcile the interests of all parties*] unusual to say the least but you might be pleasantly surprised by the reception you would receive from us.

The organisers did not respond. Waddington has observed that a feature of 1990s public order policing was the charm offensive that the police launched to win over demonstrators during the negotiations leading up to, and during, an event (Waddington 1998: 120–1). Naturally this tactic will not succeed if the protesters do not engage in negotiation. In these circumstances the police had to plan for a demonstration they knew would happen and which was intended to bring traffic in Sheffield to a stand-still for several hours. They were faced with the task of balancing the rights of the protesters to demonstrate peacefully with the expectations of shoppers and car users and also those of retailers and other businesses in the city centre that wished to go about their normal work. In order to analyse how the police balanced these different interests and managed their image through the potential difficulties and tensions, it is instructive to consider the day's events, from the morning's preparations and briefings through to the gathering of the demonstrators and the protest event itself.

The main briefing was undertaken by the 'Gold' commander to the 60 officers on duty for the day. He explained the broad intentions of the policing operation were:

1. To maintain public order and ensure the safety of the demonstrators and members of the public.
2. To allow the protesters to exercise their democratic right to demonstrate in a peaceful manner.
3. To minimise disruption to residents, commuters and the people of Sheffield.
4. To respond firmly but fairly to any criminal offences or outbreak of disorder.

5. To act in a professional manner in accordance with our statement of purpose and values ('I' *District operational order 29/97*).

The commander reported that SYP had sent officers with camcorders to earlier demonstrations in other cities, observing the policing tactics adopted and in the light of this information they determined their own policy. Building on this, a video tape was shown of the demonstration in Leeds. This showed protesters blocking a road and then erecting a scaffolding tower. The police moved in and a tug-of-war ensued which became a focus of media attention. The police lost the tug-of-war and, claiming a symbolic victory, the protesters scaled their tower.

Having shown the video, the commander asked his officers to put aside any possible prejudices against protesters with unusual styles of clothing and hair and to police the event in an unobtrusive and relaxed manner. The command team had determined not to be confrontational (which had failed for West Yorkshire Police in Leeds), and to adopt a non-aggressive, 'softly, softly' approach. In particular, the police commander ordered his officers not to attempt to prevent the erection of scaffolding. He did not want them to get 'wound up, involved in a symbolic tug-of-war – let it happen and don't sully the name of South Yorkshire Police'. Instead they should stand back and let the demonstrators protest, but at the same time keep the peace and minimise disruption to residents, commuters and shoppers. Whilst the commander instructed his officers to avoid arrests as far as possible, he had determined to maintain a high visibility of officers as intelligence received suggested that high visibility policing deterred trouble. It was his intention therefore to demonstrate large numbers of officers – an obvious show of strength, but of a restrained force.

The main theme and the repeated message of the briefing was to police the event in a restrained way which would not damage the image of SYP. To reinforce this the commander warned the officers of the presence of many cameras filming their actions. These would include regional television representatives (from *Look North, Calendar*), the city's CCTV system, the demonstrators' own filming team and the police 'Evidence Gatherers' (EGs). The SYP evidence gatherers comprised two officers, one using a camcorder, the other a 35mm camera. It was their role to film public order events, capturing images of demonstrators and flashpoints. The filming is undertaken overtly and the officers wear fluorescent yellow bibs bearing the initials 'EG'.

Following the briefing the police evidence gatherers made their way to Devonshire Green where the protesters were due to assemble. For the hour before the assembly time they wandered around the square and its surrounding streets filming the comings and goings. The protesters who arrived were diverse, including middle-class families, 'eco-warriors', pedal cyclists in colourful lycra sportswear and less conventional cyclists on 1970s 'chopper' style bikes. As the crowd grew the police heightened their presence, motor-cyclists circling the green and transit vans parking up along one side of the green. All the time the evidence gatherers kept filming, not standing on the sidelines capturing passers-by, but walking up to people and focusing their cameras on them. The protesters largely laughed off this intrusion. To the protesters, the practice of being filmed seemed to be accepted as part of the territory and none questioned the reasons. The highly surveilled nature of events such as these was encapsulated by one incident, namely the police evidence gatherer filming a protester official photographer as the protester in turn filmed the police officer. At the same time a television camera operator was filming the two of them filming each other. A resonating image taking in both the synoptic and panoptic (Mathiesen 1997).

The blowing of a hunting horn attracted the attention of the gathered throng (later estimated to be 500 by newspaper reporters and to be 1,000 by a protest spokesperson) and the organisers led the protesters on a short march into the city centre until they reached Charter Row, an arterial road. At this point two canvas-sided lorries stopped in the road, blocking it. The canvas sides were drawn back to reveal sound systems and the street was filled with music. A good humoured demonstration ensued. The blocking of Charter Row was disruptive but inadequate to gridlock the city centre. However further disruption was created by cyclists in large numbers cycling slowly around the Charter Square roundabout at the head of Charter Row. As the afternoon progressed groups of cyclists periodically broke away from Charter Square round-about to target other city centre roundabouts. This tactic almost succeeded in gridlocking the centre. The good humour of the day evaporated at the roundabouts as motorists became increasingly frustrated by cyclists impeding their progress through the roundabout. On several occasions the cyclists stopped on the roundabouts forcing cars to halt. Police motorcyclists and mounted officers then intervened, extricating the cars and admonishing the protesters, moving them on. These incidents did not escalate despite a number of flashpoints, for example, one protester jumped on the roof of a stranded car and smashed its windscreen before the police could rescue the motorist. The protest ended at 17:00 hours following negotiations between the police and protesters.

On the day, it appeared that SYP had met their objectives of maintaining the peace whilst allowing the protesters to demonstrate. At the same time they had responded firmly when necessary and in accordance with the instructions of the district commander they had not got drawn into confrontations and had not sullied the image of the force. The event passed off with only one arrest. To all appearances the force image was maintained on the day. However, this interpretation is questioned in the light of examination of the local newspapers and information from later interviews with officers who had been involved.

Examination of the newspaper reports which followed the demonstration shows that the police were criticised for the disruption which resulted from the blocked roads. *The Star* (19/5/97), under the headline *Dancing in the streets,* reported 'Police come under fire after anti-road protest party gridlocks traffic' and detailed criticisms of the police by city centre traders. As a result the police were on the defensive in the report, having to justify their tactics. Their spokesperson blamed the lack of cooperation from the protesters for the disruption 'Our intention was simply to minimise disruption to the public. We were not looking for confrontation'. The *Sheffield Telegraph (23/5/97)* was more critical leading with '*Eco party holds city to ransom'.* The story detailed irate traders and interviewed the city centre manager, who confirmed he would be complaining to the chief constable. There were also allegations that some protesters had continued to party into the night in a house in Broomhall and the police had ignored blatant drug-taking. The police spokesperson, again on the defensive, justified police tactics and criticised the protesters' lack of cooperation. In summary these media reports portrayed the police as ineffective in preventing the disruption and as failing to enforce the law.

Despite the official police stance in the media, interviews with officers who had been involved suggested that the force was far from satisfied with the day. One inspector advised that although the senior officers had insisted on restraint the officers on duty had been extremely frustrated at having to stand back and watch disruption when their natural instincts were to act to maintain order and to enforce the law. The low-key approach had evidently not been popular with these rank and file officers. An operational inspector who had been in the background during the day confirmed this. He and his officers were positioned in vans on the outskirts of the city, held in reserve and ready to support their colleagues if necessary. This officer had been listening to the operation on the short-wave radio and he had been 'bristling at the leniency allowed ... some of my lads were spitting feathers, they wanted to do something!' They had been called in to relieve congestion at a roundabout and the official non-confrontational approach went 'against the grain to let disorder rule, to stand by and do nothing'. The inspector was clearly exasperated by the tactics determined by the command team.

Therefore despite the official line that the police operation had gone to plan, it appears that the police tactics on the day had not only angered city centre traders and shoppers, but also the rank and file police officers who were on duty. These different attitudes towards the policing of the demonstration highlight the tensions contesting the different meanings of policing. Whilst the rank and file officers wanted to engage in 'real policing' by confronting the protesters, the command team was anxious to avoid confrontation which would possibly amplify this local event to national mass mediated theatre and damage the image of the force. Nevertheless it is clear that the command team was sensitive to the criticism the police received both externally and from within. Although the official line of a successful operation was maintained in the media, behind the scenes, debriefings were occurring to review the general strategy adopted.

Observation of the policing of the Reclaim the Streets demonstration and subsequent interviews with a number of the officers involved suggest that the police managers determined a 'win-win' strategy and had clearly considered the implications for their image of the different policing strategies that they could implement.[2] Waddington (1998: 120–1) has argued that the police will endeavour to negotiate and to contain disorder even at a cost of antagonising those in positions of authority. In this way such events become struggles for the meaning of policing in time and space between the different actors involved. It is reasonable to assume that the SYP command team had considered the 'what-ifs?', for example, what if they adopted a hard-line enforcement policy which led to disorder, with shoppers caught up in the confrontations? The police might have then been portrayed as confrontational with the image as effective but aggressive, thereby alienating neutral onlookers and gaining additional sympathy for the protesters and their cause. In addition. with the number of media agencies in attendance, any violent confrontations would propel the story into the regional and possibly the national media, with SYP adding to its catalogue of non-glorious involvement in public disorder events. In contrast the adoption of a softly-softly approach kept the event, its aftermath and its potential discontents local. On this level the police operation was just as much an exercise in the regulation and containment of the meaning and images of policing as an exercise to control an unpredictable demonstration.

In the event, if the police had estimated that local shoppers and traders would accept the disruption stoically they were mistaken. This was an exercise in risk management that did not work entirely successfully. Although the strategy of the command team had kept the event at a local level, it had under-estimated the ire of local traders and the local media backlash which this generated. Despite adopting a strategy which had the intention of maintaining their dignity and reputation, their image locally was influenced adversely as they were perceived as ineffective by local people and also as managerially weak by the rank and file.

Routine operational police work

The public order events described above involve specific events, conflicting issues and many people. They are highly visible and there is always going to be a media presence. There are other sides to operational policing and this next section examines images created and communicated during what might be called routine operational police work. Specifically I want to consider the work of patrol officers and traffic officers. Whilst the meaning of public order policing is highly visible involving highly surveilled many-to-many relationships, routine operational police work has limited and unmediated visibility most often involving one-to-one relationships.[3] This is a different way of controlling the meanings of policing and the associated images. Operational officers have daily numerous encounters with people in need of help and people breaking the law. These officers are not so visible in media terms as those involved in public order policing but to the people of South Yorkshire, they are the police they are most likely to meet and the encounters will create impressions, influencing the image and reputation of the force. The following sections seek to explore and explain the images and meanings of policing being communicated and promoted in this type of work.

Patrol

This part of the research involved accompanying single-crewed patrol cars during 'quick-turnaround' shifts from 1400–2200 and 0600–1400. I accompanied officers in their routine work, driving around a beat in a patrol car responding to calls from the area control room, following up enquiries and reacting to events as they happened. The officers were based at a small station on the outskirts of the town and their beat areas took in the edges of the town centre and residential areas, including a run-down council estate which had a reputation for domestic violence problems and had also seen public order incidents.

The patrol officers created different impressions over a number of situations. During one shift the first call was to a house on a council estate where a mother had reported a missing one-year-old child. The property was poorly maintained with an overgrown garden and we entered to find the house was filthy and sparsely furnished. There were two dogs in the kitchen and dog urine over the flooring. Amidst this, a young mother was distraught, her baby daughter had been taken out by her lodger and had not been seen for hours. The officer took the details, listened and reassured, obtained a photograph. He told the mother that he would alert the town centre CCTV control room and circulate a description to all patrol officers. Ten minutes after leaving, by chance, the officer spotted the missing child on the outskirts of town and returned her to the mother. Later, reflecting on the call, the officer remarked that the people on the estate didn't like the police:

'... we're a necessary evil to some of the people we deal with here – they don't like us, but we're the first people they contact when they're in bother'.

This call was an example of the officer providing service to members of the local community. The following day involved a return trip to the estate, with another officer, to attend a 'domestic'. Inside the house a young woman was in tears. She had a swollen lip and one of her front teeth was missing. Her partner, a heroin addict in need of money for drugs, had asked her for cash. When she refused, he attacked her, took £40 from her purse and left. The officer painstakingly led her through a statement, but she was in a dilemma over whether to press charges. The officer showed concern, advising her that the only way to stop the beatings (her partner had previously kicked out four of her teeth) was to prosecute. He made sure she had a safe house and access to a phone for the night and made her an appointment with the domestic violence officer. Leaving the house some two hours later, he predicted that she would drop the charges. The assailant was apprehended in town within the hour, minus the money.

These are two examples of the police as 'the social service with force' (Punch 1979a). I also observed confrontation. During the early evening whilst driving around a council estate the officer stopped an old Ford Escort XR3 which had no tax. The five youths inside were hostile and the officer dealt with them firmly. A computer check revealed that the car was stolen and the 'owner' was handcuffed and put in the police car. At this point the other youths became louder and a crowd of curious locals gathered, prompting the officer to call for back-up and a car transporter. After a short while two police cars arrived with three officers. One got out and sat on a wall, chatting to the watching residents. The other officers stayed in the cars to prevent the situation seeming heavy handed. These officers consciously constructed an image of support without seeking to escalate the tension. The situation dissolved once the recovery vehicle arrived and the XR3 was taken away. Its 'owner' was charged with theft.

The above are clear examples of service and force, but there is a middle ground where the attitude adopted by an officer will determine whether an encounter is confrontational. This particularly applies to those situations where patrol officers make 'discretional' stops and can decide whether to lecture or report their 'victim'. In this category during one shift an officer stopped two cars whose drivers were not wearing seat belts. Both drivers smiled in good-humoured embarrassment, presumably thinking it was a trivial matter. The smiles dropped from their faces as the officer sternly took them to task. The lecture finished, both drivers escaped without a fine and drove off suitably humbled. They were not happy and SYP, through these instances, may have lost potential supporters.

Traffic

These incidents involving patrol officers and motorists largely contrasted with those involving traffic division officers and motorists. During a shift with an officer in an unmarked video car, I observed him stopping and questioning, sometimes booking, speeding drivers, bad drivers and red light jumpers. The stops were mostly non-confrontational. The victims usually knew they were at fault and most accepted their fate with good grace. The officer had found that the on-board video camera had made his job less confrontational in that drivers were able to watch the video and see why they were at fault. They were less likely to question the propriety of the stop and fewer cases were contested through to court hearings.

Through the shift the officer stopped nine drivers for differing offences. Each driver was shown the video tape of their offence and seven accepted the criticism and/or the fixed penalty ticket. Two were less compliant. The officer's attitude to the drivers was always polite and never sarcastic. However, if drivers made excuses or were disrespectful or inattentive, he became more assertive, less friendly and emphasised the danger of their actions. Most people got out of the car saying thank you and good-bye.

The traffic officer believed that the nature of his role had changed in the 20 years he had been in the traffic division. On joining traffic he was warned by colleagues that all his encounters would be confrontational; it was the nature of the job. He had developed a cynical attitude towards the excuses that drivers made and carried a packet of tissues, which he handed to drivers who had 'sob-stories' to excuse their driving offence. Yet he now accepted that his role had become education- as much as enforcement-based and he believed that the on-board video was just as valuable to show drivers their mistakes and to educate them, as to prosecute them.

Reinforcing the educational role that the traffic division can perform, under a new manager the traffic division had worked with the force public relations officer and attended a number of public events, demonstrating the traffic vehicles at local shows. The vehicles had attracted considerable interest from the public, encouraging the officers to do more. In addition to the occasional show days, the traffic officers had become involved in giving talks to groups, using videos which they had recorded in the course of their daily work to illustrate safer driving. Traffic officers were visiting schools and targeting 17-year-olds, communicating safe driving messages to those having started, or about to embark on, driving lessons. These examples of proactive communication illustrated the shift of the traffic division from an ethos of enforcement and punishment towards one of education and deterrence.

Rural policing

Observing the routine work of officers in a rural location provided a further perspective on operational police work. From a village station, an inspector, one sergeant and nine constables policed a large rural area comprising expanses of moorland and a number of small residential areas. Operating three shifts of three PCs, there were frequently only two officers on duty due to sickness, holidays and training and on occasions this reduced to one officer. Although the area is somewhat isolated and in policing terms relatively quiet, if support was required, the nearest help was 20 minutes' driving distance away. These factors encouraged the officers to cultivate relationships within the community. One police officer advised that the quiet atmosphere within the district allowed them to spend more time on the jobs which arose, for example spending more time trying to help victims of crime. In their isolated geographical location they were aware that they needed communication skills to deal with potentially dangerous situations. Officers working the area had to be able to communicate to diffuse and resolve situations rather than act aggressively and rely on back-up.

It was evident that communication and creating appropriate impressions were important to these rural officers and they pitched their communication differently to the different groups they interacted with. The groups themselves had different expectations of the police. The rural beat, for example, included a wealthy land-owner with an aristocratic background. In the past he had summoned the sector inspector to meetings and asked him for an update on his plans for policing the area. The inspector respectfully attended and reported the local policing priorities. The communications with the land-owner and the impressions the police were seeking to create with him were very different to those developed with other sections of the community. For example, the area had an active 'pub-watch' whose membership comprised the area's 12 landlords. They met regularly with the sector inspector to discuss common issues such as known trouble makers, the theft of aluminium beer barrels and any public order or drugs problems. This was one of several communication networks that the inspector engaged with. At one of their meetings the inspector, acting as chairperson, pitched at an appropriate level, beginning with a joke delivered in bar-room language. To this group he was not some remote police inspector, but promoted himself as their local bobby, who lived locally, drank in their pubs and understood their problems. The level of trust that the inspector had developed with the group was illustrated at the end of the meeting when one of the licensees requested a discreet word and confided that an embryonic drug dealing problem was developing in his pub.

In a rural sector such as this, force headquarters and the policies and decrees of senior management can seem far away. Corporate messages do not always seem relevant. However, the inspector was aware of the chief constable's promotion of an 'open and honest' approach and when the *Six Hill Horizon* and the *Statement of Purpose and Values* were issued, he admitted to reading them and thinking they were something that could guide him through his work. This was a significant admission from this practical officer who had strong views about embedding policing within local communities rather than management strategies.

Observation of the operational work of patrol and traffic officers provides empirical evidence that many encounters start 'image neutral' and the attitude of the officer will determine the impression that is made. In neutral situations police have a choice of communication approaches and of conveying different meanings of policing, for example, the traffic officers most clearly have a choice to communicate enforcement and censure or education and encouragement. On the urban beat patrol, the patrol officers weighed up the people they were dealing with and determined their communications and image strategy from the way they read the situation. Different classes of people will receive different service. This has been documented elsewhere, for example Ericson reports patrol officers classifying groups and individuals by 'political' and 'minority' characteristics and according to whether they are 'for' or 'against' the police (Ericson 1982: 66–7; see also Skolnick 1966, Holdaway 1983). In contrast with the urban patrols, in the rural areas of South Yorkshire the police operate differently communicating meanings of policing which stress that they are of the local community and fostering an image which encourages the cooperation of the community. The urban patrols were more indifferent (*cf.* Maureen Cain's comparison of rural and urban policing in Cain 1971: 77–81 and in Cain 1973). What these observations of operational work have in common is that in contrast to highly visible and mediated public order policing, the encounters are often one-to-ones or one-to-few and highly invisible, but nevertheless the individual encounters build up and create an overall impression of what SYP is. It is also significant that the motivation of communicating and projecting different images is primarily instrumental and related to achieving the desired objective. For operational officers it is about accomplishing the task, getting the job done and covering their backs. Any image considerations in this respect are likely to relate to the 'presentation of self' (Goffman 1959) rather than the corporate preference. The prime motivation is not to implement the latest managerial initiative from headquarters nor to consider the public relations value of their work and its impact on the force image. Nevertheless, many officers did endorse the 'open and honest' corporate message that the chief constable had promoted since his appointment in 1990.

Community involvement

Police forces have departments which are responsible for community involvement through community-based initiatives, consultation forums, crime prevention (including the various 'Watch' schemes), schools and youth liaison, race relations and victim support. In SYP this work was the responsibility of the Crime and Community Services Department.

Whilst the policing of public order has a high profile and operational patrol and traffic work has numerous spontaneous public contacts, the work of the community services officers has a direct purpose to engage with the public in a planned manner and in this way its officers are also engaged in image work. Indeed it is in this arena that routine policing is closest to public relations work. This section considers the image work of the schools liaison officers, the community constables and also the work of the police community consultative committees. This arena of police work has been described as one in which:

> the police join with other corporate bodies culturally charged with the task of socialization into the consensus. Considerable resources are expended on police visits to school classrooms for lessons in public safety and for propagating the view that the police officer 'is part of your community, he's one of you.' Students are put to work making pictures or writing essays which reinforce these images of police work (Ericson *et al.* 1989: 168).

Not only through their work in schools, but also their work with community groups and on the community beat, this section illustrates the ways in which the police use these opportunities to communicate meanings of policing which are benign and reassuring, which position the police as guardians and a primary source of knowledge concerning community safety. In so doing this form of image work is a primary aid to police legitimacy.

The officers of SYP's crime and community services departments in each district undertook a variety of functions and these included crime prevention, neighbourhood watch coordination, schools liaison, the development of partnership activities and the organisation of initiatives, for example, *Lifestyle*. To undertake these functions, a number of officers performed specific jobs, for example as crime prevention or schools liaison officers. In addition, in each district there were a number of generalist 'community constables'. The terms of reference for these officers were agreed at district level, but their broad responsibility was for school liaison, neighbourhood watch, cycling proficiency, crime prevention surveys and for developing community relations initiatives.

Community constables' away-day

Observation of a community constables' away-day provided an insight into the work of these officers and how it helped to build the image of the force. The away-day agenda included the planning of initiatives and presentations from guests. A representative from the local Business Education Board gave a presentation and encouraged the officers to complete NVQs and to train as mentors for school pupils. The schools focus of this group was quite prominent, for example, on receiving a presentation from a sergeant of the mounted section, a discussion generated around using the horses for educational purposes. The possibility of establishing an 'adopt a police horse' scheme for schools to complement the existing 'adopt a police dog' scheme was considered. The officers discussed in some depth how it would fit the school curriculum, how it would help the learning process and how possible injury and death to the animals would be dealt with. At the same time the mounted section had been set the objective of increasing their schools liaison work as a public relations venture and a comprehensive discussion included the media paybacks involved. Image work was clearly a prime consideration of this exercise.

It was evident from the conduct of the away-day that the community constables were committed to their work in their neighbourhoods. The officers selected to be community constables were experienced officers, mainly with 20 years' or longer service. Talking informally to these officers, they spoke of their role as part of the balance between the 'force' and 'service' elements of policing. They spoke with some nostalgia of times they remembered when the police and public had a closer relationship. This had been eroded, they believed, as the police became more remote through various management initiatives and technological developments such as motorised patrols. They considered that they needed to rebuild respect for the police and they believed that their role was part of this process. This emphasis was summed up by a chief inspector who described their role and their community responsibilities as the 'history and backbone of policing'.

The positive messages of the day were balanced by one agenda item which illustrated the managerialist trends in police management. The community constables' supervisor, a sergeant, advised the officers that henceforth they would have to complete monthly reports of their activities in order that these could be aligned with the district policing objectives. The gathered officers reacted negatively to this monitoring process, believing that they were being victimised, influenced by some views within the district that the community constable's role was a soft option. The constables present did not exhibit any detailed knowledge of the district policing objectives and there was an obvious division here between the managerial knowledge and approach of the supervisor and the practical 'working rules' of the constables, who perceived the imposition of objectives and monitoring as a threat to their work in schools and in the community generally.

Observation of the away-day suggested that the community constables believed that their work was valuable in recreating images of
policing that are more usually associated with 'golden age' policing
(Weinberger 1995). Indeed one officer (with 25 years' service) recalled
that the uniform itself once commanded respect – 'it was just like
Heartbeat when I started, you only had to put on the uniform to get
respect'. These officers were not buffing the image but believed they
were benefiting the community through their work with children, by
which they also hoped to influence the parents. This meaning of policing,
communicated by officers working at a practical level, threatened to come
into tension with the managerialist vision of policing (strategy, measurement, effectiveness) as represented by the supervising sergeant. Just as
the beat officers put covering their backs above implementing initiatives
from headquarters, these community constables had a local perspective
which was about to clash with the management's systemic perspective.
Such tensions between the occupational culture of policing and the more
recent management culture encouraged throughout the public sector has
been characterised by Reuss-Ianni as a clash between 'Street Cops and
Management Cops' (Reuss-Ianni 1983, see also Bittner 1990: 367–76 and
Hunt and Magenau 1993: 78–83). In the context of this research the
'management cops' are not only the supervising officers, but also civilians
with systemic responsibilities, such as headquarters-based media and PR
officers with objectives of promoting the force's image. Whilst press
officers are looking (as a prime goal) for the cooperation of officers to
promote the force and its image, for the officers themselves, whether
community constables, traffic or urban patrol officers, their perspective is
local and related to accomplishing the task in hand. Any resultant image
pay-off is not unimportant to them, indeed image considerations
permeated the away-day agenda, but it is secondary.

Having discussed this backstage setting, the following sections
consider aspects of the formal frontstage work that community
involvement officers undertake, namely schools liaison and community
consultative committee meetings.

Schools liaison

During the community constables' away-day, working with school
children had been a consistent theme. The officers believed their work
in schools could build pupils' self-esteem and influence young persons
with negative attitudes towards the police. How the police conduct this
work in schools is now considered. One observational visit centred
around the visit of a dance group to a middle school. The schools liaison

officer facilitated the visit, which was also attended by three community constables.

The group performed a dance routine based on vandalism and then broke the pupils into two discussion circles run by the group, but each included one or more local community constables. The discussion centred on vandalism, why people might do it and what could be done about it. The pupils spoke about knowing vandalism to be wrong, but they were afraid of being beaten up and ostracised for 'grassing'. At these junctures the police officers made interventions, telling the pupils that sometimes people have to make a stand. The officers did not preach but offered advice and information with a moral overtone. The pupils were respectful well-dressed 12 year olds. Some were side tracked by the police presence asking about CCTV and traffic cameras. They had their own images of police work. For the second session the police officers changed from their uniforms into track suits. This was to counterpoint the official and 'normal' sides of police officers – the second session emphasising the ordinary person behind the uniform. The pupils split up into twos and each officer partnered a pupil through dance and movement exercises.

The formal object of the day was to raise the pupils' self esteem and the police presence was supplementary. It was not a central part of the day's activities which could have proceeded with or without the police presence. The police rode in on the wave and used the day to get to know the pupils, to build relationships and to establish an image of police officers being normal people.

In another district, the visits of a schools liaison officer to an infants' school and a senior school provided a contrast to the event described above. In these visits the officer addressed individual classes about specific subjects negotiated with the schools and which were related to aspects of the curriculum. At the infants' school the officer first addressed a year-one class (five-year-olds) about road safety and after break repeated the lesson to an older group. The children received the officer with complete attention, hanging on to her every word. The complete emphasis of the talk was safety, policing was hardly mentioned. In the yard afterwards, at break time, the young children swarmed all over the officer, delighted to see her, asking questions, telling her things. She was a familiar and welcome figure.

This idyllic reception was not repeated in a visit to a senior school on a subsequent day. The object of the visit was to address the year-eight pupils on the dangers of electricity. This audience were not so receptive, their attention was not guaranteed and the respect for authority, so evident at the infants' school, was undetectable. The pupils were less obviously enthusiastic than the younger classes about a police visit. To capture their attention, the officer showed a graphic video, *Electric Graffiti,* based around rival gangs with a den in an electricity sub-station. It featured the electrocution of one of the gang members and the police investigation which followed, generating some debate about electricity and its dangers. This video was noteworthy as it featured bad actors as police officers adopting aggressive attitudes. This video image of the police (loud, abrasive, unfriendly, investigative) introduced by a real officer was completely at odds with her own image (approachable, friendly, informative). It was the antithesis of the images that these school visits were intended to promulgate.

Police community consultative groups

The final area I want to consider in terms of image is that of the police community consultative groups (PCCGs). As discussed in chapter 3, these were established under section 106 of PACE with the vision of improving local accountability and consultation. These forums project images of policing, albeit to a limited audience.

PCCG meetings in three districts of South Yorkshire projected different images of policing. One meeting projected images of a public company's shareholders' meeting. This was held in a school hall and the district served a suburban area. The police team of eight sat at a top table facing the audience and in the manner of a company chairman the district commander formally presented his report. Following presentations from other officers, a question and answer session ensued. In contrast to this suburban community meeting, the second meeting was held in a rural village hall. This was a smaller gathering and the local officers knew and greeted the members of the public as they arrived. The audience sat patiently through presentations from the district commander and a headquarters corporate development officer, but did not become engaged until the local officers and local reports replaced talk of plans and strategy. The local sergeant spoke the language of his audience. He spoke about local issues, car crime, burglaries and community. He explained that with 17 officers and a huge area to police they relied on information and support from the public and could not manage without it. He closed his report by emphasising the local nature of policing – 'we are a *local* station, with *local* bobbies, there to serve – please keep in touch' (original emphasis retained).

The third consultation forum was a 'police/minorities liaison forum'. The purpose of the forum was to provide an arena where minority ethnic communities could meet local police officers and discuss issues of mutual concern. This meeting was more informal and less stage managed than the two already mentioned, for example, most officers were in civilian clothing and sat amongst the audience rather than in a group at the front. The forum was introduced by a chief inspector who conveyed the police messages of wanting to understand this section of the community, of making efforts to meet minorities' needs and asserting that ethnic minorities were one of many publics that the police encounter and want to work closely with. The forum did not have a formal agenda and the subject matter developed from questions from the audience or prompted questions from the police to the audience.

Although the three consultative meetings were different in terms of the policing locations they were set in, the audiences they addressed and the way in which they were managed by the police, common images of policing emerged through the observations. The police confirmed the expectations of the audiences by promoting policing that was concerned with crime detection and prevention. They also took account of the managerialist performance framework by emphasising effectiveness and efficiency. Accountability and consultation were addressed both through presentations on the strategic process of compiling the policing plan and also by the local sergeant committing his locally-based officers to serve and consult with the community. Also running through the meetings was that community safety was a partnership, and SYP were willing partners of local people and agencies.

In communicating such images of policing and controlling the meanings of policing through the work of officers in schools, in partnership work in the community and through the community consultative committees, the police are acting as knowledge workers (Ericson 1994, Ericson and Haggerty 1997). They act as experts on community safety, collecting and distributing information and knowledge which define crime and public safety debates and which can facilitate and support community partnerships. The domain of the community relations officer is also a legitimating one in that as we have seen in the work of the schools liaison officers, it provides opportunities for SYP to reinforce the 'meanings and symbols and representations that construe its own actions and weave them into the belief-systems, sensibilities, and cultural narratives of the social actors and audiences involved' (Garland 1991: 192–3).

The empirical data presented and discussed in this chapter provides some evidence that in the operational and community involvement spheres, image work has become embedded in police work. This is often unconscious and is most latent in the work of urban patrols, many of whom would no doubt scoff at the very suggestion. It is more obvious in the work of the traffic division who quite calculatedly have changed emphasis from pure enforcement to enforcement with education. The evidence also suggests that in public order policing, the image of the force is a factor considered in planning, even if it is the negative area of damage limitation rather than image promotion. Image work operates at a different level in the community involvement arena where police officers engage with local people and agencies and control the meanings of policing through the established systems of schools liaison and public consultation which operate as 'self-confirming processes ... to reproduce and consolidate their legitimacy' (Beetham 1991: 99).

Notes

1 Recognising the difficulty of facilitating an operation that was perceived by many as morally wrong, Sussex and Essex police devised media strategies that had the objective of not alienating public opinion against the police. These included such aspects as divorcing the force from the issue, emphasising that the police on duty were local police and not drafted-in riot police and identifying as the key message the paramount importance of public safety. A publicity campaign was also mounted which included sending police news-letters to residents which outlined the police role in the operation.

2 Recent research suggests the policing of protest in Western democracies during the 1990s was characterised by 'under-enforcement of the law', i.e. an emphasis on peace keeping rather than law enforcement, and 'the search to negotiate' which involves a growing role for public relations officers as mediators (della Porter and Reiter 1998).

3 The covert filming of LAPD officers beating Rodney King in March 1991 is a rare example of operational policing becoming mass mediated. It also provided a shocking image and a meaning of policing that was not intended for mass consumption. In tension with controlled promotional images of policing it achieved international infamy and undermined the legitimacy of the LAPD.

Chapter 8

Image work, police work and legitimacy

'I would far rather learn about police work from accompanying officers than listening to a force press officer.' (Peter Manning, Keele University, 1998)

Peter Manning's comment suggests that the role of police press officers is marginal to real 'police work'. At the very least it implies a distinction between the work of police officers (*police* work?) and the work of press officers (*image* work?). My aim in this chapter is to re-examine this distinction and to consider whether image is now at the core of police work. In doing so, I want to consider both the implications for policing of an increasingly mass-mediated society and also the relationship between police image work and legitimacy.

The altering significance of image work

In our mass-mediated world the management of visibility assumes great importance (Thompson 1995) and in this context we need to consider the impact of police image work and its significance for the shape and contours of public policing. Analysis of the full range of data gathered throughout this research suggests there are at least three plausible possibilities, or emergent scenarios, concerning the significance of image work. I will demonstrate in the following sections that examples, or traces, of each possibility exist in contemporary policing. I will also argue, drawing on the work of others to situate police image work within the wider context of a mass-mediated society, that the research evidence suggests that the scenarios co-exist, but some will be undercut by these wider processes, whilst others will be reinforced by them.

Scenario 1: marginal image work

The first possibility is that image work is marginal or insignificant, that it comprises nothing more than 'buffing of the image', auxiliary to and far removed from, real police work. In this scenario, image work is the territory of police press officers who service the news media with police stories, appeal through the media for information and publicise the promotional activities of the chief constable. Press and media relations occupy a low place in the hierarchy of organisational priorities and are regarded as peripheral to and distinct from core policing activities. This is reflected by the relatively low level of resources allocated to media relations, the basic quality of the press office's accommodation and equipment and the absence of detailed and implemented external communication policies.

Vestiges and advocates of this scenario remain in forces where ACPO teams are suspicious of the media, where press offices are regarded as 'bolt-on' peripherals, non-essential for real policing and where police officers are unlikely to place image work amongst their priorities or even to know the names of their own press officers. During the case study fieldwork it existed in pockets within South Yorkshire Police (SYP), for example, amongst a group of operational officers who expressed surprise that the headquarters deputy head of press and media was a civilian journalist and not a sworn officer. It was also evident in the policing district where the DPO was an image work 'spectator'. At a national level it was evident in the reaction to the ACPO Media Advisory Group (MAG) circular of May 1999 concerning the naming of victims involved in crime and traffic incidents. This was seen in a small number of forces as a sanctioned way of limiting external communications and keeping the media at arms length. Journalists too continue to argue that the police are persistently uncooperative and excessively suspicious (Campbell 1999, Stern 1999). To sum up this scenario, it is to argue that image work *is low in the organisational consciousness*. However, the signs are that the game may be up for this scenario. It is indicative of the earlier phases of police image work and the research evidence suggests some forces have moved through this situation and others, in their documentation and rhetoric, aspire beyond it. It characterises the status of police image work of the 1980s and earlier, not the late 1990s and beyond.

The denial of this scenario as a feasible long-term possibility is not based solely on the stated intentions and observed practices of police forces, it is also the implication of mass-mediated conditions and the pressures on police forces to be seen to be seeking effectiveness and efficiency which mitigate against this as a plausible scenario. In this respect, as noted previously, Thompson (1995) has argued that the development of communications media shape the evolution of society and its institutions. Equally Castells has argued that the conditions of the 'information age' create media-driven, knowledge-dependent 'network' societies (Castells 1996, 1997). The implication of the conditions described by Thompson and Castells is that organisations, particularly those such as the police which experience high visibility, have little option but to address image work. If 'we live with the media and by the media' (Castells 1996: 336), it is no longer tenable to opt out of image work or to ignore its significance. Whilst this might appear to be self-evident for a large, capital city force such as the Met., events of recent years show that 'sleepy' provincial forces are not immune. Examples include: a) the tragic murder in March 1996 of schoolchildren in Dunblane that created media interest with which the small Central Scotland Police force could not cope (McPherson 1997: 29–31); b) the media interest in the 1994 Fred and Rose West murder investigation by Gloucestershire police which became a media story in itself (Mawby 1999: 277–8); c) during April 2000 Norfolk Constabulary were besieged by media interest during the trial and conviction for murder of Tony Martin, a farmer who shot and killed a teenage burglar. This media swamping of Norfolk was not an isolated one-off example, the press office (comprising two staff) had experienced similar levels of media interest following the disappearance of two children from a Norfolk beach in August 1996. These provincial examples suggest that no police forces are immune from developments in the media which have the potential to propel local events into regional and national theatre. Therefore, although vestiges of the marginal scenario still exist, its proponents are, I would argue, swimming against the tide.

Scenario 2: supportive image work

The second scenario is one in which the impact of image work is formally recognised and harnessed by the police service to assist forces in coping with an external environment which the mass media pervade. Image work is significant and sits higher in the organisational consciousness than in the scenario described above. In this scenario, the police service recognises the technical and specialist skills of image workers and puts them to work in the interests of the policing organisation. This includes not only the recruitment of journalists, public relations specialists and marketers as effective practitioners, but also the deployment of professional communicators as middle and senior management staff, heading 'corporate communications' departments and integrated into the policy-making committees of forces. Greater resources are dedicated to press and media relations in order to maintain an adequate press office in reasonable accommodation and with the necessary range of technical equipment. The greater resources and higher organisational status of image work is embodied in media strategies and policies which impact on all staff, including the provision of media training to operational officers. In contrast to the first possibility the police service accepts that *image work is a necessary part of twenty-first century policing*, if not its core.

My surveys and interviews across the police service suggest aspects of this scenario in the ambitions, policies and practices of a number of police forces and staff associations. Evidence of this is the recognition by policing policy makers that the media play an important role in shaping images of policing and that external communication needs to be effective when policing is subject to scrutiny and criticism. In forces, senior management teams have identified the need to recruit professional image makers, to adequately resource 'press office' (or corporate communications) departments and to integrate these departments into the organisational hierarchy and decision-making processes. The practitioners are expected to be proactive, eschewing the reactive tendencies of the traditional 'press bureau'. For example, forces will identify issues concerning known events and prepare a media policy to project the desired police image.[1]

This scenario signifies the strategic importance of image work and its identification as such by police forces. However, image work is still seen as separate from police work, there to serve and support the needs of 'real' police work (as suggested by Manning's comment). One example of this was found in a force in which the press office was symbolically located next to the ACPO suite of offices (in a separate building from other headquarters staff). This denoted the importance of the department and yet the head of the department was not a member of the force policy-making team – he was consulted when it was considered appropriate and his professional advice was not always acted upon. In short, this trajectory sees image work as accepted, as necessary and important, but as separate and in support of real policing.

Although trends across the police service suggest that this scenario best describes the current situation, there is also a pattern of unevenness, across and within forces. The constituent elements of this scenario have not permeated all forces. Some forces have shown counter-tendencies and within forces attitudes towards, and commitment to, image work vary as illustrated in the case study. Nevertheless, given the external conditions already discussed, this scenario appears to have the inevitably of a rising tide which will in time sweep all before it.

Scenario 3: image at the core

The third scenario is the most far-reaching and it is to suggest that image is at the core of policing, such that 'police work' becomes 'image work'. Whilst the possibilities above promote formal specialist communicators as the prime image makers who are accepted more or less by senior officers and operational police officers, this scenario emphasises the creeping role (intended and unintended) of operational officers as agents of image work. It also suggests that press officers and operational officers will work in an integrated way, collapsing the demarcation between operational policing and 'bolt-on' image work, such that *all* are image workers, who shape what policing is in the mass-mediated environment. Image work in this scenario is not merely significant, it becomes *the defining institutional logic* of the police organisation.

In positing this as a potential scenario I draw on interview data and observational fieldwork. First, it became evident during the empirical work that image work had become an integral part of policing. Two of the interviewed ACPO officers touched on this when deliberating upon the image of their force. Both made comments suggesting that the image was generated from locally developed relationships between officers and publics, one commenting 'the image *is* the service they [local communities] get' (emphasis added). Secondly, as I have suggested in chapter 7, observational fieldwork suggested that routine operational policing was infused with considerations of image. Running through the observed police work was a concern with projecting particular and appropriate images, whether this was during routine patrol work or during the planning of initiatives at community constables' away-days. It was also evident in the planning and implementation of those operations which were most likely to attract media attention, namely the public order operation for the Reclaim the Streets demonstration and the entirety of events surrounding the policing of the Hillsborough football match. Central to these events was not only the policing of order, but also the policing of meaning.

I am not suggesting that this conception of image work is completely novel. Indeed I have argued earlier that considerations of image have existed at least since 1829 and that the nature of image work emerges in different forms at different times to meet different needs. In addition, the occupational culture of policing and the 'presentation of self' implies the constant projection of particular images (Goffman 1959, Holdaway 1983, Brown 1988, Fielding 1994, Reiner 2000a: ch. 3). What is different, arguably, is that a consciousness of image awareness infuses police organisations, running through all policing activities to the extent that image now orders police work. An analogy can be drawn here with Ericson and Haggerty's research (Ericson and Haggerty 1997). Based on fieldwork undertaken in Canada, they developed the thesis that in late modern society the core organising principle of policing is risk (external danger). The thesis suggests that policing is best understood in terms of a paradigm of risk rather than in terms of law enforcement, order maintenance and service provision (*ibid*: 11). These traditional policing activities do not disappear, but continue, subsumed by the logic of risk management. Within this model the public police coordinate their own activities with policing agents in other public and private institutions to provide a society-wide basis for risk management and security (*ibid*: 1). Policing is therefore part of 'risk communications' in which the police participate by collecting, managing and distributing knowledge, both for their own purposes and increasingly on behalf of other institutions. In doing so the police are part of a network of organisations and institutions enmeshed in 'complex webs of internal and external expectations' (*ibid*: 446) and are constrained by 'rule-governed frameworks' (*ibid*: 9).

Ericson and Haggerty's thesis has been contested on the grounds of its limited empirical research and its claim to cover all facets of social and technical development. However, for my purposes their thesis suggests a potentially fruitful analogy, substituting 'image' for 'risk'. In this reading image becomes the central organising feature of policing. This is to suggest that image work has become all-important, that image considerations run through and order police policy making and all aspects of operational work. Let us now consider some of the empirical evidence in relation to this scenario. First and most obviously, the two public order events described in chapter 7, namely the policing of a sensitive football match and the policing of a peaceful, but disruptive demonstration, were planned and executed by the police as exercises in image management in ways which dictated what was, and what was not, operationally acceptable on the day. Both were attempts to influence the social meaning of policing in potentially 'flashpoint' situations in which the meaning of policing was contested, not only by the main protagonists, but also within the police organisation.

Secondly, image considerations were not limited to those policing operations which involved high visibility and the potential for amplification to national mass-mediated events. They also infused less visible routine police work. For example, the traffic division of SYP had made a conscious change in its mode of operation in order to project positive images of policing. It had eschewed the lecture and punish approach to improving the behaviour of drivers in favour of advice and education, extending this to working closely with the headquarters public relations officer to arrange promotional activities. The community services officers, particularly the community constables, were consistently engaged in image work. Image underpinned their very function – providing a visible reassuring police presence in local communities. Their schools liaison colleagues also conducted image work projecting benign images of policing and good citizenship into welcoming class-rooms. The front-line patrol officers too, working both in the rural and urban environment, were image workers, whether communicating messages of law enforcement (whilst arresting car thieves), guardianship (recovering lost children, protecting victims of domestic violence) or policing embedded in local communities (rural patrol). Image work pervaded this police work.

In this scenario, image work is central to policing as part of the process of fulfilling the police mandate – preventing and detecting crime, maintaining order and providing service. Operational officers become the principal image makers, one expression of this being the encouragement of all police personnel to engage in promotional activities and media activities. This includes both the organisation of local public relations events such as police station open days and the launching of initiatives and also direct media liaison, from involvement with radio programmes to targeting local newspapers with police 'good news' stories. Whilst it is not novel for police officers to develop working relationships with local crime correspondents, it is novel that their active development of media relations and public relations activities is implemented as approved policy. The professional communicators continue to play a key role in this scenario – namely through the trend identified of their increasingly facilitative, enabling role rather than their deployment as up-front spokespersons or in 'spin doctor' type roles.

In a 'media laden society' (Webster 1994) in which an embattled public service institution is attempting to come to terms with the environmental conditions described by Castells and Thompson and at the same time respond to threats to its legitimacy, this third scenario is sociologically plausible; arguably the tide is pushing in this direction. However, it is questionable whether it is yet organisationally feasible. Although there are traces of image work at the core of contemporary policing, there is currently insufficient evidence to support the argument that police work has uniformly become image work. It is one tendency amongst others and, as demonstrated through the case study, co-exists with the other scenarios. Indeed there is evidence that image work in places is having difficulty gaining hold, where the encouragement of police officers to engage in image work through 'honest and open' external communications has encountered implementation difficulties. The encouragement of officers to speak openly to the media invariably leads to the centre (force management, the professional communicators at headquarters) exercising less control over the information released into the public sphere. Apocryphal stories circulate about the 'open' and 'enlightened' force in which the management encourage their staff to communicate and then have to be restrained to prevent them reprimanding the first officer whose ill-chosen or naive words to the media embarrass the force. At force level, the weakening of central control can influence the ability of the professional communicators to ensure that their key messages are communicated at the right times and in the approved way. This despite the efforts of the professional communicators to act as facilitators and coaches to maintain a corporate approach.

In summary, at the outset of the twenty-first century there was evidence of all three of the outlined scenarios across the police service which again highlights the complex nature of image work and the scope for convergence and divergence in the practice of 43 different organisations (plus the staff associations and the non-Home Office police). Yet this divergence represents not only complexity but also reflects the situation that image work is developing at varying rates. There are vestiges of the 'marginal' scenario, there are toe-holds of the 'core' scenario, but on the basis of this research and in the wider context of continuing communications developments, the 'supportive' scenario currently best describes contemporary policing. This is to argue that image work is pervading police work, the data suggesting that it is far from irrelevant (scenario 1) and has been harnessed by the police service as one means of coping with its altered external environment (scenario 2). Although there is insufficient evidence to date to support the argument that police work *is* image work (scenario 3), there are sufficient traces to suggest that this should not be overlooked as a possible future. Indeed image work's development thus far, together with the nature of the external environment, indicate that it may be headed this way.

Image work and legitimacy

I have argued above that although there is divergence evident in the image work practised by police forces, the underlying trend, supported by the pressures of the external environment, is towards a future in which image work is significant to the shape of policing. This is to theorise image work at the level of the relationship between policing and the increasingly mass-mediated environment. This, however, is linked to another dimension, that of the relationship between image work and police legitimacy. Thompson has argued that in late modern society the media can play an important role in realising democratic values as media institutions and technologies are a means by which individuals acquire information and they also provide a potential mechanism for articulating views (1995: 257).[2] The media create 'the non-localized, non-dialogical, open-ended space of the visible in which mediated symbolic forms can be expressed and received by a plurality of non-present others' (*ibid*: 245). This allows for what might be described as 'mediated accountability'.[3] In this section I draw on the fieldwork data to consider how police image work interacts with this 'space of the visible' in order to address the underlying theoretical concern with the relationship between image work and police legitimacy.

To reiterate, legitimacy is associated with the rightful exercise of authority or use of power. Has image work anything to offer police legitimacy? Is image work deployed by the police in the service of society as a whole by demonstrating the accountability and transparency of the police or is it a mechanism utilised for organisational advantage where legitimacy is lacking? To answer this at one level, analysis of the official documentation and the comments of the interviewees suggests that policy makers and practitioners believe that image work can contribute to accountable and transparent policing. The written media and public relations strategies discussed in chapter 4 suggest that image work should promote and support accountable policing, though a number suggested that positive images were the prime consideration rather than democratic accountability. So much for the level of official documentation, what about practice? This can be considered, drawing on the observational fieldwork of image work in practice, in relation to Beetham's legitimacy framework with its dimensions of legal validity, shared beliefs and expressed consent.

In terms of legal validity, as noted in chapter 3, it is in this area that police legitimacy has declined due to miscarriages of justice, proven police corruption and the apparent inability of the police to apply the law fairly or to act within it. What difference can image work make to this dimension of legitimacy? This can be considered drawing on the experiences of SYP and the 1989 Hillsborough disaster. As documented in chapter 5, SYP achieved notoriety for its involvement in the tragedy and was accused of acting illegitimately in respect of conduct on the day and activities afterwards which were perceived as spoiling tactics to avoid responsibility (Scraton 1999). Different versions of events leading up to the disaster were developed in the media and one version blamed drunken supporters for rushing into the ground. It was subsequently alleged that SYP had fed to the media messages relating to drunken Liverpool supporters to deflect the blame away from the police. When doubt was cast on the truth of these stories, the integrity of SYP was further questioned, compounding mistakes which Lord Justice Taylor identified. On this occasion it would appear that image work had not been deployed in the interests of legitimacy and, on the contrary, had been used negatively to mask illegitimacy. In particular, and referring back to the communications approaches outlined in chapter 3, this is one example of how the adoption of a misrepresentative approach is not sustainable in the long-term and is ultimately self-defeating. SYP allegedly provided a misleading interpretation of the events of 15 April 1989 and as a result is still having to deal with the consequences of not only the disaster but also the communications approach adopted that day and in the weeks following.

In the wake of the criticism of SYP emanating from the tragedy, the reaction of the senior management was to 'batten down the hatches' and to adopt a closed approach to external communication through the media. Following the appointment of a new chief constable in June 1990, the communication approach changed to one of espoused 'honesty and openness' in an attempt to rebuild the external image and internal identity of the force and to seek to re-legitimate it. Whilst this approach seemed a genuine attempt to provide transparency and accountability, the process of re-legitimation takes time and is multi-layered. At the time of the fieldwork although SYP's image had generally improved and the force's self-confidence had grown, the process was incomplete. The force's confidence was fragile and the image remained dogged by the legacy of the Hillsborough disaster.

Another example from the fieldwork provides a contrast. One of the ACPO officers interviewed discussed his media policy whilst acting as the investigating officer in the conviction of a corrupt regional crime squad detective. His approach was to acknowledge the existence of police corruption, to condemn it and to use the media interest to warn others against corruption, whilst at the same time signalling that the police service was actively pursuing and prosecuting those who succumbed. Image work was deployed not to cover-up or excuse police illegitimacy but to illustrate how the police themselves were combating it. It demonstrated transparency and accountability.

I will turn now to Beetham's second dimension of legitimacy, that of shared values, justification through reference to beliefs shared by those in the power relationship. This requires a minimum commonality of appropriate beliefs to be held by the parties in the relationship. In a multi-cultural, socially and economically diverse society different attitudes towards policing exist and to maintain legitimacy the police need to identify common ground and shared values with the different groups. The fieldwork provides examples of the police projecting and promoting images as binding agents which seek to legitimate the police role and the police institution.

At national and local levels the police draw on their history and traditions to appeal to groups within society. The myths of 'traditional British policing' still resonate and are used in contemporary image work to elicit favourable responses to the idea of policing (Loader 1997a: 4). This is precisely why one interviewed ACPO officer referred to the Dixon legacy as 'the family silver', namely a binding agent sending messages of security and reassurance. The Police Federation regularly draws on historic references and warns of threats to traditional policing in its campaigns – as Beetham has noted such practices help to 'reproduce and consolidate' legitimacy (1991: 99). This rich vein has also been mined by politicians, for example, the Home Secretary advocating Dixon of Dock Green as a role model (*Sunday Times* 8/2/98). It was also recognised at local level – the SYP community constables spoke of their pride in the uniform and their chief inspector praised their role as 'the history and back-bone of policing'. This, despite, as Reiner has argued, the traditional characteristics of British policing having little application in contemporary policing (Reiner 1995c).

The fieldwork also provided examples of the benefits of promoting a multi-functional image of the police, which served to create links with different groups within society. In this respect, whilst accompanying patrol officers it became evident that groups within the community who often had an adversarial relationship with the police acknowledged the value of the police in their service capacity, for example, in helping to locate missing children and in providing a minimum of protection to victims of domestic abuse. Conversely, burgled residents of a nearby leafier neighbourhood valued the crime detection role of the police. By portraying an image of a 24-hour multi-functional emergency service, the police are able to appeal to particular shared values with different sections of communities. Arguably a logical extension of this is the recommendation from a Home Office report that police forces should apply marketing principles to segment and target audiences with 'group specific communication approaches' (Bradley 1998: 14). It is perhaps ironic that parts of the service role, often derided by the police culture as low value and 'not real policing' perform image work as valuable in terms of legitimacy as the mythical crime fighting role.

The observed proactive publicity events and the staged conferences were also platforms for SYP to appeal to, and seek to forge, shared values. This was evident at the *Lifestyle* launch, when the police orchestrated a community-wide initiative which re-affirmed the perceived shared values of model communities, including charitable works, helping the disadvantaged and encouraging young people to be good citizens. Such community values were consistently promoted by SYP officers in their involvement with multi-agency initiatives including anti-drugs schemes and safety in the community events. In these examples police officers engaged in image work to communicate social meanings of policing and there were media 'pay-offs' in the form of newspaper, radio and television features which promoted police involvement in such community building, projecting favourable and benign images of the police. In other circumstances, however, the police role is more controversial or potentially adversarial and although the police may appeal to shared values, they will not always be successful. For example, in the planning for the Reclaim the Streets demonstration, the police commander attempted to gain the cooperation of the organisers by appealing to shared values in his letter – professing empathy and even support for the aims of the demonstration. His appeal went unheeded and the subsequent policing of the demonstration, as analysed in chapter 7, received criticism as the police were unable to motivate a minimum commonality of views between the protagonists – shoppers, retailers and protesters.

During the Reclaim the Streets demonstration, the SYP press officers were not actively deployed, but in the course of the fieldwork it became evident that professional image makers in other forces were taking on increasingly active roles in the policing of protest events. For example during the series of live animal export protests in 1995 police press officers were used operationally in Essex and Sussex to formulate and direct strategies and tactics to project appropriate images of the police. This included press officers being placed at strategic roadside locations in order to offer on-the-spot interpretations to journalists in attendance as police officers took action to remove protesters. The way in which press officers were utilised contrasts with their deployment in earlier public order policing (*cf.* Murdock 1984, Waddington 1994). Such tactics helped the police to balance the adverse publicity that the operation generated. In these different ways the police use image work to appeal to shared values and thus legitimate their operations.

The third component of Beetham's legitimacy framework is the dimension of expressed consent and as previously mentioned the notion of 'policing by consent' has become a mantra of police legitimacy. This criterion operates at the level of actions and as discussed in chapter 3 can be related to policing in terms of mechanisms of accountability and consultation. The observational fieldwork engaged with how image work interacted with this dimension of legitimacy. As described in chapters 6 and 7 at a number of events SYP submitted itself to the scrutiny of the public. These included Police Community Consultative Group (PCCG) meetings, the launch of SYP's annual report for 1996–97 (the annual report was originally a mechanism of accountability), and the media launch of Doncaster's CCTV evaluation. All these events included opportunities for the media and a limited cross-section of South Yorkshire people to question, hold to account, and express consent or dissent to, members of SYP.

Although research suggests that PCCGs are limited in their effectiveness, they provided opportunities to observe how the police approached these forums for accountability in terms of projecting images of policing. Although the different PCCG meetings were managed in contrasting ways, SYP communicated similar messages at each, projecting an image of a force that was committed to crime prevention and detection and to working in partnership with its local communities. Engaging with local people and working in conjunction with other agencies to resolve problems was affirmed. Accountability was also stressed in the form of presenting statistics and reporting progress against targets, mostly crime related. Similar messages were conveyed at the launch of the annual report and of the CCTV evaluation report – of a police force explaining its actions, justifying its policies, submitting itself to the sometimes probing questions of the assembled media representatives and thereby accepting the vicarious scrutiny of the public through the mass mediation of the events. On these occasions the police representatives were willing to enter into dialogue with their audiences, though commonly a missionary approach was adopted. In seeking the consent of their publics, and hence legitimacy, the messages communicated were often those that appealed to shared values, providing a link to the previously discussed criterion of legitimacy.

The data generated through the fieldwork illustrates how image work can contribute to or undermine accountable policing through the dimensions of Beetham's legitimacy framework. It suggests that the police have used image work instrumentally in order to compensate for illegitimacy (Hillsborough and its aftermath) and to facilitate the discharge of policing responsibilities where legitimacy deficits lurk (animal exports operations), sometimes unsuccessfully (attempts to identify shared values with the Reclaim the Streets protagonists). The fieldwork data indicates that the way in which police image work emerges, and how it contributes to policing, differs over time and space. The police service can and does utilise image work in different ways at different times which serves both to legitimate policing and to attempt to compensate for a lack of legitimacy. In the case of SYP and Hillsborough, for example, the police initially (and allegedly) attempted to legitimate their misconduct using image work, before moving through a 'no comment' phase, then finally adopting an 'open and honest' approach to their communications as a re-legitimation mechanism.

Controlling the police image?

In the preceding section I have argued that in the context in which image work permeates police work, it interacts with Thompson's 'space of the visible' in ways which can both support legitimate policing, but can also be used to attempt to compensate for problems of legitimacy. This suggests that the effects of mediated accountability (and the role of image work in the legitimation process) depend on the extent to which the police are able to control their image through the media. Therefore the question of the degree to which image work serves legitimacy or arises as a symptom or product of legitimation problems requires consideration not only of police motives and intentions but also must take account of issues of control.

Although the police cannot control the reception and interpretation of their communications activities, they are to some extent able to influence how their image is communicated and projected through their relationship with media organisations. The balance of power between the police and the media accordingly requires consideration. If the police are able to control this relationship then there arises opportunities for manipulation and distortion at the expense of dialogue and transparency. On the other hand if there is equilibrium in the balance of power then this can encourage dialogue and can enhance democratic policing through the transparency and accountability it brings. Therefore it is apt to consider the issue of control in the police–media relationship in the light of the evidence generated through the research.

One theme running through literature on the police–media relationship is that the police are the dominant party. The police are in a position to provide access to information, to select and filter information, such that this places them in a position of dominance in relation to media agencies (Hall *et al.* 1978, Ericson *et al.* 1989, Ericson 1995). Proponents of this view believe that the relationship is driven by the police. They are the gatekeepers to information, they recognise the media's needs and use them to the police advantage, defining reality in terms of images of policing. Crandon and Dunne fear that this is dangerous for democracy and reduces the media to vassals, a 'police press office can... produce messages that are more in keeping with the wishes of the police than the free flow of information which a democracy implies' (Crandon and Dunne 1997: 84). I have argued elsewhere that there are reasons to doubt this view (Mawby 1999). At the national level interviews with press officers in different police forces suggested that in their experience they could not set the policing media agenda, that they were not dominant in the relationship. At the local level this view was held in SYP's headquarters press office. At this level there was a belief, however, that compared to the situation in the 1980s they could influence the relationship sufficiently to manage the force image. This was due partly to their appreciation that they were gatekeepers to information. By providing access and information they expected reciprocation in terms of balanced media coverage. They had also become more adept at getting messages across. In the face of media criticism, they were better equipped to liaise with the media organisations, for example, they would ensure that several key messages were communicated to the media, even if these were not eventually run by media organisations. They would now defend themselves rather than batten down the hatches and return to the 'no comment' days. Instead they would have a planned response and would mobilise to convey the force's side of the story.

Within SYP, at a district level, two press officers, those that were most active, felt they controlled the local media relationship. This suggests that where long-term relationships exist (local level) rather than ephemeral relationships (national level) then the police are more able to control the relationship as the local media are more dependent on the police for a consistent supply of news. It is significant also that the impact of national media developments (technological and organisational) had not noticeably impacted on the work of DPOs with their essentially local relationships. This contrasted with the headquarters press office which, dealing with regional and national media outlets, had experienced the impact of the developments (as had force press offices across the police service – see chapter 4). However, even in the districts where the press officers considered they were in control, the press officers recognised the symbiotic nature of the relationship and observation of their news selection suggested that it was undertaken in a way which aimed to meet the media organisations' values and communication formats as much as the force's needs (cf. Ericson and Haggerty 1997).

The ebb and flow of control in the police–media relationship highlights the complexity of image work. As detailed above there were mixed feelings amongst press officers about the balance of power. At one extreme a number of district police officers felt they were in control and at the other extreme some headquarters-based press officers (not only in SYP) denied any ability to control what got into the media and relied on matching their key messages to the media's agenda. Yet police press officers at both ends of this continuum operated within the constraints of the media world and consciously or unconsciously fed the media with information in subjects they were interested in and in formats which suited the medium in question. There was an impression of police control (for some) and yet there was constraint. A similar situation was noted in a different jurisdiction, Canada, where researchers noted that the police could control access to information, but were less able to control the storyline and editing process 'ultimately police–reporter transactions entail controls from both sides, and interdependency' (Ericson et al. 1989: 125). The constraints on the police to produce information in formats and within frameworks determined by outside organisations has been alluded to by Ericson and Haggerty (1997). Although their perspective is different in that their thesis concerns risk rather than image management they argue that one current feature of policing is that the police are put under increasing pressure to supply information in formats shaped by other organisations (ibid: 18, 358–9, 433, 436).

A second aspect of the complexity lies in the notion held by headquarters press officers and some DPOs that the need to be open and honest was partly driven by a fear that less than honest or full information would be recognised and investigated by journalists. In tension with this was the belief on the part of (the same) headquarters press officers that the professionalism of the journalists they dealt with was in decline. This arose from the documented advances in media technology and capacity having led to the situation in which there is a constant demand for police news. Whilst these changes place additional pressure on police press officers to provide a service to the media, the same changes have placed increased demands on journalists. As Martin Bell argued in the BBC2 programme *Breaking the News,* the technology of electronic news gathering has led to a battle between journalists to be 'first and fastest rather than best and most accurate' (*Breaking the News,* 6 July 1997). A number of interviewees had noted that this meant that journalists were less likely to research and investigate their own stories. One press officer had found that in this environment it had become easier to place unedited and uncriticised police press releases in newspapers and radio news. It was felt that the recipient news agencies had got neither the time nor inclination to investigate the press releases further and criticise or confirm their accuracy. Another press officer referred to 'supermarket journalism', namely the situation in which the police press officers prepare the stories they want to promote and then offer them to the media, who choose which story or stories they will take. In this situation, there is no real journalism, the media select pre-prepared stories ready for consumption.[4]

It is testimony to the complexity of the police–media relationship that, operating at different levels, it is possible that all these aspects of control, and the impression of control, exist in the same force in different places at varying times. For example, the police may be able to package a story for consumption on a routine subject but as the events surrounding the Macpherson Inquiry of 1998 and its report of 1999 have shown, it is less easy to package a story involving a bungled murder investigation. Control of the police image is fluid, conditional and variable and this restricts the potential for police forces to use image work as a means of manufacturing legitimacy where it is lacking. Mediated accountability, it would appear from the evidence, can work to hold the police accountable, but is it sufficient?

Into the future

I have argued in this chapter that image work now pervades police work, whether in the guise of formal image management by professional communicators or in the form of operational officers becoming more engaged in communicating particular images. Having analysed image work at a national level and at the detailed level of a case study, I have suggested that although there is divergence in practice, image work has become significant in the shaping of police work. Further I have argued that in the mass mediated context it is necessary to consider the relationship between image work and police legitimacy. I have concluded from the research evidence that on occasions image work can enhance police legitimacy by contributing to police accountability through transparency and open communications. At other times image work is deployed as a means of coping with illegitimacy, legitimacy deficit and delegitimation.

Although this research suggests that image work is complex, multi-layered and diverse in its application, I have also argued that there are underlying trends evident which situate image work within wider transformations of policing and society in which the mass media, and communication generally, occupy a central location (Thompson 1995, Castells 1997). This is an intriguing situation whose trajectory is uncertain as twenty-first century policing grapples with adapting to managerial and social pressures at a national level and to transnational and globalising pressures at an international level (Reiner 1992b, 1997a: 1038–9, Sheptycki 1997, 1998, 2000, de Lint 1999, Taylor 1999, Johnston 2000, Wright 2000). Given the prominence of the media within these debates, as a technological tool, as a catalyst and as local and global institutions, it is clear that image work will continue to be prominent both as a means of acquiring and transferring information about policing and also as one means by which the police are scrutinised and held accountable. Image work will, in short, remain a significant aspect of policing and its legitimation. Given this, how can police image work best be developed in support of accountable policing, namely policing which embodies democratic principles including adherence to the rule of law and meaningful engagement (consultation and dialogue) with different publics to provide an accessible, responsive police service? I will outline three possible ways forward and the relationship of each to democratic policing.

The first possible way forward draws on the 'marginal image work' scenario. As discussed above image work under this scenario is marginal and low in the organisational consciousness of the police force. In the form described, with its culture of closure, this scenario would appear to have little to offer accountable policing. It is associated with the 'no comment' days when police external communications were distinguished by mistrust and the withholding of, rather than the disclosing of, information. Characterised by suspicion of communicating with the outside world and a lack of cooperation with media organisations, it is difficult to envisage that this scenario can contribute positively to accessible, transparent policing. However, it is important to note that where image work is insignificant and marginal this does not necessarily imply that policing is undemocratic and unaccountable. It is possible that a police force might choose to ignore image work with the intention of proving its democratic credentials through concrete actions rather than 'buffing the image'. In this respect it is theoretically conceivable for democratic structures of police accountability to co-exist with a minimal public relations operation. However, whilst this has normative attractions, it is sociologically untenable given the mass mediated context in which police forces now operate and in which they are compelled to manage their visibility.

The second outlined scenario, 'supportive image work', could feasibly contribute to accountable policing but as a way forward brings with it a dilemma. Its presence signals the recognition by the police service of the need to respond to the mass-mediated conditions of the external environment. In practice this scenario maintains the high visibility of policing and it can contribute to the transparency of policing. It provides a form of mediated accountability, albeit accountability acted out between the police and media agencies with little active participation of the wider population. This option has the potential for selective communication, to bring about 'the dramatic management of the *appearance* of effectiveness' (Manning 1997: 32, original emphasis). Herein lies the dilemma for democratic and accountable policing. If the police continue to develop sophisticated means of image work, this will not be in the interests of accountable policing if misrepresentative communication approaches are adopted. However, the fieldwork suggests that often missionary approaches are in fact used, and that commonly a managerial approach will be pursued, particularly in the pragmatic sphere of news management. Such communication might be conducted in the name of accountable policing but in practice tends to be directed to promoting the reputation of, and limiting the damage to, the police organisation. Culturally and organisationally, therefore, this approach is not conducive to transparency and whilst sociologically plausible, it remains normatively problematic.

To develop and engage image work in support of accountable policing, there is at least one other alternative which projects a way forward which is both sociologically feasible and also normatively desirable. This would be to work towards the alignment, and indeed integration, of the processes of accountability and the processes of image work. The starting point for this would be to commend the documented moves by the police service towards policies, initiatives and practices which promote greater openness and transparency, but also to deepen and extend these. To this end the police service should be further encouraged to embed such image work in democratic processes, aligning communication activities with systems of accountability. It is beyond the scope of this work to develop here what such arrangements might look like in any detail. However, one example would be to consider the requirements for crime audits, consultation and community safety plans under the Crime and Disorder Act 1998. This is one area in which the processes of image work could enhance the processes of accountability, not only by publicising the statutory requirements and their implementation but by helping to create the conditions whereby these processes are transparent and inclusive, for example by instigating and facilitating dialogical communication and consultation with different groups within communities. Pursuing such an approach would involve the development of press and public relations offices not as optional 'bolt-on' auxiliary departments which 'manage' the media and undertake public relations tasks when the need arises, but to use their communications skills in an integrated manner across policing functions to develop communication channels which allow for consultation and dialogue and make transparent the processes of policing. This aspires to a dialogical approach to communication and has the potential to be developed in conjunction with forms of deliberative democracy advocated by Thompson (1995: 255) or alongside recommendations for wider participation in policing accountability as advocated by Jefferson and Grimshaw (1984: 176–8) and, more recently, by Loader (1996: 162–76).

This way forward is the most conducive to democratic, accountable policing. It would enhance police communication and yet reduce the need for a specialist and separate public relations resource within forces as, if meaningful communication and transparency were built into all policing activities, then there would be less pressure to practise overt public relations. To develop image work in this direction is without doubt the most challenging way forward for the police, requiring them to adopt an organisational culture which promotes and accepts openness and trust. Although policy makers have periodically advocated such values without them being widely taken up, the fieldwork identified sufficient traces to suggest that the pursuit of this scenario is not a hopeless utopian cause. Where such traces exist, there is the potential to develop image work that serves not only the organisational needs of the police service, but also the wider public interest. Whether image work in its future development serves the interests of democratic accountable policing or the restricted interests of the police service remains to be seen. But properly integrated with systems of democratic accountability, image work can be engaged in the service of legitimate policing. It does not have to serve narrow organisational interests.

Notes

1   During a fieldwork visit to one force three somewhat controversial cases were about to come to court. For each case a press officer had undertaken a 'what-if?' exercise, anticipating the number of different case outcomes and planning the media messages and responses for each. In this way the force were prepared for whichever outcome and had worked out a considered approach, keeping to the fore messages of a) reassurance for the public (i.e. maintaining public faith in the police), and b) deterrence.

2   Thompson argues that in mass mediated societies, classical participatory democracy is impractical and promises 'too much' and existing representative democracy is remote and delivers 'too little'. To resolve this he supports 'deliberative democracy' in which individuals make judgements on the basis of information provided (1995: 255). In this vision the media have a principal role as information suppliers and as conduits for feedback and the expression of marginalised views (*ibid.* 257).

3   The 'space of the visible' is open-ended in that it is a creative space where images appear suddenly, unexpectedly and the consequences cannot be anticipated or controlled (Thompson 1995: 246–7). In the policing context the Rodney King beating provides a prime example of such mediated account-ability.

4   The police press officers' collective recognition at practitioner level of deteriorating professionalism within the media is supported by papers on related developments (Bardoel 1996, Brants 1998, Franklin 1998, Kilborn 1998). In the mainstream national media a number of articles have reported the growing sense that journalism, particularly investigative and news journalism, is declining in standards ('Non-stop TV news bad for journalism', *Guardian* 28/6/97, 'Now for the bad news', Ian Jack, *Guardian* 8/8/98; see also Cohen 1998 and Gardam 1998).

References

ACPO (1990) *Strategic Policy Document: Setting the Standards for Policing: Meeting Community Expectation*, London: New Scotland Yard.

ACPO (1993) *Your police: the facts*, London: New Scotland Yard.

ACPO (1994) *Your police: a service to value*, London: New Scotland Yard.

ACPO (1996) *Your police are making a difference*, Policing Factsheet no. 4, London: ACPO.

ACPO Quality of Service Sub-Committee (1991) *Meeting Community Expectation: 'Making it Work' – Key operational service areas*, London: New Scotland Yard.

Adorno, T. (1991) *The Culture Industry: Selected Essays on Mass Culture*, London: Routledge.

Alderson, J. (1979) *Policing Freedom*, Plymouth: Mcdonald and Evans.

Alderson, J. (1984) *Law and Disorder*, London: Hamish Hamilton.

Alderson, J. (1998) *Principled Policing*, Winchester: Waterside Press.

Allen, J., Livingstone, S., and Reiner, R. (1998) 'True Lies: Changing Images of Crime in British Postwar Cinema', *European Journal of Communication*, vol. 13(1): 53–75.

Arendt, H. (1970) *On Violence*, London: Allen Lane, The Penguin Press.

Ascoli, D. (1979) *The Queen's Peace*, London: Hamish Hamilton.

Audit Commission (1988) *Administrative support for operational police officers*, London: Audit Commission.

Audit Commission (1993) *Helping with Enquiries*, London: Audit Commission.

Audit Commission (1996) *Streetwise*, London: Audit Commission.

Audit Commission (1998) *Better by far: preparing for Best Value*, London: Audit Commission.

Baldwin, J. and Bottoms, A.E. (1976) *The Urban Criminal: A Study in Sheffield*, London: Tavistock Publications.

Banton, M. (1964) *The Policeman in the Community*, London: Tavistock.

Baker, M. (1996) 'On What Authority?', *Policing Today*, vol. 2, no. 3, pp. 10–13.

Barak, G. (1997) 'Between the Waves: Mass-Mediated Themes of Crime and Justice' in Scheingold, S.A. (ed.) *Politics, Crime Control and Culture*, Aldershot: Ashgate Dartmouth.

Bardoel, J. (1996) 'Beyond Journalism: A Profession between Information Society and Civil Society', *European Journal of Communication*, vol. 11(3): 283–302.

Barton, M. (1996) 'Double vision' in *Policing Today*, April, vol. 2, no. 1, pp. 8–9.

Bean, J. P. (1981) *The Sheffield Gang Wars*, Sheffield: D & D Publications.

Bean, J. P. (1987) *Crime in Sheffield: from deer poachers to gangsters, 1300 to the 1980s*, Sheffield: Sheffield City Libraries.

Beetham, D. (1991) *The Legitimation of Power*, London: Macmillan.

Belson, W.A. (1975) *The Public and the Police*, London: Harper and Row.

Benke, M., Buzas, P., Finszter, G., Szkinger, I., Mawby, R.C., Wright, A. (1997) *Developing Civilian Oversight of the Hungarian Police*, Brussels: European Commission.

Berkley, G.E. (1969) *The Democratic Policeman*, Boston: Beacon Press.

Berry, G., Izat, J., Mawby, R., Walley, L. and Wright, A. (1998) *Practical Police Management* (2nd edn), London: Police Review Publishing Co. Ltd.

Bittner, E. (1967) 'The Police on Skid Row: A Study in Peace-keeping', *American Sociological Review*, 32, no. 5, pp. 699–715.

Bittner, E. (1980) *The Functions of the Police in Modern Society*, Cambridge, MA: Oelgeschlager, Gunn and Hain.

Bittner, E. (1990) *Aspects of Police Work*, Boston: Northeastern University Press.

Blair, I. (1985) *Investigating Rape*, London: Croon Helm and Police Foundation.

Bland, L. (1984) 'The Case of the Yorkshire Ripper: Mad, Bad, Beast or Male?' in Scraton, P. and Gordon, P. (eds.) *Causes for Concern*, Harmondsworth: Penguin.

Bourdieu, P. (1977) *Outline of a Theory in Practice*, Cambridge: Cambridge University Press.

Boyle, R. (1999) 'Spotlighting the Police: Changing UK Police–Media Relations in the 1990s' in the *International Journal of the Sociology of Law*, 27, pp. 229–50.

Bozovic, M. (ed.) (1995) *The Panopticon Writings of Jeremy Bentham*, London: Verso.

Bradley, R. (1998) *Public Expectations and Perceptions of Policing*, Police Research Series Paper 36, Policing and Reducing Crime Unit, London: Home Office.

Brake, M. and Hale, C. (1989) 'Law and Order' in Brown, P. and Sparks, R. (eds.) *Beyond Thatcherism*, Buckingham: Open University Press.

Brants, K. (1998) 'Who's Afraid of Infotainment?' *European Journal of Communication*, vol. 13(3): 315–35.

Brogden, M. (1982) *Autonomy and Consent*, London: Academic Press.

Brogden, M. (1991) *On the Mersey Beat: Policing Liverpool between the Wars*, Oxford: Oxford University Press.

Brown, A. (1988) *Watching the Detectives*, Sevenoaks: Hodder and Stoughton.

Brown, P. and Sparks, R. (eds.) (1989) *Beyond Thatcherism*, Buckingham: Open University Press.

Bunyan, T. (1977) *The History and Practice of the Political Police in Britain*, London: Quartet.

Butler, A.J.P. (1996) 'Managing the future: a chief constable's view' in Leishman, F., Loveday, B. and Savage, S.P. (eds.) *Core Issues in Policing*, London: Longman.

Cain, M. (1971) 'On the beat: Interactions and Relations in Rural and Urban Police Forces' in Cohen, S. (ed.) *Images of Deviance*, Harmondsworth: Penguin.

Cain, M. (1973) *Society and the Policeman's Role*, London: Routledge and Kegan Paul.

Calhoun, C. (1992) *Habermas and the Public Sphere*, Cambridge, Mass.: MIT Press.

Campbell, D. (1999) 'Behind closed doors' in *Policing Today*, vol. 5, no. 1, pp. 14–16.

Cannadine, D. (1992) 'Gilbert and Sullivan: The Making and Unmaking of a British "Tradition"' in Porter, R. (ed. 1992) *Myths of the English*, Cambridge: Polity Press.

Cashmore, E. (1994) *. . . and there was television*, London: Routledge.

Cassels, J. (1996) (Chairman) *Independent Committee of Inquiry into the Role and Responsibilities of the Police*, London: Police Foundation/Policy Studies Institute.

Castells, M. (1996) *The Information Age: Economy, Society and Culture, vol. 1: The Rise of the Network Society*, Oxford: Blackwell.

Castells, M. (1997) 'An introduction to the information age' in *City*, 7, pp. 6–16.

Chapman, B. (1970) *Police State*, London: Macmillan.

Chibnall, S. (1977) *Law-and-Order News: An analysis of crime reporting in the British Press*, London: Tavistock.

Chibnall, S. (1979) 'The Metropolitan Police and the News Media' in Holdaway, S. (ed.) *The British Police*, London: Edward Arnold.

Clarke, A.(1992) 'You're nicked!' TV Police series & the fictional representation of Law and Order' in Strinati, D. and Wragg, S. (eds.) *Come on Down? Popular media culture in post war Britain*, London: Routledge.

Clarke, J., Cochrane A., and McLaughlin, E. (eds.) (1994) *Managing Social Policy*, London: Sage.

Clarke, R. and Mayhew, P. (eds.) (1980) *Designing Out Crime*, London: Home Office Research Unit.

Clutterbuck, R. (1980) *Britain in Agony: The Growth of Political Violence*, Harmondsworth: Penguin.

Coatman, J. (1959) *Police*, London: Oxford University Press.

Cockerill, A.W. (1975) *Sir Percy Sillitoe*, London: W.H. Allen.

Cohen, N. (1998) 'The death of news', *New Statesman*, 22 May.

Cohen, P. (1979) 'Policing the working-class city' in Fine, B., Kinsey, R., Lea, J., Picciotto, S. and Young, J. (eds.) *Capitalism and the Rule of Law: From deviancy theory to Marxism*, London: Hutchinson and Co.

Committee of Inquiry into the Police (1978) *Report on Negotiations, Machinery and Pay*, cmnd. 7283, London: HMSO.

Conservative Party (1979) *Conservative Manifesto*, London: Conservative Central Office.

Coulter J., Miller, S. and Walker, M. (1984) *State of siege – Miners' Strike 1984: Politics and Policing in the Coal Fields*, London: Canary Press.

Cox, B., Shirley, J. and Short, M. (1977) *The Fall of Scotland Yard*, Harmondsworth: Penguin.

Cox, M. (ed.) (1992) *Victorian Tales of Mystery and Detection*, Oxford: Oxford University Press.

Crandon, G. and Dunne, S. (1997) 'Symbiosis or vassalage? The media and the law enforcers – the case of Avon and Somerset Police', *Policing and Society*, vol. 8, pp. 77–91.

Crawford, A. (1998) 'Community safety partnerships' in *Criminal Justice Matters*, no. 33, pp. 4–5.

Critchley, T. A. (1973) 'The Idea of Policing in Britain: Success or Failure?' in Alderson, J.C. and Stead, P.J. (eds.) *The Police We Deserve*, London: Wolfe Publishing Ltd.

Critchley, T. A. (1978) *A History of Police in England and Wales*, London: Constable.

Davies, H. (1992) *Fighting Leviathan*, London: Social Market Institute.

de Lint, W. (1999) 'A Post-modern Turn in Policing: Policing as Pastiche?' in *International Journal of the Sociology of Law*, 1999, 27, pp. 127–52.

della Porter, D. and Reiter, H. (eds.) (1998) *Policing Protest: The Control of Mass Demonstrations in Western Democracies*, Minneapolis: University of Minnesota Press.

DETR (1998) *Modern Local Government: in touch with the people*, White Paper, July. Cm 4013. London: Home Office.

Downes, D. and Morgan, R. (1997) 'Dumping the "Hostages to Fortune"? The Politics of Law and Order in Post-War Britain' in Maguire, M., Morgan R. and Reiner, R. (eds.) *The Oxford Handbook of Criminology* (2nd edn), Oxford: Clarendon Press.

Emsley, C. (1992) 'The English Bobby: An Indulgent Tradition' in Porter, R. (ed.) *Myths of the English*, Cambridge: Polity Press.

Emsley, C. (1996) *The English Police: A Political and Social History* (2nd edn), London: Longman.

Ericson, R. (1982) *Reproducing Order: A Study of Police Patrol Work*, Toronto: University of Toronto Press.

Ericson, R.V. (1994) 'The division of expert knowledge in policing and security', *British Journal of Sociology*, vol. 45, no. 2, pp. 149–75.

Ericson, R.V. (1995) 'The News Media and Account Ability' in Stenning, P.C. (ed.) *Accountability for Criminal Justice*, Toronto: University of Toronto Press.

Ericson, R.V., Baranek, P.M. and Chan, J.B.L. (1989) *Negotiating Control – a study of news sources*, Toronto: University of Toronto Press.

Ericson, R.V., Baranek, P.M. and Chan, J.B.L. (1991) *Representing Order: Crime, Law, and Justice in the News Media*, Buckingham: Open University Press.

Ericson, R.V. and Haggerty, P. (1997) *Policing the Risk Society*, Oxford: Clarendon.

Evans, D.J. (1995) *Crime and Policing: Spatial Approaches*, Aldershot: Avebury.

Fabian, R. (1955) *Fabian of the Yard*, Heirloom Modern World Library.

Fairclough, N. (1995) *Media Discourse*, London: Edward Arnold.

Feist, A. (1999) *The Effective Use of the Media in Serious Crime Investigations*, Policing and Reducing Crime Unit paper 120, London: Home Office.

Fielding, N.G. (1991) *The Police and Social Conflict: Rhetoric and Reality*, London: The Athlone Press.

Fielding, N.G. (1994) 'Cop canteen culture' in Newburn, T. and Stanko, B. (eds.) *Just boys doing business*, London: Routledge.

Fine, B. and Millar, R. (eds.) (1985) *Policing the miners' strike*, London: Lawrence and Wishart Ltd.

Fleming, R. (1994) *Scotland Yard*, London: Signet.

Foucault, M. (1977) *Disicpline and Punish: The birth of the Prison*, London: Allen Lane.

Franklin, B. (1998) *Tough on soundbites, tough on the causes of soundbites*, London: Catalyst.

Gardam, T. (1998) 'Television's true lies', *New Statesman*, 15 May.

Garland, D. (1990) *Punishment and Modern Society*, Oxford: Oxford University Press.

Garland, D. (1991) 'Punishment and Culture: the symbolic dimension of criminal justice' in *Studies in Law, Politics and Society*, vol. 11, pp. 191–222.

Gerth, H.H. and Wright Mills, C. (eds.) (1948) *From Max Weber: Essays in Sociology*, London: RKP.

Giddens, A. (1994) 'Living in a post-traditional society' in Giddens, A., Beck, U. and Lasch, S. (eds.) *Reflexive Modernization: Politics, Tradition and Aesthetics in the Modern Social Order*, Cambridge: Polity Press.

Gifford, Lord (1986) *The Broadwater Farm Inquiry: Report of the Independent Inquiry into disturbances of October 1985 at the Broadwater Farm Estate*, London: Karia Press.

Goffman, E. (1959) *The Presentation of Self in Everyday Life*, Harmondsworth: Penguin.

Gouldner, A.W. (1976) *The dialectic of ideology and technology*, London: Macmillan.

Graef, R. (1989) *Talking Blues*, London: Fontana.

Green, P. (1990) *The enemy without: policing and class consciousness in the miners' strike*, Buckingham: Open University Press.

Grunig, J.E., and Grunig, L.S. (1989) 'Toward a theory of the Public Relations Behaviour of Organizations: Review of a Program of Research' in Grunig, J.E., and Grunig, L.S. (eds.) *Public Relations Research Annual*, (pp. 27–63), Hillsdale, NJ: Lawrence Erlbaum Associates.

Habermas, J. (1984) *The Theory of Communicative Action, volume 1: Reason and the Rationalisation of Society*, Cambridge: Polity Press.

Habermas, J. (1987) *The Theory of Communicative Action, volume 2: Lifeworld and System: A Critique of Functionalist Reason*, Cambridge: Polity Press.

Habermas, J. (1989) *The Structural Transformation of the Public Sphere*, Cambridge: Polity Press.

Habermas, J. (1992) 'Concluding Remarks' in Calhoun, C. (ed.) *Habermas and the Public Sphere*, Cambridge, Mass.: MIT Press.

Habermas, J. (1996) *Between facts and norms*, Cambridge: Polity Press.

Hall, S., Critcher, C., Jefferson, T., Clarke, J., and Roberts, B. (1978) *Policing the Crisis: Mugging, the State, and Law and Order*, London: Macmillan.

Harding, T. (1997) *The Video Activist Handbook*, London: Pluto Press.

Harfield, C.G. (1997) 'Consent, Consensus or the Management of Dissent?: Challenges to Community Consultation in a New Policing Environment', *Policing and Society*, vol. 7, pp. 271–89.

Harvey-Jones, J. (1992) *Trouble Shooter 2*, Harmondsworth: Penguin.

Haseler, S. (1996) *The English Tribe: Identity, Nation and Europe*, London: Macmillan.

Heward, T. (1994) 'Retailing the Police: Corporate identity and the Met.' in Keat, R., Whitely, N., and Abercrombie, N. (eds.) *The Authority of the Consumer*, London: Routledge.

Highmore, S. (1993) *The Integration of police officers and civilian staff*, London: Home Office.

HM Inspectorate of Constabulary (1998) *What Price Policing?: A Study of Efficiency and Value for Money in the Police Service*, London: Home Office.

HM Inspectorate of Constabulary (1999) *Police Integrity – securing and maintaining public confidence*, London: Home Office.

Hobsbawm, E. (1983) 'Inventing Traditions' in Hobsbawm, E. and Range, T. (eds.) *The Invention of Tradition*, Cambridge: Cambridge University Press.

Holdaway, S. (ed.) (1979) *The British Police*, London: Edward Arnold.

Holdaway, S. (1983) *Inside the British Police*, Oxford: Basil Blackwell.

Home Office (1982) *Byford Report Briefing Note* (unpublished) – A summary of the main conclusions and recommendations of Mr Byford's report on his review of the police investigation of the Yorkshire Ripper case, 19 January, London: Home Office.

Home Office (1983) Circular 114/83, *Manpower, Effectiveness and Efficiency in the Police Service*, London: HMSO.

Home Office (1988) Circular 105/88, *Civilian Staff in the Police Service*, London: HMSO.

Home Office (1997) *Policing and the Public: findings from the 1996 British Crime Survey*, Home Office Research and Statistics Directorate Research Findings no. 60. London: Home Office.

Howgrave-Graham, H.M. (1947) *Light and Shade at Scotland Yard*, London: John Murray.

Hunt, R.G. and Magenau, J.M. (1993) *Power and the Police Chief: An Institutional and Organizational Analysis*, London: Sage.

Hurd, G. (1979) 'The TV presentation of the Police' in Holdaway, S. (ed.) *The British Police*, London: Edward Arnold.

Innes, M. (1999) 'The media as an investigative resource in murder enquiries' in the *British Journal of Criminology*, vol. 39, no. 2, pp. 269–86.

Jackson, B. with Wardle, T. (1986) *The Battle for Orgreave*, Brighton: Vanson Wardle Productions.

Jefferson, T. and Grimshaw, R. (1984) *Controlling the Constable*, London: Frederick Muller Ltd and the Cobden Trust.

Johnston, L. (2000) *Policing Britain: Risk, Security and Governance*, London: Longman.

Joint Consultative Committee (1990) *Operational Policing Review*, Surbiton: Joint Consultative Committee.

Jones, T., Newburn, T. and Smith, D.J. (1994) *Democracy and Policing*, London: Policy Studies Institute.

Jones, T., Newburn, T. and Smith, D.J. (1996) 'Policing and the idea of democracy', *British Journal of Criminology*, vol. 36, no. 2, pp. 182–98.

Judge, T. (1994) *The Force of Persuasion*, Surbiton: The Police Federation.

Keating, J. (1991) *Counting the cost,* Barnsley: Wharncliffe Publicity Ltd.

Kettle, M. (1985) 'The National Reporting Centre and the 1984 Miners' Strike' in Fine, B. and Millar, R. (eds.) *Policing the miners' strike*, London: Lawrence and Wishart Ltd.

Kilborn, R.W. (1998) 'Shaping the Real: Democratization and Commodification in UK Factual Broadcasting' in the *European Journal of Communication*, vol. 13(2): 201–18.

Laing, S. (1991) 'Banging in some reality: the original Z Cars' in Corner, J. (ed.) *Popular Television in Britain*, London: BFI.

Laurie, P. (1970) *Scotland Yard. A Personal Inquiry*, London: The Bodley Head.

Layder, D. (1993) *New Strategies in Social Research*, Cambridge: Polity Press.

Leigh, A., Mundy, G. and Tuffin, R. (1999) *Best value policing: making preparations*, Policing and Reducing Crime Unit Police Research Series Paper 116, London: Home Office.

Leishman, F., Cope, S. and Starie P. (1996) 'Reinventing and restructuring: towards a "new policing order"' in Leishman, F., Loveday, B. and Savage, S.P. (eds.) *Core Issues in Policing*, London: Longman.

Loader, I. (1996) *Youth, Policing and Democracy*, London: Macmillan.

Loader, I. (1997a) 'Policing and the social: questions of symbolic power', *British Journal of Sociology*, vol. 48, no. 1, pp. 1–18, March.

Loader, I. (1997b) 'Private security and the demand for protection in contemporary Britain', *Policing and Society*, vol. 7, pp. 143–62.

Loader, I. and Mulcahy, A. (2001a) 'The Power of Legitimate Naming, Part I: Chief Constables as Social Commentators in Post-War England', *British Journal of Criminology*, vol. 41, no. 1, pp. 41–55.

Loader, I. and Mulcahy, A. (2001b) 'The Power of Legitimate Naming, Part II: Making Sense of the Elite Police Voice', *British Journal of Criminology*, vol. 41, no. 2, pp. 252–65.

Locke, J. (1960) *Two treatises of Government*, edited by Laslett, J., Cambridge: Cambridge University Press.

Loveday, B. (1993) *Civilian Staff in the Police Force: Competences and conflict in the Police Force*, Leicester: CSPO.

Loveday, B. (1994) 'The Police and Magistrates' Court Act', *Policing*, 10, 4, pp. 221–23 Winter.

Lukes, S. (ed.) (1986) *Power*, Oxford: Blackwell.

Macready, Sir N. (1924) *Annals of an active life, volume 2*, London: Hutchinson.

Macpherson of Cluny, Sir William (1999) *The Stephen Lawrence Inquiry*, cm 4262-1, London: HMSO.

Manning, P.K. (1971) 'The Police: Mandate, Strategies and Appearances', in Douglas, J.D. (ed.) *Crime and Justice in American Society*, Indianapolis: Bobbs-Merrill.

Manning, P.K. (1988) *Symbolic Communication,*, Cambridge, MA.: MIT Press.

Manning, P.K. (1996) 'Dramaturgy, Politics and the Axial Media Event', in *The Sociological Quarterly*, vol. 37, no. 2, pp. 101–18.

Manning, P.K. (1997) *Police Work: The Social Organization of Policing* (2nd edn), Illinois: Waveland Press.

Manning, P.K. (2001) 'Theorizing Policing: The drama and myth of crime control in the NYPD', *Theoretical Criminology*, vol. 5, no. 3, August.

Mark, R. (1977) *Policing a Perplexed Society*, London: George Allen & Unwin Ltd.

Mark, R. (1978) *In the office of Constable*, London: Collins and Son.

Mathiesen, T. (1997) 'The Viewer Society: Michel Foucault's "Panopticon" revisited', *Theoretical Criminology*, vol. 1, no. 2, pp. 215–34.

Mawby, R. I. (1979) *Policing the City*, Saxon House: Farnborough.

Mawby, R.C. (1997a) *Survey of police service media and public relations offices*, Stafford: CPSMR, Staffordshire University.

Mawby, R.C. (1997b) 'Managing media and public relations in the police service', *Police Management and Research*, vol. 1, no. 1, pp. 67–80. London: Goodrich.

Mawby, R.C. (1999) 'Visibility, Transparency and Police Media Relations' in *Policing and Society*, vol. 9, pp. 263–86.

Mawby, R.C. (2001) *Survey of police service media and public relations offices 2000–2001*, Stafford: CPSMR, Staffordshire University.

McCabe, S., and Wallington, P. (1988) *The Police, Public Order, and Civil Liberties: Legacies of the Miners' Strike*, London: Routledge.

McLaughlin, E. (1994) *Community, Policing and Accountability: The politics of policing Manchester in the 1980s*, Aldershot: Avebury.

McLaughlin, E. and Muncie, J. (1994) 'Managing the Criminal Justice System' in Clarke, J., Cochrane, A. and McLaughlin, E. (eds.) *Managing Social Policy*, London: Sage.

McLaughlin, E. and Murji, K. (1997) 'The Future Lasts a Long Time: Public Policework and the Managerialist Paradox', in Francis, P., Davies, P. and Jupp, V. (eds.) *Policing Futures: The Police, Law Enforcement and the Twenty-First Century*, London: Macmillan.

McLaughlin, E. and Murji, K. (1998) 'Resistance through representation: "Storylines", advertising and Police Federation campaigns', *Policing and Society*, vol. 8, pp. 367–99.

McLaughlin, E. and Murji, K. (2001) 'Lost connections and new directions: neo-liberalism, new public managerialism, and the "modernization" of the British police' in Stenson, K. and Sullivan, R.R. (eds.) *Crime, Risk and Justice: the politics of crime control in liberal democracies*, Cullompton: Willan Publishing.

McNee, D. (1983) *McNee's Law*, London: Collins.

McPherson, D. (1997) 'A shadow police press team for major incidents' in *FOCUS*, no. 9, pp. 29–31, London: Home Office Police Research Group.

Metropolitan Police (1851) *General Regulations, Instructions and Orders, for the Government and Guidance of the Metropolitan Police Force*, London: W Clowes and Sons for HMSO.

Michie, D. (1998) *The Invisible Persuaders: How Britain's Spin Doctors Manipulate the Media*, London: Bantam.

Moores, G.H. (1979, chairman) *Report on relationships between the police and the public in South Yorkshire*, Barnsley: South Yorkshire County Council.

Morgan, R. (1989) 'Policing by consent: legitimating the doctrine' in Morgan, R. and Smith, D.J. *Coming to Terms with Policing*, London: Routledge.

Morgan, R. (1992) 'Talking About Policing', in Downes, D. (ed.) *Unravelling Criminal Justice*, London: Macmillan.

Morgan, R. (1995) *Making Consultation Work: A Handbook for Those Involved in Police Community Consultation Arrangements*, London: Police Foundation.

Morgan, R. and Maggs, C. (1985) *Setting the PACE: Police-Community Consultation Arrangements in England and Wales*, Bath Social Policy Papers 4, Bath: Bath University.

Morris, P. and Heal, K. (1981) *Crime Control and the Police*, London: Home Office Research Unit.

Motschall, M.F. (1995) *The Role and Rhetorical Strategies of Police Public Information Officers in Law Enforcement Agencies*, doctoral dissertation, Wayne State University, Detroit, Michigan.

Moylan, Sir J. (1934) *Scotland Yard and the Metropolitan Police*, London: Putnam and Co.

Mulcahy, A. (2000) 'Policing History: The Official Discourse and Organizational Memory of the Royal Ulster Constabulary', *British Journal of Criminology*, vol. 40, no. 1, pp. 68–87.

Murdock, G. (1984) 'Reporting the riots: images and impact' in Benyon, J. (ed.) *Scarman and After*, Oxford: Pergamon.

Newburn, T. (1995) *Crime and Criminal Justice Policy*, London: Longman.

Newburn, T. and Jones, T. (1996) 'Police Accountability', in Saulsbury, W., Mott, J., and Newburn, T. (eds.) *Themes in Contemporary Policing*, London: Police Foundation and the Policy Studies Institute.

Norris, C. (1993) 'Some Ethical Considerations on Field-work with the police' in Hobbs, D. and May, T. (eds.) *Interpreting the Field*, Oxford: Clarendon Press.

Northam, G. (1988) *Shooting in the Dark: Riot Police in Britain*, London: Faber and Faber.

Olins, W. (1988) 'Identity – the corporation's hidden resource' in Gorb, P. and Schneider, E. (eds.) *Design Talks!* London: Design Council.

Olins, W. (1989) *Corporate Identity – Making business strategy visible through Design*, London: Thames and Hudson.

Oliver, I. (1997) *Police, Government and Accountability* (2nd edition), London: Macmillan.

Outhwaite, W. (1994) *Habermas – A critical introduction*, Cambridge: Polity Press.

Perlmutter, D. (2000) *Policing the Media: Street Cops and Public Perceptions of Law Enforcement*, London: Sage.

Police Federation (1996) *Where we stand on ... community involvement*, Surbiton: Police Federation.

Police Federation (undated) *The Policing Agenda: A Message from the Federation*, Surbiton: Police Federation.

Pollitt, C. (1993) *Managerialism and the Public Services*, (2nd edn), Oxford: Blackwell.

Posen, I. (1995) (Chair) *Home Office Review of Police Core and Ancillary Tasks*, London: HMSO.

Poster, M. (1995) *The Second Media Age*, Cambridge, Polity Press.

Pringle, P. (1955) *Hue and Cry: The Birth of the British Police*, London: Museum Press Limited.

Punch, M. (1979a) 'The Secret Social Service' in Holdaway, S. (ed.) *The British Police*, London: Edward Arnold.

Punch, M. (1979b) *Policing the inner city*, London: Macmillan.

Rawlings, P. (1995) 'The Idea of Policing: A History', *Policing and Society*, vol. 5, pp. 129–49.

Reiner, R. (1978) *The Blue-Coated Worker*, Cambridge: Cambridge University Press.

Reiner, R. (1991) *Chief Constables: Bobbies, Bosses or Bureaucrats?*, Oxford: Oxford University Press.

Reiner, R. (1992a), *The Politics of the Police* (2nd edn), Hemel Hempstead: Harvester Wheatsheaf.

Reiner, R. (1992b) 'Policing a Postmodern Society', *The Modern Law Review*, vol. 55, no. 6, pp. 761–81.

Reiner, R. (1994a) 'The Dialectics of Dixon: The Changing Image of the TV Cop' in Stephens, M. and Becker, S. (eds.) *Police Force Police Service*, London: Macmillan.

Reiner, R. (1994b) 'What should the police be doing?' *Policing*, vol. 10, no. 3, pp. 151–7, Autumn.

Reiner, R. (1995a) 'From Sacred to Profane: The Thirty Years' War of the British Police' in *Policing and Society*, vol. 5, no. 2, pp. 121–28.

Reiner, R. (1995b) 'Counting the Coppers: Antinomies of Accountability in Policing' in Stenning, P.C. (ed.) *Accountability for Criminal Justice*, Toronto: University of Toronto Press.

Reiner, R. (1995c) 'Myth vs. modernity: Reality and unreality in the English model of policing' in Brodeur, J.-P. (ed.) *Comparisons in Policing: An International Perspective*, Aldershot: Avebury.

Reiner, R. (1997a) 'Policing and the Police' in Maguire, M., Morgan R. and Reiner, R. (eds.) *The Oxford Handbook of Criminology* (2nd edn), Oxford: Clarendon Press.

Reiner, R. (1997b) 'Media Made Criminality: The Representation of Crime in the Mass Media' in Maguire, M., Morgan, R. and Reiner, R. (eds.) *The Oxford Handbook of Criminology* (2nd edn), Oxford: Clarendon Press.

Reiner, R. (1998) 'Policing Protest and disorder in Britain' in della Porter, D. and Reiter, H. (eds.) *Policing Protest: The Control of Mass Demonstrations in Western Democracies*, Minneapolis: University of Minnesota Press.

Reiner, R. (2000a) *The Politics of the Police* (3rd ed.), Oxford: Oxford University Press.

Reiner, R. (2000b) 'Romantic realism: policing and the media' in Leishman, F., Loveday, B. and Savage, S.P. (eds.) *Core Issues in Policing* (2nd edn), London: Longman.

Reiner, R., Livingstone, S., and Allen, J. (1998) 'Discipline or Desurbordination? Changing Images of Crime in the Media Since World War II', paper presented to International Sociological Association World congress of Sociology, Montreal, Canada, 31 July.

Reiner, R. and Spencer, S. (eds.) (1993) *Accountable Policing*, London: IPPR.

Reith, C. (1938) *The Police Idea*, Oxford: Oxford University Press.

Reith, C. (1943) *British Police and the Democratic Ideal*, Oxford: Oxford University Press.

Reith, C. (1948) *A Short History of the Police*, Oxford: Oxford University Press.

Reith, C. (1952) *The Blind Eye of History*, London: Faber and Faber.

Reuss-Ianni, E. (1983) *Two Cultures of Policing: Street Cops and Management Cops*, New Brunswick, NJ: Transaction Books.

Rolph, C.H. (1973) 'Police and the Public' in Alderson, J.C. and Stead, P.J. (eds.) *The Police We Deserve*, London: Wolfe Publishing Ltd.

Rousseau, J.J. (1946) *The Social Contract and Discourses*, London: J.M. Dent and Sons Ltd.

Royal Commission on Police Powers and Procedures (1929) *Final Report*, cmd 3297, London: HMSO.

Russell, B. (1938) *Power: A New Social Analysis*, London: Allen and Unwin.

Samuel R., Bloomfield, B. and Boanas, G. (eds.) (1986) *The Enemy Within: Pit villages and the miners' strike of 1984*, London: RKP.

Savage, S. and Charman, S. (1996a) 'In favour of compliance' in *Policing Today*, vol. 2, 1, pp. 10–17, April.

Savage, S. and Charman, S. (1996b) 'Managing Change' in Leishman, F., Loveday, B. and Savage, S.P. (eds.) *Core Issues in Policing*, London: Longman.

Savage, S., Charman, S. and Cope, S. (1998) 'The role of ACPO: Choosing the way ahead', *Policing Today* vol. 4, no. 2, pp. 38–40.

Savage, S., Charman, S. and Cope, S. (1999) 'The State of Independence: The Discourse of Constabulary Independence', paper presented to the British Criminology Conference, Liverpool, July.

Savage, S., Charman, S. and Cope, S. (2000) *Policing and the Power of Persuasion: The Changing Role of the Association of Chief Police Officers*, London: Blackstone Press.

Scarman, Lord (1981) *Report of an Inquiry: The Brixton Disorders, 10–12 April 1981*, cmnd 8427, London: HMSO.

Schlesinger, P. and Tumber, H. (1992) 'Crime and Criminal Justice in the Media' in Downes, D. (ed.) *Unravelling Criminal Justice*, London: Macmillan.

Schlesinger, P. and Tumber, H. (1994) *Reporting Crime: The Media Politics of Criminal Justice*, Oxford: Oxford University Press.

Scott, Sir H. (1954) *Scotland Yard*, Harmondsworth: Penguin.

Scott, J. (1990) *A Matter of Record: Documentary Sources in Social Research*, Cambridge: Polity Press.

Scraton, P. (1999) 'Policing with Contempt: The Degrading of Truth and Denial of Justice in the Aftermath of the Hillsborough Disaster', *Journal of Law and Society*, vol. 26, no. 3, pp. 273–97.

Shapland, J. and Hobbs, D. (1989) 'Looking at Policing' in Hood, R. (ed.) *Crime and Criminal Policy in Europe*, Oxford: Centre for Criminological Research, Oxford University.

Sheehy, P. (1993) (Chairman) *Inquiry into Police Responsibilities and Rewards*, cm 2280.1 London: HMSO.

Sheffield Borough Watch Committee (1844) *Rules orders and regulations for the guidance of the officers and constables of the police*, Sheffield: J. H. Greaves.

Sheptycki, J. (1997) 'Insecurity, risk suppression and segregation: some reflections on policing in the transnational age', *Theoretical Criminology*, vol. 1, no. 3, pp. 303–15, August.

Sheptycki, J. (1998) 'Policing, Postmodernism and Transnationalization', *British Journal of Criminology*, vol. 38, no. 3, pp. 485–503, Summer.

Sheptycki, J. (ed.) (2000) *Issues in Transnational Policing*, London: Routledge.

Sillitoe, P. (1955) *Cloak without dagger*, London: Pan Books Ltd.

Skogan, W. (1990) *The Police and the Public in England and Wales: A British Crime Survey Report*, Home Office Research Study 117, London: HMSO.

Skogan, W. (1994) *Contacts between Police and Public: findings from the 1992 British Crime Survey*, Home Office Research Study 134, London: HMSO.

Skogan, W. (1996) 'Public Opinion and the Police' in Saulsbury, W., Mott, J., and Newburn, T. (eds.) *Themes in Contemporary Policing*, London: Police Foundation and the Policy Studies Institute.

Skolnick, J. (1966) *Justice Without Trial*, New York: Wiley.

Smith, D.J., Gray, J. and Small, S. (1983) *Police and the People in London*, vols. 1–4., London: Policy Studies Institute.

South Yorkshire Police (1991) *Media Strategy – Into the Light*, Sheffield: South Yorkshire Police.

South Yorkshire Police (1996a) *Strategic Plan 1996–2001*, Sheffield: South Yorkshire Police.

South Yorkshire Police (1996b) *Annual Report of the chief constable 1995–96*, Chesterfield: Philip Dent Public Relations.

South Yorkshire Police (1996c) *Media & Public Relations Strategy – 'Reality and Reputation'*, Sheffield: South Yorkshire Police.

South Yorkshire Police (1996d) *Press & Public Relations Department Media Survey 1996*, Sheffield: South Yorkshire Police.

South Yorkshire Police (1997a) *Strategic Plan 1997–2002*, Sheffield: South Yorkshire Police.

South Yorkshire Police (1997b) *Annual Report of the chief constable 1996–97*, Chesterfield: Philip Dent Public Relations.

South Yorkshire Police (1998) *Annual Report of the chief constable 1997–98*, Huddersfield: Pluto Design.

Sparks, R. (1990) 'Dramatic power: television, images of crime and law enforcement' in Sumner, C. (ed.) *Censure, Politics and Criminal Justice*, Buckingham: Open University Press.

Sparks, R. (1992) *Television and the drama of crime*, Buckingham: Open University Press.

Sparks, R. (1993) 'Inspector Morse: The Last Enemy' in Brandt, G.W. (ed.) *British Television Drama in the 1980s*, Cambridge: Cambridge University Press.

Sparks, R. and Bottoms, A.E. (1995) 'Legitimacy and Order in Prisons', *British Journal of Sociology*, 46, 1, pp. 45–62, March.

Sparks, R., Bottoms, A.E. and Hay, W. (1996) *Prisons and the Problem of Order*, Oxford: Clarendon Press.

Stansfield, W. (1973) 'Being a Chief Constable' in Alderson, J.C. and Stead, P.J. (eds.) *The Police We Deserve*, London: Wolfe Publishing Ltd.

Stern, C. (1999) 'Verbals', *Police Review*, 19 March.

Steedman, C. (1984) *Policing the Victorian Community: The formation of an English provincial police force 1856-80*, London: Routledge and Kegan Paul.

Stephens, M. and Becker, S. (eds.) (1994) *Police Force, Police Service*, London: Macmillan.

Stockdale, J.E., Whitehead, C.M.E. and Gresham, P.J. (1999) *Applying Economic Evaluation to Policing Activity*, Policing and Reducing Crime Unit Police Research Series Paper 103, London: Home Office.

Storch, R.D. (1975) 'The plague of the blue locusts' in Fitzgerald, M., McLennan, G. and Pawson, J. (eds.) (1981) *Crime and Society*, Milton Keynes: Open University.

Taylor, I. (1989) 'Hillsborough, 15 April 1989: Some Personal Contemplations', *New Left Review*, 177, pp. 89–110, September/October.

Taylor, I. (1997) 'Crime, anxiety and locality: responding to the "condition of England" at the end of the century', *Theoretical Criminology*, vol. 1, no. 1, pp. 53–75.

Taylor, I. (1999) *Crime in Context: A Critical Criminology of Market Societies*, Cambridge: Polity Press.

Taylor, I., Evans, K. and Fraser, P. (1996) *A Tale of Two Cities. Global Change, Local Feeling and Everyday Life in the North of England: A Study in Manchester and Sheffield*, Routledge: London.

Thompson, E.P. (1980) *Writing by Candlelight*, London: Merlin.

Thompson, J.B. (1990) *Ideology and Modern Culture*, Cambridge: Polity Press.

Thompson, J.B. (1993) Review article of Habermas's Structural Transformation of the Public Sphere in *Theory, Culture and Society*, 10, 3, pp. 173–89.

Thompson, J. B. (1995) *The Media and Modernity: A Social Theory of the Media*, Cambridge: Polity Press.

Tobias, J.J. (1975) 'Police and Public in the United Kingdom' in Mosse, G.L. (ed.) *Police Forces in History*, London: Sage.

van Riel, C.B.M. (1995) *Principles of Corporate Communication*, London: Prentice Hall.

Waddington, D., Jones, K. and Critcher, C. (1989) *Flashpoints: Studies in public disorder*, London: Routledge.

Waddington, P.A.J. (1991) *The Strong Arm of the Law: Armed and Public Order Policing*, Oxford: Clarendon Press.

Waddington, P.A.J. (1994) *Liberty and Order*, London: UCL Press.

Waddington, P.A.J. (1998) 'Controlling Protest in Contemporary Historical and Comparative Perspective' in della Porter, D. and Reiter, H. (eds.) *Policing Protest: The Control of Mass Demonstrations in Western Democracies*, Minneapolis: University of Minnesota Press.

Waddington, P.A.J. (1999a) *Policing Citizens: Authority and Rights*, London: UCL Press.

Waddington, P.A.J. (1999b) 'Police (Canteen) Sub-culture: An Appreciation', *British Journal of Criminology*, vol. 39, no. 2, pp. 287–309.

Waddington, P.A.J. (2000) 'Public order policing: citizenship and moral ambiguity' in Leishman, F., Loveday, B. and Savage, S.P. (eds.) *Core Issues in Policing* (2nd edn), London: Longman.

Wall, D. (1998) *The Chief Constables of England and Wales: The Socio-Legal History of a Criminal Justice Elite*, Aldershot: Dartmouth.

Waters, I. (1996) 'Quality of service: politics or paradigm shift?' in Leishman, F. Loveday, B. and Savage, S.P. (eds.) *Core Issues in Policing*, London: Longman.

Waters, I. (2000) 'Quality and performance monitoring' in Leishman, F. Loveday, B. and Savage, S.P. (eds.) *Core Issues in Policing* (2nd edn), London: Longman.

Weatheritt, M. (1993) 'Measuring Police Performance: Accounting or Accountability?' in Reiner, R. and Spencer, S. (eds.) *Accountable Policing*, London: IPPR.

Webster, F. (1994) 'What information society?', *The Information Society*, 10, pp. 1–23.

Weinberger, B. (1995) *The Best Police in the World: An Oral History of English Policing from the 1930s to the 1960s*, Aldershot: Scholar Press.

Whitaker, B. (1964) *The Police*, Harmondsworth: Penguin.

Williams, R. (1961) *The Long Revolution*, Harmondsworth: Penguin.

Wilsher, P., Macinytre, D. and Jones, M. (1985) *Strike: Thatcher, Scargill and the Miners*, Sevenoaks: Coronet.

Worsborough Community Group (1985) *The Heart and Soul of it*, Barnsley: Self published.

Wolff Olins (1988) *A Force for Change: A report on the corporate identity of the Metropolitan Police*, London: Wolff Olins Corporate Identity.

Wright, A. (1996) 'Accountability and the management of coercive power', COLPI Conference paper, Budapest, February.

Wright, A. (2000) 'Managing the future: an academic's view' in Leishman, F., Loveday, B. and Savage, S.P. (eds.) *Core Issues in Policing* (2nd edn), London: Longman.

Wright, A. (2002) *Policing: an introduction to concepts and practice*, Cullompton: Willan Publishing.

Young, M. (1991) *An Inside Job*, Oxford: Clarendon Press.

Index